WORKING-CLASS GIRLS IN NINETEENTH-CENTURY ENGLAND

Working-class Girls in Nineteenth-century England

Life, Work and Schooling

Meg Gomersall

Consultant Editor: Jo Campling

First published in Great Britain 1997 by
MACMILLAN PRESS LTD
Houndmills, Basingstoke, Hampshire RG21 6XS
and London
Companies and representatives
throughout the world

A catalogue record for this book is available
from the British Library.

ISBN 0–333–62200–6 hardcover
ISBN 0–333–62201–4 paperback

First published in the United States of America 1997 by
ST. MARTIN'S PRESS, INC.,
Scholarly and Reference Division,
175 Fifth Avenue,
New York, N.Y. 10010

ISBN 0–312–12970–X

Library of Congress Cataloging-in-Publication Data
Gomersall, Meg.
Working-class girls in nineteenth-century England : life, work and
schooling / Meg Gomersall.
p.   cm.
Includes bibliographical references and index.
ISBN 0–312–12970–X (cloth)
1. Girls—England—History—19th century.   2. Women—Education–
–England—History—19th century.   3. Working class families–
–England—History—19th century.   I. Title.
HQ1229.G66   1996
305.4'0942—dc20   95–51280
                                                                          CIP

10   9   8   7   6   5   4   3   2   1
06   05   04   03   02   01   00   99   98   97

Printed and bound in Great Britain by
Antony Rowe Ltd, Chippenham, Wiltshire

Contents

List of Tables

Acknowledgements

My mother was an intelligent girl who grew up in rural Suffolk in the 1930s. She passed what was then known as the scholarship examination and, had she been allowed to attend grammar school, she would have enjoyed an extended academic education and may even have gone on to attend university. Unfortunately, my grandfather thought that a grammar school education was wasted on a girl, who after all would only be a housewife. Finishing elementary school at the earliest possible leaving age, she became a domestic servant, a job which was still the main occupational destination for working-class country girls in the region. She did not remain a servant for long and her story of being dismissed for eating the master's dinner was one I always cherished, but though she eventually achieved a responsible post in the Civil Service and gained some qualifications through study at evening classes, she always saw her limited schooling as a major deprivation.

All-age elementary schools such as the one my mother attended disappeared after the 1944 Education Act and my brother and I both went to state grammar schools at the age of 11. My father's ill health meant that money was tight but my mother insisted that I should stay on at school and have the chance to go to college. Thanks to the state education sytem and my mother's encouragement, I did achieve this goal. But, rather than the glittering career (and marriage to a middle-class man with good prospects) that my mother thought my university education would bring me, I became a teacher. This was because by the time I got my degree I had a young family and needed a job that could be 'fitted in' around my domestic commitments. Despite my superior educational opportunities, my adult life became very similar to my mother's. I had a better job in terms of status and earnings, but, like her, I was employed in a traditional area of 'women's work' and, like her, spent most of my 'leisure' time cooking, cleaning, washing and all the other thousand and one things that women do.

All these experiences have informed the research that led to this book. It took me many years to complete in between the demands of full-time work and home and family and the practical and moral support of my husband Tom has always been important. And, though my son's domestic skills may have been encouraged more by his dissatisfaction with the quality of my ironing than the persuasive powers of my feminist beliefs, he deserves particular thanks for keeping the house going when I was working away from home. I also owe special thanks to Richard Aldrich at

London University Institute of Education. He supervised the Ph.D. thesis from which this book evolved and managed to combine patience with rigorous and constructive criticism, when long stretches of silence were followed by a mass of often only half-digested material from me. His belief in my capabilities was also a great support when I despaired of ever finishing the work. And finally, I owe thanks to Nathan, who let me have a computer on long-term loan when mine crashed and only asked for this acknowledgement in payment. So thanks Nathan.

Introduction

Why is it, asked an Inspector of elementary schools in 1856, that, 'in pamphlets and speeches and schemes of so-called national education, they (girls) are almost uniformly ignored?'[1] This was a question that until recently might also have been asked by anyone with a familiarity with twentieth-century publications on the history of English education, as the experiences of women and girls remained largely unexplored. But although this area has received some attention in the last ten years,[2] several major challenges still remain. Very little has been published, for example, on the nineteenth-century education of working-class[3] women and girls, despite the fact of this being a crucial period in the development of mass elementary (working-class) schooling. With the exception of Gomersall and Purvis,[4] those with an interest in this period have focused on the experiences of women and girls from higher social groups or on the post-1870 period. Indeed, though several writers have put forward viewpoints regarding working-class female education in the earlier part of the century, these are largely unsubstantiated, with very little evidence given to support arguments.[5] There is a need, therefore, for detailed evidence on the schooling of working-class girls in this period, particularly that which goes beyond statements of policy and intent to investigate the realities of female educational experiences and their causes and consequences.

Perhaps even more significantly, there are unresolved challenges in the construction of theoretical frameworks which recognise the multifaceted nature of these experiences, and the complexities of the relationship between gender and schooling and other social institutions, events and processes. Purvis's model of a 'double burden'[6] of class and gender operating to limit the educational opportunities available to working-class women and girls has some explanatory usefulness, for example, but it does not recognise the often very considerable variety in those experiences over place, time and circumstance – or the fact that girls could actually enjoy educational advantages over their male peers. Similarly, her identification of bourgeois class and gender ideologies as the prime shaping determinant of female education underestimates the significance of the material contexts of working-class life and the often complex ways in which economics and ideologies were intertwined and interdependent in a constantly changing relationship of conflict and accommodation.

Both these challenges have informed the research and the writing of this book. For, although the presentation of detailed evidence of the

1

nineteenth-century schooling experiences of girls from the lower socio-economic ranks would have gone some way towards emending previous neglect, it would have added little to our understanding of the causes and consequences of such schooling or of its significance in the adult lives of women. The questions I pursue here, therefore, relate to gender differences in the relationship between social and educational ideals and purposes, to their influence on schooling practices, to the tensions between a whole range of economic, cultural and social factors which influenced both the provision of schooling and 'consumer' responses, and the relative significance of schooling in shaping attitudes and informing wider experiences. My intention, in short, is to view the education of working-class girls as being 'in society, as something of society, as forming and being formed by society'.[7]

The society in which these girls lived was, however, one in which all social relations, including economic relations, were informed by considerations of gender, with 'common sense' understandings of what it meant to be a woman or a man expressed in practices which defined their different social positions and structured their lived experiences in different ways.[8] Ideas about and experiences of gender, however, were neither singular nor static during this period. They influenced and were influenced by developments in capitalist economic organisation and were mediated by cross and inter-class differences and by differences in occupation and material circumstances. Nor, as will be shown, were ideas of gender always consistent with people's lived experiences, and there were often considerable disparities between gender orthodoxies and perceptions of the naturally ordained 'roles' of working-class women and between actual lives and behaviours.

PATRIARCHAL PROCESSES

If concepts of gender roles were subject to challenge and change, the basic principle of patriarchy, that is, of male domination over women, remained a constant shaping factor in nineteenth-century English society, representing what Lown has called a 'pivotal organising principle'[9] in responses to social and economic developments.

The concept of patriarchy has been developed by feminist historians as an interpretive framework that encompasses the basis and structure of relations between men and women and the interaction between these and social and economic organisation and institutional arrangements. It recognises that the concepts and analyses of mainstream ('male-stream'[10]) history are posited on a male paradigm and can operate to preclude discussion – even recognition – of issues of women's experiences. The concept is not without its own difficulties, however, as it is informed by many, sometimes conflicting theoretical perspectives and, as Lown has warned, 'to start talking in terms of patriarchy is to enter a conceptual minefield'.[11] Critics of the concept have also argued that it is insufficiently sensitive to the variety of women's experiences over time and place and within different classes, cultures and ethnic groups.[12]

In a comprehensive overview of these many different analyses of patriarchy, Walby defines it as 'a system of social structures and practices in which men dominate, oppress and exploit women'. Rather than there being a single source of male oppression, she argues, male domination is located in six social structures; patriarchal production relations in the household, patriarchal relations in paid labour, the patriarchal state, male violence, patriarchal relations in sexuality and patriarchal cultural institutions, including education. The term 'social structures' is used to reject biological determinism and the idea that every man is dominant and every woman subordinate.[13] In Walby's analysis, individual experiences are mediated by the intensity of and balance between the six structures of patriarchy. Similarly, changes in the degree and form of patriarchal oppression over time also arise from shifts in the balance between and intensity of these structures.[14]

The dominant form of patriarchy through much of nineteenth-century England was private patriarchy, where the expropriation of women's labour in the household by husbands, cohabitees and fathers represented the dominant patriarchal structure. Many working-class women in the period experienced more public forms of patriarchy, however, particularly in their paid work where, as will be shown in the following two chapters, strategies of exclusion and segregation were used to reinforce male power and control. Further, though Victorian domestic patriarchy is frequently seen as 'traditional' patriarchy, the culture of domestic ideology that developed in the early nineteenth century represented a redefinition of patriarchy, linked to the socio-economic changes associated with the development of industrial capitalism.

The onset of mechanised production introduced a new element into pre-existing divisions of labour between men and women, by threatening the material base of the traditional, male dominated, hierarchy of labour. This offered the possibility of more equitable relations between the sexes. Marx, for example, anticipated that increased use of machinery would dispense with the need for the physical strength and skills that gave a rationale to adult male domination of manufacture, and suggested that 'modern industry' had created a 'new economic foundation for a higher form of the family and relations between the sexes'.[15]

The economic foundations of patriarchy may have been eroded by the use of female labour in the cotton factories of early industrial England, but the cultural and ideological bases of unequal relations between men and women nevertheless remained firm. The consciousness of working people was not derived directly from their experience of the factory system but was the product of reflection on experience informed by traditional value systems.[16] These traditional values were derived from patriarchy, with social relations based on male superiority and female inferiority operating as a major cultural precondition for the accommodation of family values and structures with the organisation of economic production.

Changes in the organisation of labour in textile production, however, rode roughshod over traditional family values, to present a major challenge to patriarchal principles. The problem was not simply that of the factory employment of women as such. The concepts of gender held by working people in the early part of the century defined an engagement in economic activity as customary for women, with an axiomatic expectation that they would contribute to family earnings wherever possible. 'None but a fool', advised *A Present for a Serving Maid*, published in 1743, 'will take a wife whose bread must be earned solely by his labour, and who will contribute nothing towards it herself.'[17] But the conditions under which such work was acceptable were also defined by gender values. The economically productive work of women should be carried on within a familial context, with women either working at home or as part of the family team.

By employing women as independent workers, the factory system flouted the cultural norms of women's social position within the working-class family and, as it was widely perceived, threatened the very structure of family life. The cheap 'competition' of working women also threatened – or was seen to threaten – the job security, wage levels and the status of men, both as workers and as 'honourable' men and husbands and fathers.[18]

Such changes were not accepted without protest. Nor was such protest ineffectual. The organisation of labour under capitalism involved more than a straightforward imposition of changing employment conditions on a passive labour force as the economic needs of capitalism dictated, and there was a need for manufacturers to employ strategies of labour recruitment which did not interfere too drastically with the values and customary expectations of the labour force.[19] Rather than being a one-way affair, the relationship between manufacturers and the factory labour force developed through relations of coercion, resistance and negotiation between employers and employees and between men and women via a complex interaction between cultural values and economic forces. In my argument, therefore, changes in the mode of production and the organisation of labour were defined as tolerable or intolerable according to the degree in which they challenged or supported patriarchal social relations of male superiority and female inferiority. Hence the tensions which characterised the development of early industrial capitalism, as the organisation of factory labour challenged the gender divisions of labour in the home and the workplace that were the material base of patriarchy and attacked working people's understanding of what it meant to be masculine or feminine. Hence also the easing of tensions from around mid-century, as the reassertion of patriarchal principles across a variety of sites reconciled cultural values and economic organisation in an harmonious accommodation of interests. In sum, patriarchy provided both the model for such accommodation and the means towards hegemonic ends, operating as a 'major mediator of harmony and order'[20] in the re-establishment of an equilibrium between economic and familial relations disturbed by the growth of industrial capitalism.

Education was central to this process. As an explicit instrument of socialisation, the provision of formal schooling took a gendered form. As part of their lived experiences, the broader educative experiences of family, community and workplace also took a gendered form, to teach boys and girls and men and women about their respective social positions, to inform their ideas about people and about themselves and how life 'ought' to be.

This broad approach and the identification of the paid and unpaid work of women as a key issue shaped this study in several ways. Firstly, it informed the initial focus for research, with the decision to locate this in geographical regions where the paid work of women and girls showed substantial variation; that is, in the cotton textile regions of industrial Lancashire and the agricultural districts of rural Norfolk and Suffolk. This was then followed by investigation of the lives and work of women in industrial West Yorkshire and Derbyshire, in the mixed economy of greater London and in urban and rural Somerset in the west of England, to see if initial and tentative conclusions held true in the broader picture thus obtained.

Secondly, the approach adopted here is very different to that conventionally employed by historians of education. Detailed attention to schooling is combined with detailed attention to changes in the organisation of agricultural and industrial production and to developments and tensions in responses to social change, to chart the complex and multiple realities that informed the context of women's lives and education. Only in this way can we explore beyond 'ideological stereotypes'[21] of working-class women in this period, to recognise similarities and differences in their experiences and to identify common factors of cause and consequence.

Thirdly, this dimension has informed the organisation of the book, as the evidence reveals patterns of change within the century that falls into three broad periods. Thus the development of industrial capitalism and changes in the organisation of agricultural production meant that the first four decades of the century were marked by considerable social tension with major implications for schooling and for the lives and work of women. This was followed by a period of accommodation from around the middle of the century, with the values of 'reformism and respectability' placing an increased importance on formal schooling and on the domestic responsibilities of working-class women. Finally, the later part of the century was marked by what Walby has referred to as 'first wave' feminism involving women from all social classes,[22] but where the involvement of the state gave an increasing emphasis to the schooling of girls as preparation for a domestic future.

Chapter 1 thus develops the theoretical models which have informed this work, to chart changes in the lives and work of women in the nineteenth-century industrial districts of Lancashire and to explore interconnections between the cultural values of patriarchy and economic and social organisation. This is further developed in Chapter 2, through an examination of the very different experiences of women living in the agricultural districts of Norfolk and Suffolk in the East of England. Chapters 3 and 4 then relate this to the purposes and practices of schooling in this early part of the century, both that provided for the working classes and the 'alternative' forms of schooling originating within the working class. This is followed in Chapters 5 and 6 by a discussion of developments in formal schooling in the later part of the century, including the increasing influence of the state on the nature and quality of elementary schooling. Chapter 7 then focuses on the impact of schooling on the lives of working-class women, with an evaluation of their educative experiences in schooling and in family and community life in a concluding discussion of the causes and consequences of nineteenth-century elementary schooling for girls. The final chapter then moves from the past to the present, to consider the implications of the 'lessons of history' for analysis of current developments in the schooling of girls in the later twentieth century.

One final point remains to be made. I have already referred to the dearth of research and publication on the subject of working-class girls' schooling in this period. This stands in contrast to the extensive scholarship that has been undertaken in the area of women's work, with the rediscovery of an earlier generation of writers such as Alice Clark and Ivy Pinchbeck and more recent publications by writers such as Sally Alexander, Maxine Berg, Judy Lown, Sonya Rose, K. D. M. Snell[23] and many others. For this reason it was decided to concentrate specifically local research on the schooling experiences of girls, whilst relying on more easily accessible and published materials, both contemporary and recent, to investigate the lives and work of women. Inevitably, therefore, though the study contains new evidence hitherto unpublished, it also draws heavily on more familiar sources such as official state publications and contemporary writings as well as recent publications. In bringing together new research into the schooling experiences of girls in this period with detailed evidence of women's lives and work, the book is able to offer new and more critical ways of understanding the causes and consequences of women's schooling – or a lack of it – in relation to their lives and experiences, to illuminate both the nineteenth-century past and the twentieth-century present.

1 Patriarchy Challenged? Women and Work in Nineteenth-century Industrial Lancashire

THE EARLY STAGES OF INDUSTRIALISATION

The organisation of labour in proto-industrial textile production foreshadowed its organisation in capitalist industrial production, with an occupational interchange between the work of men and women that defined spinning as 'skilled' male work and weaving as 'unskilled' women's work. Pinchbeck explained this in simple terms, suggesting that it was their physical strength that made male spinners numerically dominant and 'skilled' workers.[1] But a singular explanation of physical strength as the sole criterion of occupational competence fails to recognise the significance of ascriptive criteria in defining the respective capabilities of men and women and the ways in which the advantages enjoyed by some workers, mainly men, can be utilised to reinforce and gain advantage, often at the expense of more vulnerable workers, mainly women. As the spinning machines became more complex, a sub-contracting system of labour organisation developed whereby the spinner directly employed several assistants (piecers), often his wife and/or children, paying for this out of his own piece-rate earnings. It was the replication of his paternal authority within the family within this supervisory role which defined the adult male as a spinner, and it was essentially their control over the recruitment to the 'skilled' ranks of the spinners that the direct employment of the piecers gave them that confirmed the spinners' well paid and skilled status. Women spinners also recruited their own piecers, but although they were said to do their work 'as well as men'[2] they were not seen to possess the same authority and, therefore, were not accorded the same status. Through this enhancement of the paternal authority of the male spinner, the early factories thus supported traditional family gender relations, with a tolerable alignment of cultural values and the organisation of production.

The characteristic factory employment for women in textile production was that of weaving, but this did not become a 'skilled' factory occupation. For the conditions of eroded apprenticeship regulation and worker control that eased the entry of women into weaving were also the conditions that marked the long and painful decline of hand weaving from an artisan craft skill to the debased trade that it had become by the 1830s. And it was the competition of the handloom that led to the tight profit margins and low wages of factory weaving and contributed to its definition as 'women's work'. For if mechanised factory production was to be profitable it also had to be cheap. As Factory Inspector Saunders recognised,

> The small amount of wages paid to women acts as a strong inducement to employ them instead of men, and in power loom shops this has been the case to a very great extent.[3]

Receiving only 'supplementary' wages, women weavers were not only cheaper to employ, they were also seen to be more amenable to the discipline of the factory and less able to resist the loss of the autonomous work habits that they had enjoyed under the domestic system of production. Women were also seen to lack the physical strength and technical skills needed for supervisory work as tacklers and overlookers. Nor was it general for them directly to recruit their assistants, though these were paid from the women's piece-rate earnings, and no apprenticeship system developed, such as that associated with spinning. Despite their numerical dominance and the economic importance of their labour, female weavers were not, therefore, accorded the authority and status enjoyed by the male spinners and represented no direct threat to the spinners' patriarchal authority in the factory.

Despite this, the organisation of factory weaving as a predominantly female occupation led to an increasingly vociferous outcry against the employment of 'factory girls' in the 1830s. It was here, in the 'unnatural' reversal of family roles and responsibilities apparently caused by the factory employment of women weavers, while male handloom weavers experienced ever lower wages and declining employment, that working-class family life was seen to be 'turned upside down'. Here that the 'inversion of the existing social order' was causing 'ruinous consequences', with children growing up 'like wild weeds' and husbands 'condemned to domestic occupations' while 'the wife supports the family'.[4]

Many such complaints were heard from many different groups; from working men to aristocrats such as Lord Ashley,[5] from the Utilitarian philosophers to the Evangelical Christians, from male spinners, male weavers, working men in a variety of occupations and sometimes from women themselves. But there was no common origin or pattern to such complaints in the 1830s, nor were they by any means universal. Beyond a broad adherence to general principles of patriarchy, there was no cross-class or proletariat intra-class consensus as to the nature of these complaints, or, as yet, as to proposed remedies. The issue of what the social and economic roles of working-class women 'ought' to be under industrial capitalism remained open at this point.

Male handloom weavers, for example, bitterly resented the factory employment of women as weavers and actively sought the imposition of legal limits on their hours of work. But they seem to have regarded the work of women as a symptom of their problems as much as a cause. It was the greedy exploitation of employers and the failure of the government to honour its responsibility to protect working people against such exploitation that forced men, women and children to work ever longer hours in competition with each other and against the weaving machines. Conversely, the solution to the problems of the hand weavers was for the government to impose wage controls and limit the hours of *all* factory labour, and thus control this destructive competition. As the handloom weavers understood it, the appropriate role of women weavers was one where they worked alongside their husbands, fathers and families, fitting in paid work with domestic work as they had done in the former 'golden age' of domestic production.

In contrast, the 1820s saw a hardening of the male spinners' attitudes and the development of a systematic, sustained (and sometimes vicious) campaign of opposition against women's factory employment, supported by an increasingly explicit gender-defined rationale. Their immediate opposition was directed against the increased employment of female spinners in the factories. This was a cost-cutting strategy adopted by Lancashire manufacturers in the later 1820s, with 'whole mills' being said to be operated by female mule spinners working at half the piece-work rates previously paid to men.[6] In response, male spinners adopted specific policies to exclude women from the trade, barring them from membership of the amalgamated Union in 1829 and excluding female piecers from the training that would enable them to become skilled spinners. It was the perceived unfairness of women's 'competition' and the threat that this presented to their job security and wage levels and to their 'right', as men and as the fathers of families to be paid more than women, that galvanised male spinners into defensive action. As a union official explained in the *Manchester Guardian* in 1824,

We do not stand opposed to women working, but we do enter our protest against the principle on which they are employed. The women, in nine cases out of ten, have only themselves to support, while the men generally have families. This the employers know, and of this the unprincipled take advantage.[7]

The immediate threat presented by female competition had declined by the later 1830s, as increasing use of long and double mules placed a premium on physical strength, and productivity and profitability were seen to be increased by the employment of male spinners.[8] The male spinners' fear of such competition nevertheless remained potent whilst at the same time changes in the organisation of production presented additional threats to their authority and status. The development of large urban factories after 1825, where the spinning and weaving processes were combined under one roof, brought large numbers of women weavers into the workplace who were outside the supervisory authority of the spinners. Increased production on the long and double mules also meant unemployment for numbers of spinners while those who retained their jobs experienced heavier work loads at reduced rates.[9] Even more significantly in this context, an increase in the number of piecers needed to operate these machines simultaneously undermined the apprenticeship system of recruitment and the spinners' control over entry to the trade. To the adult male spinners of the 1820s and 1930s, therefore, working women represented both a direct threat to employment and an indirect threat to their 'paternal' authority when both were also under attack from other developments. Smelser's argument, that it was the erosion of the close working relationship between the adult male spinner and his piecer son that largely caused the dissatisfactions evident amongst the spinners, has been convincingly attacked, but his contention that the 1820s saw 'an array of threats to the family's traditional organisation'[10] has considerable validity if reexamined from the perspective of family gender relations and working-class notions of masculinity. So, a policy of occupational segregation by gender, involving the exclusion of women from an areas of work where they competed directly with male workers represented a strategy utilised by the spinners – and by other groups of male workers – in the struggle against new conditions of economic exploitation as well as a defence of the traditional authority of the male as the head of the working-class family. In such instances class struggle took a gendered form.

This was not universally the case. There were those who argued the importance of collective action, with men and women of the working classes joining together in a defence of cultural values and ways of life and against exploitation. This view found its strongest expression amongst the Owenites. In an editorial in *The Pioneer* in 1834, for example, James

Morrison argued that equal pay for male and female tailors could eliminate the problem of cheap female labour undercutting male earnings and employment:

> since man has deemed her (the working woman) to inferiority, and stamped an inferior value upon all the products of her industry, the low wages of woman are not so much the voluntary price that she sets upon her labour, as the price which is fixed by the tyrannical influence of male supremacy. To make the two sexes equal, and to reward them equally, would settle the matter amicably; but any attempt to settle it otherwise will prove an act of gross tyranny.[11]

Yet even amongst the Owenites opinions were divided. The majority of Owenite tailors, for example, supported exclusionist rather than co-operative policies as a defence against female 'competition', with strikes against the employment of women in 1827 and 1830 and a declaration of 'war against the female tailors' in the strike of 1834.[12] For the majority of working men, principles of gender equality and co-operation had little substance when they came into conflict with deeply felt notions of masculinity, and well-tested exclusionist strategies against the encroachments of cheap competition seemed to offer a more immediate defence than the long-term, untested and intangible benefits of co-operation with female workers.

If the disturbances of the 1820s and 1830s had at their heart a defence of working-class family and gender values, wider political dimensions also intruded to make the industrial districts a prime site of what Perkin has called 'the struggle between the ideals' that marked the transition to an industrialised and class-segregated society.[13] Thus, the work of the 1832 Committee of Inquiry into the factory system was also seized upon as an opportunity to revive the 'true Tory principles' of aristocratic paternalism as a panacea for social ills. As a vehicle for high Tory propaganda, it was therefore inevitable that Sadler's Committee of Inquiry would be affronted by any instances of cruelty, abuse and immoral behaviour found in the factories, not least because such abuses signalled the abrogation of the social responsibilities of those with power to protect and promote the well-being of working people. And in defining the factory employment of women as a major social problem, the aristocratic paternalists also sought to underline the extent to which they shared common ground with many working men. Here, therefore, can be seen an important source of the distortions, exaggerations and misrepresentations of evidence presented in the report of Sadler's Committee. Yet, though followed by a second Committee of Inquiry in 1833 which moderated many of the claims made in the first report, it was the picture drawn by Sadler that captured the public imagination. This was the 'evidence' that informed a stream of pamphlets, speeches and books to present a picture of almost unrelieved hardship and cruelty, moral degradation and abuse that signalled the supposed collapse of family life in the cotton districts of Lancashire. The central figure in this picture was the so-called 'factory girl', the ignorant and immoral wife and mother who so neglected her family responsibilities that family members were reduced to a condition of near savagery. Thus writers such as Gaskell and J. P. Kay (who as Kay-Shuttleworth was to be responsible for state educational policy from 1839), and many others, united to label the factory employment of Lancashire women as a prime cause of social problems in an outbreak of moral panic that swept the country in the 1830s.

Many factory owners and workers denied these charges with equal vehemence, not least on the grounds that very few *married* women actually were employed in the factories.[14] The 'truth' of the situation in the industrial North, however, was informed by preconception and prejudice and subjective judgements prevailed over facts and figures to give substance to fears about the deterioration of family life in the Lancashire cotton towns. The deficient and depraved factory girl thus became an established figure in popular imagination.

It must be emphasised, however, that there was no concerted movement to define the roles of women in solely domestic terms in the 1830s. Even the supporters of paternalism believed that in the interests of self-reliance, everyone in the family should undertake economically productive work, though in the case of the mother of the family this should be 'fitted in' around her primary domestic responsibilities. And, though many male workers sought to control the conditions of women's labour, the thrust of working-class political activity remained directed towards a reduction in the length of the working day for *all* workers to give some protection against exploitation and, most importantly, to preserve some semblance of family life in the new conditions of factory employment.

THE FACTORY ACTS OF 1833 AND 1844

Such hopes were disappointed by the Factory Act of 1833. Indeed, by restricting the factory employment of children but not that of adult workers the Act further exacerbated disjunctions between the organisation of factory labour and working-class family life. Evasions of the terms of the Act were widespread but many children were dismissed as being too young to work or not worth the trouble and expense of providing with schooling as the Act required, while the practice of working children in relays (shifts) became commonplace. The 1833 Act thus increased problems of child care and also encouraged the employment of adult women in compensation for the loss of child earnings.[15] That mothers might be compelled to work in the cotton factories instead of their children was 'deprecated as extremely mischievous' by the 1833 Commissioners[16] and, not surprisingly, the outcry against the factory labour of women remained vociferous. Lord Ashley, the Chairman of the Select Committee appointed to oversee the operation of the 1833 Act, for example, condemned the 'disgusting language' and behaviour of married women factory workers who, he said, neglected their family responsibilities in favour of drinking and smoking on the grounds that 'if I have the labour, I will also have the amusement'.[17] Many similar criticisms were made in the later 1830s and in the 1840s, largely repeating those made in the early 1830s but, in contrast to the earlier outcry, condemnation of the 'evils' of the factory system was now extended to include calls for legislative controls over women's work, even the exclusion of women from the factories altogether.

At the same time a new concept of working-class gender roles was emerging, with male workers claiming their moral right to a 'breadwinner' wage sufficient to maintain a family without the need for a wife's wages, and enabling married women to concentrate exclusively on domestic concerns as they 'ought' to do. The *Ten Hours Advocate*, the official mouthpiece for the campaign for shorter working hours in the textile factories expressed the argument in the following terms:

> it is needless for us to say, that all attempts to improve the moral and physical condition of female factory workers will be abortive, unless their hours are materially reduced. Indeed, ... married females would be much better occupied in performing the domestic duties of the household, than following the never-tiring motion of machinery. We therefore hope the day is not distant, when the husband will be able to provide for his wife and family, without sending the former to endure the drudgery of the cotton mill.[18]

In articulating such views the male working class neither 'colluded with pressure from the bourgeoisie', nor were they 'bought off' by the capitalists as has been suggested,[19] but were exercising choices compatible with their cultural beliefs, experiences and values. The campaign for short time, for example, was a movement to improve conditions for all workers, including male workers, and, as such, was an expression of an alternative theory of the economics of factory production against the political economy of the manufacturers. Very simply, workers believed that the amount of work available was limited and that competition between manufacturers caused over-production, declining profits and lower wage levels. Regulation of hours of work would, therefore, take the edge off this damaging competition, share out work more equitably, and help to smooth out the slumps and booms that led to rushes of work interspersed with periods of under- and unemployment. As the primary wage earner of the family, a male worker, as a husband and father, had an *a priori* right to work that was greater than that of a female worker; a 'right' that was reinforced in terms of family economics by the generally higher wage he received and by legislation such as the 1834 Poor Law which gave men the sole responsibility for the economic welfare of families. The woman worker, particularly the married woman worker, not only had less 'right' to work, she was a cause (and a consequence) of working-class poverty. Her presence in the labour market flooded the labour supply and reduced wage rates, and she took work away from those who had a greater need. As the Miners' Association bluntly expressed the argument in 1843, 'keep the women at home to look after their families ... decrease the pressure on the labour market and there is then some chance of a higher rate of wages being enforced'.[20]

Support for control of women's employment and the idea of a male breadwinner wage and the wholly domestic wife can also be seen as a logical extension of the classic exclusionist strategies employed in the early craft guilds and later worker associations to safeguard their skills and status against the encroachments of the unskilled. The period between the later 1830s and early 1840s, for example, was a period of intense industrial conflict between the spinners and their employers, with technological innovation leading to labour surplus and reduced wage rates, and with threatened job losses from increasing use of the self-acting mule, which, or so the manufacturers claimed, could be readily operated by cheap, unskilled and docile women workers. Small wonder then that, as leaders of many of the Lancashire short-time committees, the spinners were in the forefront of the campaign to exclude women from the factories or at least to restrict their employment to designated areas of 'women's work'.

Even for unskilled and semi-skilled workers, the rhetoric of the breadwinner wage had a moral validity that could be used to bolster claims for better conditions of work. Though the evidence is slight, it seems that the weaving unions also gave support to this ideal, despite the importance of women's paid work in this area. Speaking at a meeting in Clitheroe in 1853, for example, Margaret Fletcher told the young women in the audience that whenever a young man pays his address to you and wishes to make you his wife, ask if he is able to maintain you. If he says he is not, tell him to go about his business, for you never intend when married to go out to work.

Similarly, in a speech at Bolton, she urged 'all married women to stop at home, to nurse their children and keep their husbands comfortable'.[21]

The extent to which groups like the spinners and weavers were influenced by bourgeois views on the roles of women is impossible to quantify, though their expressed views were very similar. It is likely, however, that this was a deliberate policy on the part of workers. For while industrial protest was received with considerable alarm as an unwelcome manifestation of working-class recalcitrance, the articulation of demands in terms resonant of bourgeois family values was calculated to receive a far more sympathetic response from many members of the middle and upper classes. Male workers also played on public fears of social disorder and a deputation to Sir Robert Peel on 'the Ten Hours Factory Question' in 1842, for example, warned that unless women were withdrawn from the factories 'the consequences ... cannot fail to be fraught with danger to the state'.[22]

Public sensibilities continued to be assaulted throughout the 1830s by reminders of a persistent failure to subdue the working classes, as strikes followed riots and mass demonstrations of popular discontent. Even more seriously, the working classes were presenting a direct challenge against the state, through the articulation of alternative economic, social and polit- ical theories of the rights of labour through the trade union movement, within Owenism and in the mass political movement of Chartism. This was, in Schwarzkopf's terms, 'the first self-initiated and self-organised mass movement of the British working class'[23] and, through the later 1830s and 1840s the movement united a whole range of working-class struggles and aspirations in common cause within the campaign for the enfranchisement of the male working classes.[24]

Evidence of political sedition and industrial unrest amongst the working classes was viewed with profound disquiet by the middle and upper classes, with a widespread concern for 'the condition of England' in the 1840s. And here the Evangelical Christians found common ground with the Benthamite Utilitarians in seeing an extension of 'middle-class' values as the means to alleviate social ills. Both also saw working-class women as having a crucial role to play in the achievement of social well-being and harmony. The moral and spiritual regeneration of the nation and the security of the social order were thus to be furthered by legislation and other strategies designed to educate working people towards more 'intelligent' behaviours, including a 'civilised' understanding of the proper roles of women within the working-class family. If the economic doctrines of *laissez-faire* denied the complete ban on the factory work of women that the Evangelicals would have wished, restriction of their hours of work would give the protection that women's natural fragility required and would allow them to devote more time to home and family. Further, the extension of schooling to factory girls eventually would lead to the voluntary withdrawal of married women from the factories, as girls learned 'civilised' behaviours and values, with a proper appreciation of their responsibilities as wives and mothers.

Such views were not universal. There were those who recognised the benefits to women – and to society in general – of the availability of relatively well-paid work. In his report on handloom weaving in 1840, for example, Hickson argued that 'the great drawback to female happiness ... is their complete dependence and almost helplessness in securing the means of subsistence'. The availability of well-paid employment meant that Lancashire women were not forced into early marriages by the need to find a home, and, he continued,

> the consciousness of independence in being able to earn her own living, is favourable to the development of her best moral energies. It is a great error in our view of social economy to suppose that the interests of either sex requires that the other should be restricted in the right of acquiring or holding property.[25]

Such views were out of step with popular opinion, however, and though the majority of manufacturers also opposed legislative interference in their concerns, a Factory Act of 1844 officially labelled women and children as 'unfree agents' requiring the protection of the state in their relations with employers. Like that of children, the factory work of adult women became subject to regulation, with a prohibition on night work and with a limit of 12 hours on the length of the working day. The educational requirements of the 1833 Act also were strengthened to make factory children 'half-timers', with a division of their time between factory labour and the compulsory schooling that was to be the means of teaching them the desired behaviours that were to 'civilise' the industrial population.

TOWARDS CONSENSUS

By the end of the 1840s, the collapse of Chartism meant that fears of revolution had all but disappeared and the 1850s were marked by a lessening of overt class-conflict and an evident mellowing of social class relations in an era of 'reformism and respectability'.[26] Issues of gender were again fundamental to this process, with the principles and practices of patriarchy providing both the model and the means for the reconciliation of conflicting interests. Patriarchy provided, in short, a hegemonic framework for cross- and intra-class accommodation.

The immediate consequence of the 1844 Factory Act was a decline in the employment of children and a sharp *increase* in the factory work of adult women aged over 20, from around 42 per cent of female factory labour force in 1841 to 57.4 per cent in 1851. Further, according to Hewitt's estimates, this was paralleled by an increase in the employment of married women and widows from around 27 per cent of female labour in 1847 to around a third of the female workforce in 1873.[27] Yet this increase in the factory work of married women was *not* accompanied by expressions of public outrage. And here we have a curious dichotomy, with on the one hand, an apparent agreement between the male workforce, the state and paternalists such as Lord Ashley that the factory work of women, particularly of married women, was undesirable and, on the other hand, an apparent acceptance of their continuing, even increasing presence in the factories. It can be argued quite correctly that the notion of the wholly domestic wife was entirely inappropriate to the exigencies of working-class life, with a gross disjunction between the male breadwinner ideal and the failure of many male workers to earn wages sufficient to maintain a non-earning wife. Nevertheless, the question still remains, why was there no continuing furore against the factory work of women in the 1850s and 1860s on a scale of that seen in the 1830s and 1840s?

The short answer is that though women's factory work was defined as unacceptable in bourgeois and unionist rhetoric, it actually was acceptable – under the right conditions. And the right conditions were achieved when the organisation of factory labour became compatible with the organisation of family life and working-class gender concepts. Working men may or may not have achieved a breadwinner wage, women may or may not have been employed in the factories, but the equilibrium disturbed by changes in economic production in the earlier part of the century was being effectively restored as the values and interests of working people and of capital gradually became reconciled. And as accommodation was achieved and antagonistic class relations mellowed into a cross-class adherence to the mores of respectability, so also moral panic regarding the factory employment of women declined.

Contrary to the arguments of Hartmann and other exponents of the simple consensus model of mid-century patriarchy, the majority of capitalist manufacturers did not recognise that their long-term interests lay in paying 'breadwinner' wage levels to their male workers.[28] Most Lancashire industrialists were strongly of the opinion that it was the right of workers of either sex to 'dispense their labour on whatever terms and under whatever circumstances they may individually and independently see fit', were 'averse to all legislative interference in their concerns', and generally were motivated by the immediate and the expedient.[29] But if expediency denied adherence to domestic ideologies and issues of morality gave little justification for the payment of breadwinner wages, economic expediency did support an implicit process of industrial negotiation, wherein manufacturers and worker associations bargained with each other, according to the strengths and vulnerabilities of their relative positions. And, in the relatively prosperous post-1850 period, when generally booming markets and healthy profit margins, steadily improving wage levels and greater job security supported less antagonistic labour relations, both workers and their employers generally were ready to negotiate and compromise in the accommodation of their respective interests.

This is most clearly evident in the case of skilled workers such as the spinners. By mid-century, the spinners had come to terms with the new order of industrial capitalism and, as skilled workers, had developed strong and exclusive 'closed' unions strongly opposed to the employment of women in their trade. Despite the claims of the machine builders, spinning on the new self-acting mules remained a technically demanding job, with a skilled and experienced spinner making an appreciable difference to output. The spinner–piecer system also was a convenient, effective and established method of management and recruitment, and, with the former recalcitrance of the spinners much reduced by the disputes and defeats of the 1830s and early 1840s, the manufacturers were prepared to support their continuing authority within the factory. The relationship that developed was consequently one of mutual dependency as employers came to recognise that efficiency and profitability were more effectively supported by co-operative relationships with the new model, moderate unions of mid-century. And in the implicit contract developed between the spinners and manufacturers, the employers gave support to the status of spinning as a skilled, male occupation deserving of breadwinner wages sufficient to support a family. Thus, with average wages of around just under 22*s* in 1850, 24*s* in 1860 and 28*s*–30*s* in 1870,[30] a spinner was able to support a wife and two children in a respectable life-style, without the need for the wife to work in the factory. Indeed, in Joyce's analysis, there was a stigma attached to women's paid work in the spinning stricts that did not exist in the weaving areas.[31]

The case of the weavers was very different. As easily replaced unskilled and semi-skilled workers – and with male workers in a numerical minority – their unions were forced to rely on collective tactics to enhance their bargaining position. This collaboration of male and female weavers achieved some success, most notably the achievement of a standard list for wages in Blackburn in 1853, but the weak and often short-lived weaving unions were seen by the manufacturers as essentially subordinate, to be used or ignored as expediency directed. The much lower wages paid to weavers, therefore, reflect not only the cheapness of 'women's work' but also the weak bargaining position of the unions, though the two are inter-related in many complex ways. And with wage rates of around half those paid to spinners at 11s per week in 1850, 12s 6d in 1860 and 14s in 1871,[32] male weavers were most definitely not in a position to support a non-earning wife and family, except in conditions of the most grinding poverty.

Evidence of differences in the employment patterns of women between the weaving and spinning districts of Lancashire also demonstrates that the 'new model' family form of private patriarchy, with a wholly domestic wife economically dependent on her breadwinner husband, was incompat-ible with the financial circumstances of weavers. The proportion of adult women in employment in cotton in the spinning towns of Bolton and Oldham in 1861, for example, was, at 25 and 31.6 per cent respectively, appreciably lower than the 38.4 and 35.6 per cent of women employed in the textile factories in the weaving towns of Blackburn and Preston.[33] By the turn of the century, when the geographical split between weaving in the north and spinning in the south of the county was well established, only around a fifth of married women worked in the spinning mills of Bolton and Oldham but around a third were working in the weaving sheds of Blackburn, Burnley and Preston. Though it was 'almost automatic' that a working-class girl would work in the factories throughout the industrial districts, most women in the spinning towns left the factories when they married or when their first child was due. In contrast, in the weaving towns 'the married woman's "double shift" was commonplace' and in some instances 'none of the local mothers stayed at home as housewives, but each kept her job on in the nearby mill'.[34] A more traditional model of family life was therefore maintained in the weaving districts, with wives combining domestic work with earning much as they had always done.

An equal obligation to earn was matched, on the surface at least, with a rough and ready equality between male and female weavers. Male weavers possessed no special technological skills, their position as a numerical minority and union strategies of collective action operated

against explicit gender differentiation and men and women worked alóng-
side each other and were paid the same rates for the job. In the reality,
however, though relations between the weavers and their employers
were more exploitative and antagonistic than the paternalistic
employer/employee relations that seem to have been relatively common in
spinning,[35] an implicit consensus came into play which structured the
work of men and women along clearly defined gender lines. Supervisory
jobs as tacklers and overlookers were reserved for men, 'driving' and
other coercive pressures to greater productivity were more often directed
against women and a 'real, though unobtrusive segregation' operated to
deny equal earnings to women. 'There is no attempt to discriminate
between women's work and men's work as such', suggested the Webbs,

> But taking the cotton weaving trade as a whole, the great majority of
> women will be found engaged on the comparatively light work paid at
> the lower rates. On the other hand, the majority of the men will be
> found practically monopolising the heavy trade, priced at higher rates
> per yard, and resulting in higher weekly earnings.[36]

Men also dominated the leadership of the weaving unions and, though they
used gender-inclusive language that recognised the importance of women's
contributions to collective action, trade-union rhetoric constructed workers
as masculine and marginalised women.[37] In effect, though male weavers'
earnings may have been too low to allow conformity to the male breadwinner ideal, male dominance was reinforced within the factory through gender
segregation and female subordination, and, in Joyce's words, 'by unofficial
means, sanctioned by the employers, the inequality of the sexes was sym-
bolised and proclaimed to the cotton community'.[38]

   This recognition that the re-establishment of a symmetry between the
organisation of factory labour and family values and divisions of labour
allowed a variety of life-styles, and that social equilibrium could also
accommodate the factory wife, also casts new light on the notion of 'a
coincidence of interests between philanthropy, the state and the male
working class' from the 1840s.[39] If reinterpreted in terms of the
reaffirmation of *patriarchy*, with its constituent elements of male dominance and female subordination, supported and sustained by gender divisions of labour, then the consensus model makes sense. The
reinterpretation of patriarchy expressed in the ideal of the male breadwinner and the dependent housewife served an important purpose in
linking the aspirations of the working classes to the social and cultural
norms of the bourgeoisie, but this 'new model' family form within a
private form of patriarchy did not meet adequately the needs of capital or

of much of the work-force. The reinforcement of patriarchy as a fundamental principle of social organisation, however, provided an infinitely
more flexible model. For the manufacturers, utilisation of the values and
practices of patriarchy encouraged the goodwill, stability and welfare
(through improved standards of domestic care) of the skilled work-force
and the smooth operation of production. At the same time, it also maintained a supply of cheap, readily exploited, female labour that could be
used or discarded as market forces dictated. For skilled workers, 'new
model' private patriarchy supported their 'honourable' labour and pride
in skill, their masculine self-esteem and high wage levels, whilst also
providing for the full-time services of their wives at home. For the
unskilled male workers, with domestic dislocation eased somewhat by
the imposition of controls on women's labour, the reconstitution of the
traditional patriarchal family and gender differentiation in the factory
buttressed male pride, while domestic ideologies, in theory at least, gave
moral substance to claims for higher wages. Some adjustments had
proved necessary to accommodate conflicting values and concerns, but
with the acceptance of the principle of a male breadwinner wage for *key*
workers and the imposition of overt and covert limitations of women's
factory work to sustain gender divisions of labour and female dependence, the immediate and long-term interests of capital, the state[40] and
the male working class had become reconciled in a consensus that was
both ideological and pragmatic.

WOMEN'S VIEWS

Meanwhile, what of the women themselves? What were their views?
Bland assumptions that the interests of women were 'indisputably
included in those of ... their fathers ... (and) their husbands' and that their
views could be 'struck off without inconvenience'[41] were being challenged
in the early part of the century. Women were involved in all forms of
working-class protest and, as the words of a female correspondent to the
Owenite *Co-operative* magazine in 1829 demonstrates, they were beginning to question the right of men to speak for them. 'Who', she asked,
'... shall settle the question of the true social position and claims of
women?'

> Men have hitherto done it. How has it been done? They have dictated
> duties towards themselves, and, with general consent, have punished us
> severely when those duties have not been rigidly observed ... have any

of the self-named reforming parties, so vociferous now in England for their own rights, given a single thought to, or shown any desire for ... change in this helot condition of their country women?[42]

The rights of women were an important issue for debate amongst the Owenites. Yet when a female member of the audience at a meeting of the United Trades Association observed

> that a great deal was said of the slavery of the working classes, and of the inadequate wages of the men, but never a word of the slavery of the poor women, who were obliged to toil from dawn to midnight for seven or eight shillings a week

the response, as expressed in *The Crisis*, was that 'the still small voice of woman ... must be suppressed for a season till men be served'.[43]

But that voice was not altogether suppressed and in the 'Page for the Women' begun in 1834 in *The Pioneer*, the second most widely read working-class newspaper of the period, that 'still, small voice' expressed female grievance with considerable force. Nevertheless, it is difficult to sustain an argument that female involvement in protest and reform movements was marked by a desire for major change in social relations of gender or for female independence. It might be argued that the domestic perspective and self-depreciating language often employed by female protesters represented an attempt to pre-empt male hostility, but though they protested against injustice and hardships in the *operation* of gender ideologies, it would seem that women did not challenge traditional gender-based family roles and relationships of men and women. If working men were strongly defensive of their notions of masculinity, so also were women of their femininity. Speaking as 'wives, mothers and daughters', with their protests 'often couched in terms which suggest the restoration of lost rights rather than the establishment of new ones',[44] the demands expressed by women demonstrated a wish for an ideal society wherein they could meet their responsibilities towards their families, take an 'honourable' pride in their domestic skills and be treated with respect. Women also strongly defended their right to earn a decent living when compelled to do so. An early suggestion, put forward in *The Examiner* in 1832, that many of the ills of contemporary society could be solved by excluding women from factory work altogether brought this amusingly expressed, but deeply serious response from 'The Female Operatives of Todmorden'.

> You are for doing away with our services in the manufactories altogether. So much the better, if you had pointed out any more eligible and

practical employment for the surplus female labour, ... If our competition were withdrawn and short hours substituted, we have no doubt that the effects would be as you stated, 'not to lower wages, as the male branch of the family would be enabled to earn as much as the whole had done', but for the thousands of females who are employed in manufactories, who have no legitimate claim on any male relative for employment or support, ... what is to become of them? ... It is a lamentable fact, that, in these parts of the country, there is scarcely any other mode of employment for female industry, ... We see no way to escape from starvation, but ... fairly to ship ourselves off to Van Diemen's land, on the very delicate errand of husband hunting; and having safely arrived at the 'Land of Goshen', jump ashore with a 'who wants me?'[45]

Many working-class women seem therefore to have supported the ideal of a male breadwinner wage – or at least to have accepted it as the best means of improving their own position. A reliance on circumstantial evidence is unavoidable here, as women's declining participation in radical protest and political movements around the 1840s (and the marginalisation of women's concerns within Chartism[46] and unionism) means that there is little direct evidence of their views. It does seem, however, that women 'accepted an image of themselves which involved both home-centredness and inferiority' from around the 1840s.[47] It may well have been, as Dorothy Thompson also suggests, that working-class women were primarily concerned with issues of class struggle, but there were also strong incentives for women to give their support to the union ideal of the male breadwinner wage. The women of industrial Lancashire may have developed a tradition of well-paid work and enjoyed a degree of independence unmatched elsewhere in Victorian England, but it was an independence that was really only available to the young single girl.[48] Married female factory workers carried a very heavy burden and were rightly described by a contemporary observer as 'the slaves of Lancashire society'. 'On Saturday', wrote Ellen Barlee, 'the mills close at midday and the men and single women make real holiday', but

> the married women, who seem the slaves of Lancashire society, are obliged then, however, to set to work harder than ever. They have only this day to clean their houses, provide for the week's bake for the family, mend clothes, besides doing any washing that is not put out, and attend the market to purchase the Sunday's dinner ... Then there is also washing the children and setting them to rights ... so that the poor mother seldom gets a rest ere the Sabbath dawns if, indeed, she is not up all night.[49]

In Joyce's opinion, their work in the factories was a source of pride and respectability to women workers in the weaving districts,[50] and this may well have been the case. But it also seems likely that a conspicuous display of domestic excellence (and of wifely obedience) was also made necessary by the continuance of women's paid work, with women's self-respect being demonstrated and judged by the standards of domestic competence displayed in the home. Burnett has remarked, for example, on the constant concern expressed in nineteenth- and early twentieth-century autobiographies with cleanliness and order, commenting that 'this preoccupation, amounting almost to an obsession in some housewives (sic), was a distinguishing feature of the "respectable" working class, marking them off from the feckless, dirty, uncaring and undeserving poor'.[51] The respectable working wives of Lancashire may have been paid wage levels above those available to women elsewhere, but their lives were hardly enviable. As Taylor has argued,

> Perhaps in the New Moral World it would be possible, as the Owenites promised, to integrate collectivised domestic work with other productive and intellectual employments, but in the Old Immoral World housework and waged work had become a terrible double load which no woman would willingly take on so long as she had a husband (or some other conjugal partner) to support her. The 'ideology of domesticity' was not just a set of oppressive ideals foisted on a supine female population; it was an ideology actively adopted by many working-class women as the best in a very narrow range of unhappy options.[52]

The male breadwinner wage ideology unfortunately did little to emancipate women from this crippling work-load. Indeed, the reverse was often the case, with the assumption that women's wages were essentially supplementary depressing both male and female earnings. Women were trapped in a vicious circle; with employers able to pay low wages to men secure in the knowledge that the earnings of wives would bring family incomes up to subsistence level, many women had little choice but to work for wages.[53] Similarly, the assumption of female dependence ignored the plight of widows and other women supporting families, for even the relatively high wages of a weaver were, at around 11s a week in 1850, 12s 6d in 1860 and 14s in 1870, totally inadequate for family support.[54] If many women welcomed the shorter hours of work imposed by the 1844 Factory Act there were also many who were desperate to work as many hours as possible in order to earn sufficient to feed their children, and of the 1,133 workers interviewed by Factory Inspector Horner in the late 1840s, it was the men rather than the women who preferred shorter working hours.[55]

The disadvantages of the non-earning housewife's position were not so immediately apparent, particularly if she had a 'good' husband. Mary Merryweather found, however, that many women had very low expectations of their treatment by their husbands. She remarked:

If we said to a poor woman who came for relief, 'I hope your husband is kind to you', the answer often was, 'Well Ma'am, he don't pay (beat) me', implying that she was grateful for that amount of goodness.[56]

The breadwinner wage was seen to be earned by the husband, with the work of his wife being perceived, if recognised at all, as a labour of love, not deserving of any economic reward. Writing in *The Pioneer* in 1834, Frances Morrison described the 'power relations' in working-class families dependent on male wages as ones where women were subject to their husbands in 'a yoke of bondage'.

If a working man should make thirty shillings a week he may drink ten pints if he pleases; go to a coffee house and read the papers, and bring in fifteen shillings a week to keep the home and pay the rent withal. *He has the right to do this*, for he makes the money. But what is the woman doing? She is working from morning till night at housekeeping; she is bearing children, ... And all this for nothing; for she gets no wages. Her wages come from her husband; they are optional; he can give her either twenty shillings to keep house with, or he can give her only ten. If she complains, he can damn and swear, and say, like the Duke of Newcastle, 'Have I not a right to do as I please with my own?' And it is high treason for women to resist such authority and claim the privilege of a fair reward for their labour! [original emphasis][57]

We do not know how many working men may have abused their power in this way. The point is, as Morrison stressed, that men had a *right* to use 'their' wages as they wished and, indeed, there is evidence that numbers of men kept their wives in ignorance of their true earnings and that a chief cause of secondary poverty was the practice of husbands keeping a large part of their wages for personal use.[58]

This is not to imply that all working-class husbands were domestic tyrants and their wives downtrodden victims, but as the norms of 'respectability' show very clearly, the social and cultural world of the post-1850 period was constructed in line with a male view of the world, to give priority to male concerns and interests. As Kirk has commented, 'respectable workers had a strong and positive evaluation of home and family ... (but) much of the responsibility for the cultivation of "sound" and "respectable" habits within the family was placed on women'.[59]

Conversely, women were also held to be responsible for non-respectable behaviour on the part of husbands and families and male drunkenness and other disreputable behaviour, for example, was attributed to the failure of 'lazy, slovenly, mis-managing wives' to maintain expected standards of domestic comfort.[60]

Such failings were often attributed to a lack of training in domestic economy, and while education was seen as a route to independence and political and social freedom for men, for women it was the route to domestic efficiency. Similar gender-based distinctions can also be seen across all the key elements of respectability. If for men it meant self-reliance and independence, with a refusal to be 'petted, pampered and patronised' by their social superiors, it meant the exact opposite for women. They were naturally incapable of managing their own affairs beyond the care of the household, their reliance was to be placed on the superior wisdom and strength of their father or husband, and any show of independence was distinctly unwelcome. Self-respect, for men, lay in 'honest endeavour' in their employment, in providing for the economic needs of their families and in a strong commitment to personal advancement. For women it meant honest endeavour in domestic labour, in providing for the domestic, emotional and moral needs of their family and a strong commitment to the advancement and well-being of her husband, children and kin. 'Respectability' was, therefore, defined by patriarchal principles to mean, for women, the abnegation of individual rights against the higher claims of husband, home and family.[61]

The unions had come to terms with the new order of industrial capitalism and the political movement of Chartism had come to an effective end by the 1840s. At the heart of reformism lay the principles and practices of patriarchy, permeating all aspects of Lancashire life and imposing heavy burdens on women. Men had negotiated the terms of social and industrial peace in the industrial districts of Lancashire but it was largely women who paid the costs.

CONCLUSIONS

It is impossible to evaluate the impact of industrialisation on women's level of participation in paid labour but it is clear that, whether their paid work increased or decreased, the early stages of industrialisation in no way 'emancipated' the working-class women of the industrial North, or equalised relations between the sexes. Differences in task allocation, in wage levels and in status, though blurred in some areas, continued to differentiate between the work of women and men and still located women in the lower ranks of labour hierarchies inside and outside the factories. Even the 'independent' female weaver hardly was paid enough to finance a decent standard of living, let alone the dissipated life-style that was attributed to her in the popular imagination.

The 'factory girl' nevertheless was seen as a direct threat to the security, earnings, status and authority of the male work-force and, through her very visible presence in the factory, was also a symbol of the threatened or actual loss of all that working people held dear – and which they sought to defend through industrial and political action. Though the majority of female factory workers were single women, though women did not directly challenge the patriarchal status quo, the organisation of women's work in economic production was a major source of tension in inter-class conflict in the industrial North.

Concern about the factory employment of women was widespread across all social ranks. With the awful warning of where class conflict had led the French nation not many years previously, many feared the apparent depravity of factory women and the supposed collapse of family life amongst the industrial working classes as harbingers of similar events in England. For the Evangelical Christians the factory work of women signalled the moral degeneracy that was the root cause of social disorder. For the paternalistic Tories, on the other hand, issues of women's work represented an opportunity to gain the support of working people in a common defence of traditional values against the challenge to their authority presented by ascendent capitalist interests. The result was the definition of the factory employment of women and the perceived collapse of family life amongst the industrial working classes as a key issue of the 1830s, and the subject of continuing conflict, debate and negotiation between labour, capital and the state over subsequent years.

The real significance of gender issues, however, was that the utilisation of gender divisions of labour and of the cultural values of patriarchy gave power – to threaten, to undercut, to bargain, to gain support – to both manufacturers and to workers seeking control over the processes of production. For the manufacturer, the employment of women as cheap outworkers and machine operators maximised profits and attacked the skills-based monopolies of male occupational groups. On the worker side, exploitation of gender divisions was seen to support the position of skilled male labour within the factories and, ultimately, the well-being of the working classes overall, with expression of the cultural values of patriarchy giving a moral imperative to claims resonant with the values and anxieties of contemporary society. And in seeking alliance with the industrial working classes against the encroachments of the Liberals and Radicals, the Tories also recognised the political mileage to be gained from concerns of gender in establishing common cause with workers and exploiting public anxieties towards support for the paternalistic values they espoused.

Gender issues were, in sum, vulnerable to exploitation by the powerful in furtherance of their own economic, social or political ends and it was for that reason that they become highly visible and high-profile concerns.

They were also central to the reconciliation of conflicting interests that took place around mid-century. As Joyce has commented, the success of employer hegemony in the North lay not in the imposition of ideologies but through an engagement with the family values at the centre of people's lives and through a redefinition of the family economies of factory workers.[62] Whether in 'new model' form or in the traditional pattern of family life, the organisation of the working-class family and the organisation of production became reconciled in a collusion of patriarchal interests. Whilst the erosion of patriarchy was a major source of conflict in the early stages of industrialisation, its reaffirmation was a major source of the cross-class consensus that marked the second half of the century. Class struggle had taken a gendered form and so also did the hegemonic alliance between workers, capital and the state.

2 Women's Work in Agricultural Production: Nineteenth-century Norfolk and Suffolk

The Eastern counties of England have been described as 'the pioneers and centres of the new commercial agriculture'[1] in the nineteenth century and, as in the industrial districts of the north of England, the development of modern capitalism provoked far-reaching changes in the organisation of labour within agricultural production. These were changes which had a major impact on the lives and work of women and on the organisation of family life amongst the working population.

In the immediate context, perhaps the most significant effect of the intensification of capitalist farming was a drastic curtailment of the income generating opportunities available to women. In the earlier eighteenth century the wives and daughters of small owner–occupiers and those with access to common land could make an important contribution to family incomes by growing crops and raising livestock for subsistence or sale. Women also worked in domestic textile production and men, women and children all contributed to family subsistence, with family life being organised on a semi-independent basis. The relocation of textile production to the industrial North, meant, however, that this source of income was lost to women in the region. 'Some years back', reported the 1843 Commission on the Employment of Women and Children in Agriculture,

> the labouring classes of Suffolk and Norfolk were much better off than they are now, owing to the very general employment of women and children in hand spinning. That employment has been put an end to by machinery and no other domestic manufacture has been found to take its place.[2]

The enclosure of common lands and the associated spread of large farms across the East of England had also deprived rural women of many of their traditional agricultural by-employments by the early nineteenth century, forcing them and their families to an unprecedented dependence on agricultural wage labour as a means of earning a living. At the same time the loss

30

of the commons raised the costs of subsistence by making it necessary to purchase items such as fuel and food previously obtained at little or no cost.

The practice of employing single women as residential farm servants was also in decline, and by around the 1830s distinctions between the agricultural work of single and married women had largely disappeared, with both searching for work as day labourers. Changes associated with the intensification of capitalist farming in the mid-eighteenth century, however, had extended and consolidated long-standing gender divisions of labour with, in the counties of Norfolk and Suffolk, a greater concentration on cereal production reinforcing male dominance in heavy and skilled work in ploughing and harvesting.[3] Women's agricultural work was thus limited to casual and seasonal employment in haymaking and spring weeding and to relatively minor tasks in harvesting.[4] As a result, many women were forced into a situation of almost complete economic dependence, and as the 1806 report of The Society for Bettering the Condition of the Poor commented, with an implicit recognition of the customary expectation that women should have an economically productive as well as domestic role, women were often 'laid up for the Winter' and became

> a burthen on the father of the family, and in many cases on the parish. The wife is no longer able to contribute her share to the weekly expenses ... In a kind of despondency she sits down, unable to contribute anything to the general fund of the family, and conscious of rendering no other service to her husband except that of the mere care of his family.[5]

Unfortunately, all too often male workers were also unemployed or worked only on a casual basis. Some attempt was made by the Poor Law Commissioners to suggest that this was a consequence of the 'displacement' of male labour by female, with the work 'which should be performed by the men' being thrown 'on the shoulders of women',[6] but in the situation of labour surplus that prevailed in the region, there were few incentives to ignore customary gender roles. Indeed, the need to offset possible reductions in wage costs against likely rises in poor rates resulting from the unemployment of family men operated as a real disincentive to substitute female for male labour. In contrast to the situation in Lancashire, gender divisions of labour in agriculture were reinforced and extended, and while issues relating to female employment began increasingly to be seen as problematic in the industrial North, the issue of female *un*employment was seen as a major contributory factor in the conditions of poverty and high poor rates that were present in the rural East.

Rather than being displaced by the cheap competition of female labour, male workers, like female workers, were suffering the effects of a general

surplus of labour and the seasonal labour requirements of cereal production.[7] Even skilled workers such as stockmen and horsemen were
employed by the week or day and the farm labourer had become essentially a casual worker, to be hired and dismissed at the farmer's conve-
nience. As a Suffolk clergyman told the Poor Law Commissioners in
1834, 'the number of unemployed labourers is such that a farmer is always
sure of hands when he wants them. It is cheaper to hire day labourers ...
especially as they are always sent home on a rainy day.'[8] Even if men and
women were able to find work, declining wage levels and rising costs
meant that family earnings frequently were too low to meet family needs –
with a well-documented rise in parish poor rates in the later eighteenth
and early nineteenth centuries linked to a spiralling vicious circle wherein
subsidy of wages depressed wage rates and where the employment of
those on relief forced independent labourers on to the parish.

If the payment of poor relief gave families some protection against the
worst effects of underemployment, the unmarried, especially single
women, were left particularly vulnerable. Though theoretically entitled to
poor relief, single women were frequently paid a mere pittance or were
denied relief altogether, with the intention that this would force them into
domestic service – virtually the only alternative occupation open to rural
girls – thereby saving the parish the expense of their maintenance.[9] The
single woman was, to put it bluntly, 'surplus' to local needs and was seen
to be an unnecessary drain on local resources.

Rural girls were also 'devalued' by the operation of gender divisions of
labour and the limited opportunities to contribute to family incomes that
were available to them. Flora Thompson wrote of family life in
Oxfordshire in the 1880s:

> The parents did not want the boys to leave home. Later on, if they
> wished to strike out for themselves, they might even meet with opposi-
> tion, for their money, though barely sufficient to keep them in food,
> made a little more in the family purse and every shilling was precious.
> The girls, while at home, could earn nothing ... if there was any incon-
> venience it must not fall on the boys; if there was a limited quantity of
> anything the boys must still have their full share.[10]

Writing in 1892, Jeffries similarly commented on the attitudes of rural
families towards girls:

> If a thoughtful English peasant women rejoiced that in her house a son
> was born, it would be, not because 'she had gotten a man from the
> Lord', but a thanksgiving that it was not a girl ... an aged agricultural

woman said that she would rather have seven boys than one girl; for the former, when they became lads, went out and earned their own living, but the girls you never knew when they were got rid of ... the girl is made to feel every day her fault in being a girl.[11]

With little alternative work available for girls domestic service became the 'chief field of labour for young women' in the region,[12] and the out-migration of village girls became a regular feature of life in the rural communities. Typically, girls started their lives in service in the homes of the wealthier members of the community and then moved on to more distant employment after learning the basic skills of their trade. Nine-tenths of the domestic servants in the county town of Ipswich in Suffolk at mid-century, for example, were girls from the country districts, and a high proportion of the 32,000 Suffolk-born people said to be living in London at this time would have been women and girls in service.[13] Though Richards' description of domestic service as disguised underemployment aptly sums up the ways in which domestic work absorbed what gender ideologies and divisions of labour had jointly defined as the 'surplus' labour of women,[14] it still held many attractions for the country girl. Not least amongst these was the fact that, unless exceptionally unfortunate, the quality of food and accommodation in service would have been far superior to that available in the average labourer's home, and that, in comparison with other female occupations, service offered a well-paid job with some prospects.[15] Perhaps even more importantly, service offered a well-defined and easily accessible escape route away from the poverty-stricken conditions of the rural areas towards a better future.

For those unwilling or unable to enter domestic service, often the only viable alternative was marriage, and, as statistics of falling marriage ages demonstrate, many saw marriage as 'a defence against the unemployment that increasingly was the lot of women'.[16] Even where women could find work, wage levels were so low that, as Hampson has argued, often 'marriage at any price, or even illegitimate relations, seemed to women the only solution'.[17] Indeed , mothers were said to encourage the seduction of their daughters, so that they might marry and so leave the family home.[18] Parish officials were also quick to force marriages under the Bastardy Act of 1773 or even to bribe men into marrying 'troublesome females' where a woman's marriage removed parish liability for her maintenance – and the apparent willingness with which women co-operated with parish authorities is clear evidence of, as Pinchbeck put it, 'the straits to which women were reduced by the weakness of their economic and social position'.[19] The situation envisaged by the female operatives of Todmorden, where female unemployment meant that 'husband hunting' represented virtually the only 'escape from starvation',[20] was all too close to the truth for many women in Norfolk and Suffolk.

Early marriage may have eased the immediate problems of the unmarried, but the concomitant rise in the birth-rate, unmatched by any corresponding increase in employment, served only to expand the over-abundant supply of labour, with a self-sustaining impetus towards worsening under- and unemployment. And, like the handloom weavers and the disaffected factory workers of the North, the working people of Norfolk and Suffolk felt a deep sense of grievance against the new economic and social order, with a widening gulf between the work-force and their social superiors marking the dismantling of the reciprocal ties of obligation that had justified the inequalities of the old social order. The economic doctrines of *laissez-faire* had replaced paternalism as the determining principles of social organisation, leaving working people unprotected against the malevolent operation of the 'laws' of supply and demand. The lives of the rural work-force had indeed been turned 'upside down' quite as much as those of the handloom weavers of Lancashire, with the economic imperatives of capitalism riding equally roughshod over the customary ways and values of working people.

THE 1834 POOR LAW

It was, as Hobsbawm and Rudé have described 'an explosive situation',[21] with sporadic outbreaks of violent protest in 1815, 1816 and 1822. Then, in 1830–1831, grievance found expression in the protest, riots, and attacks on machinery and property that became collectively known as the 'Swing Riots'.

Riot was not without its temporary gains, but riot also bought harsh retribution, with swift and forceful reaction from the authorities quickly subduing insurrection. Unlike the recalcitrant working people of the industrial cities of the North who continued to defy all attempts to subdue protest, the working people of the rural districts had shown they were unable to sustain opposition against the forces of law and order. The failure of their protest had exposed their essential weakness and, with their last scruples removed by a sense that the labourers had forfeited any rights to paternalistic protection, the leaders of rural society were ready to endorse any scheme which promised to enforce obedience – and to reduce the payment of the poor relief which was seen to have encouraged the indolence and insolence that underpinned disaffection. The New Poor Law of 1834, with its coercive operation of imperatives towards 'independence', was seen to be the ideal instrument for the achievement of such goals.

The Poor Law Amendment Act became law in July 1834 and was swiftly implemented in the southern counties. 'Independence' was now to be encouraged by the substitution of indoor relief in a workhouse for the payment of poor relief, and with the workhouse regime nicely judged to be 'less eligible' than the standard of living enjoyed by those who worked to support themselves and their families.

Recognising that a decline in the paid work of women (and of children) was a major contributory element in rural poverty, the Poor Law Commissioners anticipated an increase in women's paid employment with approval. One witness to the 1834 Commission, for example, suggested that 'by providing work for their wives and children also, [the farmers] would contrive to make the earnings of the family adequate to their support without any allowance from the parish'.[22] The labourer also was expected to demonstrate his 'independence' by finding work 'not only for himself, but for his wife, and as many of his family as might be able to work ... seeing that nothing but the united efforts of all the family could then keep them out of the workhouse'.[23]

Literary evidence apart, there is little firm evidence from which any increase in women's agricultural work after 1834 can be gauged; the essentially casual and seasonally erratic nature of the work they did made it largely invisible and census returns seem severely to have under-estimated the size of the female work-force.[24] Nevertheless, taking Higgs's calculations as guidelines for an admittedly crude estimate of the size of the hidden female work-force, the numbers of women field-workers can be calculated at around 7,000 in Suffolk and nearly 9,000 in Norfolk in 1841, though with seasonal and regional variations in the extent of such work.[25] Many of those seeking work, however, were forced into the labour 'gangs'; a system of subcontracting labour which first appeared around the 'open' parish of Castle Acre in Norfolk in 1826, in response for a demand for labour in 'closed' parishes where strict controls over residency limited village populations. Here, long hours of hard physical labour and long journeys to and from the place of work brought small rewards. Like the putting-out system in textiles, where the sweated labour of women and children went to enhance profit margins, the gang system was, as Mr Denison commented in his report to the 1843 Commission on the Employment of Women and Children in Agriculture, 'a mode of getting out of them [the workers] the greatest possible amount of labour in a given time for the smallest amount of pay'.[26]

The 1843 Commission recognised that the 1834 Poor Law was a prime cause of the rapid expansion of this highly exploitative system.[27] Yet, as far as the majority of farmers, landowners and rural ruling classes were concerned, the effects of New Poor Law were wholly beneficial. It had achieved its aim of reducing the costs of poor relief, had encouraged desired habits of 'independence' and, as an instrument of social control, was effective in instilling attitudes of 'respect' towards their social superiors amongst working people. But though the prospect of unemployment and the workhouse meant that 'the men had to be more submissive than they used to be ... and the masters knew it',[28] the 'respect' thus exhibited was grudging, with an enforced and surface deference disguising deeply felt grievances. Indeed, by the later 1830s social relations between the farming classes and the rural proletariat had deteriorated to such an extent that Digby's description of the situation as an 'undeclared civil war' hardly exaggerates the case.[29] As a witness told the 1837 Select Committee on the Poor Law,

> the ill feeling between the labouring people and those above them is very bad; there's a very strong and ill feeling now, much more than is generally imagined, much more than I have witnessed in the North on any occasion.[30]

The coercive operation of the New Poor Law had been the final blow that had shattered the chains of social dependence. From functional protest, where working people sought to remind their social superiors of their obligations, disaffected labourers turned to covert protest to express their bitterness and alienation. This took many forms; animal maiming, poaching, the sending of threatening letters and, above all, incendiarism. And by the 1840s arson attacks had become so common across the two counties that local people wryly referred to incendiarism as 'our disease'.

TOWARDS CONSENSUS?

National interest in the situation in the region was generated by an extended investigation into the conditions of labouring families by Thomas Campbell Foster of *The Times* newspaper,[31] and for a brief period the problems of rural Suffolk were in the forefront of the 'condition of England' debates of the early 1840s. But as the radical MP John Bright observed, with a cynical appreciation of the real motivation often underlying expressions of social concern, 'If they had in Lancashire, instead of 250 fires in nine months, one in a month, much surprise would have been expressed that they (the members for the manufacturing districts) had not made a proposition for an investigation into a matter of such consequence.'[32] And when a motion was put forward for a parliamentary inquiry into the events in the region, it was easily defeated when the Home Secretary and the members for Norfolk and Suffolk denied the evidence of rural discontent and social unrest.

Unlike the threatening hordes of the industrial districts, the bovine and plodding peasantry of the East seemed to possess little real potential for disorder and violence. What did a few fires matter in comparison with mass political movements such as Chartism, which threatened the very foundations of English society? And if existing systems of social control were sufficient to contain disturbances to the locality, why bother to seek additional solutions?

Nor was the paid work of Norfolk and Suffolk women seen to be a problem. Neither farmers nor workers nor even the social arbiters of rural communities raised any objections – economic, cultural or moral – against the employment of women in field-work before the later part of the century. Not only was the 8*d* a day a woman might earn essential to the family budget, the absence of these 'supplementary' earnings would very quickly have exposed the weaknesses of the workhouse system as an instrument of social control. In almost complete reversal to the situation in Lancashire, in rural Norfolk and Suffolk the under-and unemployment of women was the problem, whilst the paid work of women was an integral part of the 'solution' to social and economic difficulties.

There was, however, some limited local interest in the benefits to be gained from a less exploitative, more paternalistic system of social relations between the classes, with the extension of a limited number of benefits to the 'deserving' members of the working population to promote feelings of gratitude and obligation. Probably the most effective paternalist strategy was the provision of small allotments of land, with the intention that working men would spend their leisure time in useful and productive labour instead of wasting time and money in the beer-shops. But rather than providing men with a useful and rewarding spare time activity, the allotment provided economically productive work for *women* as an alternative to field labour,[33] and an opportunity to re-create a way of *family* life that had been eroded by capitalist agricultural development. As the 1843 Commission recognised, the allotments were the only thing 'which at all supplies the place of spinning'[34] in providing work that allowed women to supplement family incomes without too drastic an interference with their domestic responsibilities. The allotment was thus an effective means of institutionalising agricultural paternalism as it represented and enabled, albeit in a small way, a return to 'traditional' values and ways of life across all spheres. It restored an equilibrium to the organisation of labour in production and in the family.

To this extent, the operation of paternalism in the countryside was consistent with ways in which more paternalistic industrialists sought to mute protest and control the work-force.[35] But though the gentry and clergy of Norfolk and Suffolk might have had a positive appreciation of the advantages of 'soft' forms of coercion, the farmers generally did not. The economic relationship between the labourers and farmers was not one of mutual dependency such as that enjoyed by the spinners, but was more akin to that of the weavers and their employers, with the added disadvantage to the labourers that even mass collective action was ruled out by rural isolation. In the situation of labour surplus that prevailed there was simply no need, as the farmers saw the case, to make any material, social or cultural concessions to the labourers. Paternalism was unnecessary, potentially damaging in undermining the control which forced deference and obedience, and, therefore, it should be ignored or actively subverted. Indeed, few farmers actually provided allotments or gave financial support to other services such as schooling.

There were further inconsistencies between approaches to social control in the industrial and agricultural regions, the most noticeable of which was the absence, at this point, of any attempt to structure gender relations or to control the paid work of rural women. Not surprisingly, the Commissioners inquiring into the agricultural employment of women and children in 1843 found much to deplore. Like her counterpart in the industrial North, the rural wife and mother was said to be deficient in every way. Her children were physically and morally neglected and she was ignorant. 'Even where they have been taught to read and write', stated Mr Austin,

> the women of the agricultural labouring class are in a state of ignorance, affecting the daily welfare and comfort of their families. Ignorance of the commonest things, needlework, cooking and other matters of domestic economy, is described as nearly universally prevalent.[36]

Just as in the factory districts, the supposed deficiencies of the rural housewife were held to be responsible for the undesirable behaviours exhibited by male labourers.

> The husband is also a sufferer from his wife's absence at home. There is not the same order in the cottage, nor the same attention paid to his comforts as when the wife remains at home all day ... He may come

home tired and wet; he finds his wife has arrived just before him; she must give her attention to the children; there is no fire, no supper, no comfort, and he goes to the beer shop.[37]

Unlike the case in Lancashire, however, the sheer incongruity of domestic ideologies to the economic situation of labouring families does seem to have occurred to the Commissioners, and there was some expressed ambivalence regarding the acceptability or otherwise of women's paid work. Even Mr Austin was able to appreciate that the 'moral' strengths of domestic ideologies might be undermined by the evils of poverty. 'Upon the fullest consideration', he wrote,

> I believe that the earnings of women employed in the fields are an advantage which, in the present state of the agricultural population, outweighs any of the mischiefs arising from such employments. All direct interference in the employment of women in agriculture must be deprecated at present. The evils that attend it can only be relieved by generally bettering the condition of the agricultural labouring class.

Even the injurious moral consequences of female employment in the labour gangs were counterbalanced by an awareness that, should it be curtailed, 'immorality and crime would be increased by idleness and distress'.[38]

What is apparent here is a clear appreciation of the harsh economic realities of working-class life that is noticeably absent from the majority of similar observations on the factory employment of women. Issues of scale and familiarity may well have influenced judgements; large numbers of the women of Suffolk and Norfolk were not engaged in unfamiliar and 'unnatural' work in 'competition' with men and, most importantly, the situation did not generate widespread fears of social and political revolution. With perceptions undistorted by issues of social control and moral panic, the supposed deficiencies of rural women could, therefore, safely be ignored.

In the 1850s the geographically and socially isolated world of the eastern farming communities began to open up with the coming of the railways. New opportunities became available to working people, particularly those with some education and out-migration began to accelerate. The process was often gradual and cumulative; from the village to the local town to larger urban centres or following the lead of a pathfinder from the village, but even as early as 1851, a contemporary observer calculated that 15 Suffolk-born people had moved away for every 100 still living in the county.[39] The result was a loosening of the stranglehold grip of the farmers, as labour surplus was reduced and farmers began to realise that they were in danger of losing their younger and more enterprising workers. Wages began slowly to rise and conditions slowly to improve as farmers sought to keep their labourers and as the labourers themselves began to assert a genuine independence in strike actions and occasional combinations. The gradual disappearance of the labour surplus after the 1850s meant that conditions very definitely were improving for labouring families.

Improved conditions also seem to have been accompanied by a decline in female agricultural work, with an estimated fall to only around 2,000 Suffolk women and around 3,258 Norfolk women in field-work in 1861.[40] Mr Frazer of the 1867 Commission of Enquiry on the Employment of Women and Children in Agriculture attributed this to 'natural and spontaneous influences'. 'Everywhere', he said, he 'heard the same story',

> that women are found to be less and less disposed to go out to work upon the land. They will refuse unsuitable work; they will stay at home on wet days. Whether from easier circumstances in which they live, or from their having become intelligent enough to make more accurate measure of loss and gain, there seems to be much less attraction for them in the farmer's 8d. or 9d. a day than there used to be.[41]

A further report in 1869 also commented on this trend. 'There seems to be almost everywhere, an increasing disinclination to field work on the part of women', stated Mr Norman,

> (they) told me that although they themselves had always been in the habit of working they had made up their minds that it did not answer ... They seem to be arriving at the conviction that where a cottage is to be kept clean and tidy, and a family provided for, the whole time of the mother of the family should be spent indoors, and that the money she can earn by going into the fields is insufficient to compensate her for the necessary loss which is occasioned by her absence at home.[42]

Mr Frazer confessed, however, to some real perplexity on the subject, weighing the pros and cons of women's field work in an argument which considered several aspects of the issue. There was, first of all, the now strongly established convention that women ought not to be engaged in work so inappropriate to their 'natural' sphere. 'It is universally admitted', he said,

> that such employment, ... is to a great extent demoralising. Not only does it almost unsex a woman, in dress, gait, manners, character, making her rough, coarse, clumsy, masculine; but it generates a further

very pregnant social mischief, by unfitting or indisposing her for a woman's proper duties at home.

Field-work also disinclined girls from their 'proper' work as domestic servants and dairymaids. On the other hand, women were needed on the land and it was said that Norfolk farming 'could not be effectively performed without them'. Their earnings often also were still vital to family budgets and, Mr Frazer continued,

> there is an almost universal opinion that only be a tyrannical use of power could the legislature step in and prevent, at any rate adult and married women, from gaining their livelihoods and adding to the scanty resources of their family by any means that are honest and in themselves innocent.

And if single women were excluded from field labour, what else might they do?

> if domestic service, marriage, needlework, shops and charing will absorb the women there will be no moral risk of excluding female labour from the fields ... if such exclusion narrows the range of female occupations, and a class of idle or starving women is produced, the gain to morals is doubtful enough.[43]

The solutions put forward to the 'evils' consequent on female agricultural work were the same as those employed against women's factory labour; legislation to control what were seen to be the worst abuses and the education of girls towards a proper appreciation of their womanly duties. Thus the Agricultural Gangs Act of 1867 limited the employment and labour of children and provided that gangs should be strictly segregated by sex, with women's gangs being accompanied by a licensed female as well as the gang master. The rest was left to the power of education to reinforce those 'natural and spontaneous influences' that were attracting women into domesticity.

We see here, in the reports of the Commission, a similar shift in thinking to that seen in Lancashire in the 1840s – and one with a similar alignment of cross-class interests. But unlike the case in Lancashire, where political and economic interests fused with ideology and culture to structure the perceptions and experiences of men and women, the increasingly home-centred attitudes of rural women that are signalled in these reports seem to have resulted from a situation where what suited working men and women was acceptable to employers[44] and more or less coincided with middle-class ideologies of gender. Natural and spontaneous the desire to avoid lifting turnips on a wet day may well have been, but what seems to have been the key influence here was the relative improvement in economic conditions that freed many women from a need to work in the fields to the same extent as previously. A slight rise in the proportion of boys aged 10 to 14 in paid work[45] may, possibly, represent a shift in values in line with middle-class ideologies, with the employment of boys in field-work being seen as more suitable than that of their mothers. But, though the distinction is a subtle one, it seems more plausible to suggest that an improvement in the economic position of families allowed a return to more traditional ways of life, consistent with long-held and deeply felt family values. With rising male wages, many families could now manage on the combined earnings of husbands and sons with, probably, the harvest earnings of women and possibly also the products from an allotment. The position of the husband and father as the main provider was thus restored, while the wife and mother was again able to combine her domestic responsibilities with some income generating activities. Equilibrium had been re-established.

What is particularly striking about the situation in Norfolk and Suffolk, however, is the extent to which relations between working people and their social superiors remained alienated, with a complete failure to instil any sense of working people having, in the Duke of Richmond's phrase, 'a stake in the hedge' of rural society. In their exodus from the countryside working people were voting with their feet against oppression and the 'grandmotherly control' implicit in paternalistic benevolence. As a Suffolk unionist was to put it in the further flare-up of class antagonisms in the 1870s, through their blatant economic oppression and denial of the traditional values of labouring families the leaders of rural society 'have been crushing us ever since we left Paradise. They got us down – feet, legs, hands, arms and shoulders.'[46] In the 1860s there was, almost by default, some restoration of the family values of working people and of masculine and feminine self-esteem. But, just as the labourers cried to the firemen rushing to put out fires in the 1840s, it was 'too late, too late'. Alienation had gone too far and the result was continuing class-conflict and antagonism.

CONCLUSIONS

The moral panic created by the apparent depravity of factory women contrasts rather strangely with the view that a prime solution to the problems of rural society was the employment of married women in independent labour away from the home environment. What would maintain the family

– and the socio-economic status quo – in one region was seen to threaten their very foundations in another. Married women in both regions continued to organise paid work around the demands of family and home, taking what casual, ill-paid work was available and fitting it in around child care and domestic labour, and the loss of traditional by-employments in textiles and family-based agriculture and the need to seek work away from the domestic environment probably caused greater dislocation to the organisation of family life in rural Norfolk and Suffolk. And if the unmarried factory girl was exposed to moral dangers through her 'independent' employment in the factory, what of the single female agricultural worker displaced from the familial environment of farm service into field-work or exposed to the moral dangers of extreme poverty?

Changes in the family and income-generating activities of rural women in the East of England were not seen to be problematic *per se*, because gender divisions neither offered, nor were seen to offer, any real economic or broadly political advantages to competing groups. In the situation of surplus labour that existed in the region there simply was no need to seek to erode any vocational skills that might give workers some control over the labour process or to pursue divide-and-rule strategies, setting female against male labour. Similarly, on the worker side there was little to be gained from any further extensions of gender divisions of labour. In preserving customary gender divisions of labour, the recruitment of the agricultural work-force remained congruent with the traditional value-systems of families.

Changes in the organisation of production did, nevertheless, threaten the traditional organisation of family life, did override the cultural values that located women as joint earners within a domestic context and did, in Smelser's terms, provoke an 'avalanche of disturbance' in the Norfolk and Suffolk countryside. But in flexing their collective muscles in opposition to the new order of things, the agricultural labourers had demonstrated their essential vulnerability. With acquiescence ensured by forceful coercion supplemented by the economic 'policing' of the New Poor Law, there was simply no need to seek accommodation with the work-force. Class struggle had been firmly subdued – or so it was thought – and issues of gender could be left undisturbed.

In both regions, economic changes had provoked considerable tensions in relation to the organisation of family life and traditional cultural values, but only in the industrial North, where issues relating to gender were vulnerable to exploitation by the powerful in furtherance of their own economic, social or political ends, did they become highly visible and high-profile concerns. In the agricultural regions of eastern England, the

developing class antagonisms of the early nineteenth century saw an iden-
tity of class interests uniting men and women of the rural proletariat in
common cause against the ruling and employing classes of the region. And
here the failure of hegemony lay in the failure to safeguard the family
values and 'cultural preconditions' of labouring families. In seeking to
impose control, in the rejection of the right of rural families to any 'stake
in the hedge' of agricultural capitalism, the rural classes of agrarian
society simply had denied the values at the centre of the family lives of
working people. The result was class alienation and antagonism.

3 Schooling for Social Control? The Early Nineteenth Century

Two basic questions are pursued in this chapter. Firstly, what were the purposes of schooling for working-class boys and girls? And secondly, because it cannot be assumed that intentions translated directly into practices, how were these reflected in schooling provision and enrolment? Neither question is singular in its focus; each contains a number of dimensions to include a whole variety of views on the merits (or otherwise) and purposes of schooling for girls and for boys of this class, and a whole variety of determinants, both ideological and pragmatic, that informed school provision and attendance. Stephens has warned that 'the nature and experience of elementary (working-class) education varied so much from place to place that to talk of a national condition is to distort reality',[1] and for that reason the focus on industrial Lancashire and rural Norfolk and Suffolk is continued, with comparisons between the two regions allowing commonalities of purpose and practice to be clarified, whilst also enabling the provision and operation of schooling directly to be linked to conditions of women and girls' family, community and work-place experiences discussed in Chapters 1 and 2.

THE PURPOSES AND PROVISION OF SCHOOLING

The idea that a period of formal schooling was a normal part of growing up for boys and girls of this class was not one that was general at the end of the eighteenth century. Education, work, family and community life were normally synonymous, with children learning the skills, knowledge, attitudes and behaviours of adult life through interaction with family and community members. This might include the learning of basic literacy skills, and in Lancashire there was a vigorous tradition of 'daily fireside education' where children were taught to read and sometimes also to write and to do basic arithmetic.[2] Some schooling was available and in Lancashire, the sons if not the daughters of weaving families had quite a good chance of attending school,[3] but formal schooling (or an

45

apprenticeship) essentially was a supplement to familial education or, in the case of orphans or other unfortunates, a substitute.

In equipping children for their adult roles parents inevitably were informed by the practical circumstances of their daily lives and the socio-economic and cultural status quo. Equally inevitably, therefore, the education of boys and girls encompassed gender-derived values and divisions of labour as well as class-cultural perceptions. Girls were taught spinning and husbandry skills and housework and child care by their mothers in preparation for their dual role as housewives and supplementary earners, and also that their place in the 'natural' order of things was relative to that of their father or husband and family. Boys similarly learned weaving and/or husbandry skills and were prepared for their role as chief breadwinner and 'head' of the family. Gender-based assumptions also defined the acquisition of literacy skills as being less relevant to girls, and it is doubtful whether the popular northern tradition of the educated and literate worker was ever seen to apply to girls and women at all. We do not know for certain that parents were less inclined to teach their daughters to read, but we do know that girls were much less likely to go to school, that endowments for the education of poor 'children' were used predominantly for the schooling of boys,[4] and that the curriculum of girls' charity schools gave a greater priority to the acquisition of domestic skills than to literacy. We also know that illiteracy was far more common amongst women than amongst men.[5] Differences in literacy levels were probably less acute in regions such as the east of England, where the scattered rural population rarely had access to a school and where popular cultural traditions gave little value to 'book learning', but here equality would have meant an equality of ignorance. Nevertheless, the meaning of education for the lower orders in both regions in the later eighteenth century was gender-specific, and in the bringing up and schooling of their children, the customary practices of working people assumed and replicated gender divisions and patriarchal values as the norm.

The shift to mechanised production of textiles largely worked against the educational traditions of weaving families, with increasing poverty and the need for all family members to work ever-longer hours denying the investment of time or money on education and schooling, and with existing school provision totally incapable of catering for the rapidly expanding, youthful population of Lancashire. In consequence, there was a sharp declined in literacy rates in the county after the 1770s.[6] These declining literacy levels seem to have caused little concern and, as Sanderson has commented, 'almost all the new factory jobs created by the new technology were successfully operated by sub-literate labour'.[7] While the technical skills of female weavers, for example, were much in demand and attitudes of deference and docility were seen to be vocationally relevant, an ability to read was not.

But if industrialisation helped to create a largely illiterate work-force in Lancashire, it also helped to create one that was seen to be turbulent and threatening; and if there was little concern about the illiteracy of the lower orders, there was considerable and very widespread concern about their undisciplined, 'uncivilised' and disrespectful behaviours, and the threats these were seen to present to the efficiency of production and the peace of the social order. It was fast becoming apparent that the largely amateur and parochial authority system of pre-industrial society was totally inadequate in the new social and demographic context of the rapidly expanding industrial towns. The former deference of the lower orders was beginning to give way to a new spirit of class identification with unwelcome manifestations of independence from the old social bonds, and, with an awareness of how easily antagonism and conflict could slip over into revolution, the middle and upper ranks of society became increasingly alarmed. Radical and revolutionary ideas were abroad and 'private property and public liberty' were seen to be threatened by the growth of 'a lawless and furious rabble'.[8]

A variety of palliatives and remedies were proposed and implemented; from increased philantrophy and poor relief to censorship, repression and coercion, and to calls for the moral regeneration of all ranks in society – but most particularly for the lower ranks. And one way of achieving this was to 'train up the lower classes in habits of industry and piety'[9] via the provision of schools for their children.

This was not a new idea. An enthusiasm for the establishment of charity schools in the eighteenth century had been motivated by the same zeal to rescue and reform the people. What was new in the early nineteenth century was the idea that *all* working-class children should attend school to learn 'civilised' habits of obedience – though preferably without too much expense and avoiding any encouragement to children to aspire beyond their ordained lot in life. Also new, in line with the concept of schooling as a vehicle for mass social reform, was the principle that the schooling of girls was equally, if not more important than the schooling of boys. As the wives and mothers of the future it was essential that girls should be educated in the 'correct' moral and Christian values so that they might extend a civilising and restraining influence on their husbands and children. This was emphasised by the two voluntary education societies established in the early nineteenth century, with the 1818 annual report of the parent branch of the Anglican National Society stressing the prime importance of educating girls. The Report urged that provision should be made for the instruction of as many girls as possible:

judging the right education of the female sex, even in the lower situations in life, to be of the utmost importance: it being obvious to every day's experience, that the training of younger children devolves upon the mother at an age very important for forming their principles and conduct: and in poor families where the wife has been best taught, the family is best conducted and the children brought up in the best manner.[10]

In some instances, the Society even brought financial pressures to bear to ensure that school places were provided for girls:

... where it was intended only to establish a boys' school the Committee have made their grant subject to the express condition that a girls' school also should be provided.[11]

Similarly, the largely Nonconformist British Society described educated girls as 'the leaven yearly put into the mass of human society' and urged:

however earnestly the education of boys is promoted, if we at the same time neglect the culture of the female mind, it is evident that the great object of our exertions will be very imperfectly obtained, if it should not be entirely frustrated.[12]

The part-time Sunday schools also sought actively to promote the schooling of girls. As the Stockport Church of England Sunday school declared in 1811,

Another motive that will prompt a benevolent and reflecting man to countenance Sunday schools is, that in them equal provision is made for the instruction of Girls as of Boys. Other charity schools are more designed for the education of boys; but girls have an equal, if not superior claim, because their influence is more extensive ... to correct those low and degrading practices which have prevailed in the manufacturing districts, and to raise the female character to its proper tone and influence in the lower walks of society, the instructions of the Sunday school are peculiarly well adapted.[13]

POPULAR VIEWS ON GIRLS' SCHOOLING

True to its *laissez-faire* principles the Tory government of 1807 declined an involvement in the provision of mass schooling, with Whitbread's proposal for a national system of compulsory schooling foundering on the issues of finance and control that were to block all attempts to establish a national, state system of education before 1870. And though the state became increasingly involved in educational matters after the payment of the first grant-in-aid in 1833, this reliance on voluntary provision left the way clear for a wide diversity of views to inform the purposes of working-class schooling, with a consequent wide diversity of provision apparent in the range, nature and quality of schooling available to the working classes. Though the weight of public rhetoric may have been inclined towards providing schooling as a means of creating a docile, co-operative, virtuous and loyal population of working people ready and eager to serve the needs of the economic and social order, there was no national consensus as to the advantages of mass schooling. Nor, in the voluntary context of schooling, was there any means beyond exhortation and appeals to individual generosity, of ensuring a sufficient supply of school places, nor any means of compelling working-class children to attend school. The gaps between the stated aims and intentions of the National and British Societies and the realities of provision and practice were thus often considerable – and nowhere was this more apparent than in the matter of girls' schooling.

Thus, while a rationale based on the imperatives of social reform emphasised the importance of educating girls for the moral responsibilities of marriage and motherhood, the rather more instrumental concerns of local school providers and supporters often saw the training of girls for the practical duties of domestic service as having a more immediate priority – a purpose which, particularly in this early period, attracted as much hostility as support. The 1815 annual report of Whitby British school for girls is representative of many similar, in its attempts to gain support for the school and disarm hostility.

> An institution of this kind not only recommends itself to the benevolence of the ladies of Whitby, but also to their interests. The difficulty of obtaining steady, industrious and faithful servants has long been a subject for just complaints. The school for girls can scarcely fail to have a powerful effect in removing this serious evil; for it will prove a valuable nursery for female servants trained up in habits of regularity and industry, integrity and goodness.
>
> Some, it is true, have asserted or insinuated that it is dangerous to educate the lower orders of society, particularly females: that servants who can read and write will be less dutiful and submissive that those who are ignorant, and that learning makes them arrogant, discontented and intractable.[14]

Even as late as 1833, the Ladies' Committee of the British Society still felt the need to comment on the particular difficulties that bedevilled girls' schooling. As they commented:

> Prejudices which, so far as the boys are concerned, have long since passed away, still hang around the education of girls and, it is to be feared, will not easily be dissipated.

And as they went on to say, popular views regarding the purposes of girls' schooling very definitely gave a low priority to the schooling of girls for the purposes of socialisation.

> The friends of the poor are commonly very selfish, or very shortsighted, with regard to the instruction of girls; – they forget the great majority of them will be mothers ... and mothers form the character of their offspring.[15]

WORKING-CLASS VIEWS

Similar tensions were also present in the 'alternative' educational views of the more radical elements of the working classes themselves. In the same way that unwelcome manifestations of working-class independence gave a dynamic to the provision of mass schooling, so also the narrow repressive purposes of the schools and classes provided for them by their social 'superiors' gave an impetus to alternative, indigenous counter-cultural educational theories and practices in the industrial districts of the North. It was better for working people to be without an education at all, it was argued, than to be educated by their rulers, 'for then education is but the mere breaking in of the steer to the yoke; the mere discipline of the hunting dog'.[16] The children of working people would *not* 'be taught their duties every day and all day long',[17] but, with their parents, would learn *really* useful knowledge and develop an ability to

> form right judgements, to see things as they really are, the real qualities and relations of physical objects, real facts and the real consequences of actions, it is their interests to be taught *nothing but the truth.* [original emphasis][18]

The purpose of education was universal enlightenment: because knowledge was good in itself, because it enabled individuals to develop their own talents and foster the communal good, and, above all, because the possession of knowledge and understanding would enable working people to bring about a reformed and just society. And if enlightenment was to be universal, education must be extended to all – boys and girls and men and women – and in ways that were accessible to all. And in reading and discussion groups, the circulation and reading of the working-class political press, in coffee houses, pubs and private homes, lecture halls, schools and classes, the radicals developed a varied, flexible, often haphazard and improvised but vigorous education 'network' aimed at this end.

Some radicals spoke explicitly of the equal rights of women to be educated. William Thompson, who became an Owenite in the 1820s, urged, for example:

> Let your libraries ... and your lectures ... be equally open to both sexes. Have not women an equal right to that happiness which arises from an equal cultivation of all their faculties that men have? ... Long have the rich excluded the poorer classes from knowledge: will the poorer classes now exercise the same odious power to gratify the same odious propensity – the love of domination over the physically weaker half of their race?[19]

An article in the Owenite journal *The Pioneer*, similarly gave support to women's education, stating

> While the working-classes are looking in a thousand ways for the means by which to extricate themselves from poverty ... one of the most fruitful sources ... is seldom thought of ... THE EDUCATION OF OUR FEMALE POPULATION. [original emphasis][20]

That there was a strong demand from women for education is unquestionable. Robert Raikes, who was popularly known as the founder of the Sunday School movement, said that 'mothers of the children and grown up women ... begged to be admitted'[21] to learn to read alongside the children, and, as letters to *The Pioneer* illustrate, there were many women eager to take advantage of the educational opportunities available to them. A 'Bondswoman of Birmingham' (Frances Morrison) wrote:

> it is time the working females of England began to demand their long suppressed rights. Let us, in the first place, endeavour to throw off the trammels that have so long enshackled our minds and get knowledge ... maybe the time is not distant when the superiority of educated females will be acknowledged over those who are kept in blind and stupid ignorance.

Another letter told of the efforts of the 'ladies of Leicester':

> the scandalous bye word of 'blue stocking' which has been thrown at every intelligent woman who happens to have more sense than her

stupid husband has not deterred the ladies of Leicester from uniting to obtain the advancement of themselves and their kindred.[22]

Unlike the Mechanics' Institutes of the period, the Owenite Halls included women amongst their members and these were an important, if numerically and geographically limited, venue for women's education in the 1830s and 1840s. Indeed, the issue of women's membership was used by working men as 'a handy stick with which to beat their middle-class competitors' in the struggle to wrest control of the Mechanics' Institutes from the middle classes in the 1830s.[23]

Owenite schools also catered for children of both sexes, with the constitution of Charlotte Street Owenite school, for example, displaying a specific commitment to equal opportunities, in stating that every child would be encouraged 'to express his or her opinions'. Similarly, Taylor describes the socialist infant school in Wisbech as having equal education for girls as one of its key policies in 1838, and with girls taking an energetic part in activities such as gymnastics.[24] But as the continuing debate in the pages of the socialist press illustrates, despite all the expressed commitment to the principle of gender equality, Owenite attitudes towards women's education were as double-edged and ambivalent as they were towards issues of women's paid work. 'Men tremble at the idea of a reading wife', exclaimed Frances Morrison, a working-class Owenite feminist, and though working men were said to feel that 'to read a newspaper is a want as urgent almost as the desire for food', few, it seemed, 'take any trouble to create in their wives this taste for reading'.[25] There were also those who argued that women's mental capacities were 'naturally' different from those of men and that their emotionalism denied the rational objectivity that characterised 'the cold calculations of the masculine intellect'.[26] Others put forward a rationale for women's classes that bore a striking similarity to middle-class views on working-class female education. Rather than enlightenment, the purpose of female education was the elimination of domestic thriftlessness and an improvement in standards of child care and the cleanliness and comfort of the working-class home. Thus Rowland Detrosier, the President of the breakaway 'New Mechanics' Institution' established in Manchester in 1829, described the aims underlying the classes for women in the new institute in the following terms:

> Be assured the condition of the industrious artisan can never be permanently improved until the daughter of the poor man be educated to perform with propriety and decorum the important duties of a wife and mother ... Is it of no moment to the working man that he should have a

partner who has the ability to administer to his comfort and wants ... ?
Is it of no moment that the few comforts which are still left to him
should be served up with cleanliness? Or would it ... detract from the
charms of the home, if, when returning from the labours of the day, he
found his little cot the blessed scene of cleanliness, good sense and
cheerfulness? ... With whom are passed the first years of those who are
to become the future parents of the future race? ... From woman, in that
sacred character of mother! But if that woman be ignorant, brutish and
uncleanly in her habits, what rational hope have you that her children
will make either good mothers, good wives, good husbands or good
fathers?[27]

As one woman complained bitterly,

> Even the zealous friends of female education are afraid to press its
> claims on other than utilitarian and comparatively low grounds ...
> women are to be educated in order to qualify them for the duties of
> wives and servants ... How rarely it is argued that women should be
> educated in order that whatever capacities they possess may be permit-
> ted to grow to their full height ... ![28]

The 'spearhead knowledge' sought by radical men may have centred on
'the experiences of poverty, political oppression and social and cultural
apartheid', it may have rejected the 'narrowly pragmatic' in favour of 'the
knowledge calculated to make you free'[29] – if, that is, you were male. For
women, the radical phrase 'really useful knowledge' took a different
meaning, and it was one that was 'narrowly pragmatic' and utilitarian. For
how could children be properly brought up, how could husbands be kept
content and, above all, how could society be reformed and regenerated if
working-class women lacked domestic skills? And how could this be otherwise? Both the inherited educational traditions and the indigenous educational resources which provided the basis for the informal educational
networks developed by the radicals laid stress upon the educative role of
the family, with an emphasis on 'bringing up the coming generation as
harbingers of the new society'.[30] Purvis has commented that it is often
difficult to differentiate between the views of men from different social
strata with regard to working-class female education[31] and certainly, both
the middle classes and the radical working classes emphasised the importance of women's 'natural' role in cultural reproduction. It followed, therefore, that the prime purpose of educating working-class girls and women
was to enable them to bring up their children with a 'true' understanding
of the social, economic and political order – however that 'truth' was

defined. And, all too often, such a rationale translated into female education that focused on the acquisition of domestic skills rather than the
development of the intellectual capacities of women. Women themselves
may have had an alternative version of the purposes of education, but, as
with political and industrial protest, the particular claims of women were
subsumed, marginalised or denied in an assertion of working-class ideals
defined in male terms.

ACCESS TO SCHOOLING AND EDUCATION

In contrast to the early Mechanics' Institutes, female membership of the
Owenite Halls and classes was actively encouraged. But despite the intended
universality of the enlightenment to be gained through education, it does
seem that women's access to the more informal working-class educational
activities were limited by gender divisions and behavioural conventions. It
was socially acceptable for women to go into public houses in this period,[32]
and one assumes that women were not debarred from the coffee-houses, but
all reference to the reading and discussion groups that met in such establishments suggest that these were predominately, if not exclusively, male gath-
erings. Women were less likely to be literate than men and were also less
likely, because of the conditions of their lives and work, to enjoy the discussion and debate with friends and workmates that was so important in developing education beyond basic literacy towards a real desire for knowledge
and understanding.[33] And if the obstacles faced by working people eager for
education – 'the lack of leisure, the cost of candles (or of spectacles) as well
as educational deprivation' – presented 'almost overwhelming difficulties'[34]
for men, how much more sharply they must have impinged on women who
generally had less money, less leisure and less basic education. In sum, these
more informal activities were located in male domains, based on male cultural activities, defined by male educational needs and were, whether by
cause or effect, predominantly male activities.

Boys similarly dominated the elementary day schools provided for the
working classes by the two major educational societies, despite the theoretical primacy given to the education of girls. Boys even outnumbered
girls in the National Society's model central school at Baldwin's Gardens
in London, with girls representing only around 38 per cent of pupils
admitted to the school between 1812 to 1832 (Table 3.1).

The same was generally the case in the schools run by local branches
with, in 1829, the number of boys 'on the books' of day and Sunday
schools in union with the National Society considerably outnumbering

Table 3.1 Average number of children enrolled at Baldwin's Gardens School, 1812–32[35]

	Boys	Girls
1812	610	250
1817	579	273
1822	493	232
1827	350	188
1832	310	170

Total admissions 1812–1832 Girls 4,262 *Boys* 7,089

girls, with only 74,136 girls registered as pupils compared with 100,477 boys (42.5 per cent girls).[36] Accurate evidence of enrolment at the schools in association with the British Society is unobtainable, but the Ladies' Committee of 1826 was definitely of the opinion that 'slow progress' was being made 'in the instruction of females', and that

> from all the information your committee have obtained, ... as to the average number of children in the schools, it is clear that the blessings of early instruction are provided for a far less number of girls, than that of boys.[37]

Of course, the schools of the two major education societies represented only a part of the educational provision available to the working classes. With around two-thirds of day school pupils on their books in Lancashire, Norfolk and Suffolk and with only a handful of English counties having a majority of pupils enrolled at publicly provided schools, the representative day school for working-class children in this period was a private school.[38] Run by working people, often friends and neighbours, such schools were part of working-class communities and offered a form of schooling that was compatible with the values, customary ways and exigencies of working-class life. Perhaps of greatest importance to parents was the fact that the private schools were flexible in their organisation; attendance could be casual and intermittent and, if work was available or a child's services needed at home, then they could be kept away without fuss. Possibly for this reason, the private schools seem to have been particularly popular for girls and, though statistical evidence for this period is not available, there is no reason to suppose that the high levels of girls' attendance at private schools in 1851 represented a major change in patterns of school attendance.[39] But though they may have attended private schools in large numbers, the 1833 statistics of educational enrolment strongly suggest a much lower proportion of female scholars on the books of public and private day schools together (these were not differentiated) across the country as a whole. It is impossible to be precise about these figures; even allowing for the known irregularities in their collection and errors of omission and classification, they also contain large numbers of children whose sex was 'not specified'. Assuming a proportional breakdown of this category, however, the proportion of female scholars in attendance at day school can be estimated at around 44 per cent.[40] Clearly, the importance given to the equal or superior access of girls to formal schooling by the education societies singularly had failed to translate into equalities of school attendance.

Purvis has argued that this was because the education of girls was, in practice, considered to be of less importance than that of boys and that, as a result, fewer school places were provided for them.[41] The complaints of prejudice against the schooling of girls cited earlier do support this argument, and the contrast between the lengthy and enthusiastic accounts of the progress of boys' schools and classes and the brief, often cursory attention given to those for girls in the annual reports of the two societies certainly conveys a lesser interest in the education of girls, though management procedures were also contributory.[42] Thomas Pole commented in 1814 that 'a preference seems to be generally given to boys' in education, and the educationist Samuel Wilderspin attributed the inferior levels of school attendance of working-class girls in London to the common assumption that girls as young as seven or eight could earn their own livings.[43] As Bryant has warned, however, gross generalisations based on national figures have their dangers,[44] not least in obscuring the significance of local conditions in mediating perceptions of the merits of education for boys and girls and of local cultural, social and economic influences on educational provision and school attendance.

In Norfolk and Suffolk, for example, the provision of schooling was relatively healthy in 1818, as it was in predominantly agricultural counties in general, and around 7 per cent of the population of both counties was enrolled at a day school.[45] The supply of school places was only sufficient for around 40 to 49 per cent of the child populations, however, and in Suffolk alone, 216 of 633 parishes had no day-school facilities at all at this point, thus denying any child, boy or girl, the opportunity to go to day school.[46] Expansion in school provision was relatively steady and by 1833 Norfolk and Suffolk had 9 per cent and 9.7 per cent of their respective populations registered as day-school pupils, with girls representing around 47 per cent of day scholars in Norfolk and 47.1 per cent in Suffolk.[47]

For reasons of rural poverty, local indifference and hostility and resultant limited contributions for the support of schools, however, there remained many districts and villages, where no school of any description, public or private, day or Sunday, existed at all. That prejudice was a key factor in limiting school provision in the region was plain, but it was a general prejudice against the whole notion of educating the lower orders or was one that was directed against the schooling of *boys*. As the rector of Beeston complained in 1814, all his efforts to extend schooling in his parish were hampered by 'a two-fold cause viz, the objections of the farmers to losing the labour of a boy who is capable of work, and the inability of the parents to forgo the price of that labour'.[48] Nor was there any incentive to send a boy to school. With no alternative employment to agricultural labour, what use was book learning? Indeed, in the situation of labour surplus that prevailed in the region, farmer hostility against the 'educated' labourer was a positive disincentive to boys' schooling. Even as late as the 1840s, the school Inspector, the Revd Bellairs, still encountered strong prejudice against education for boys, with the 'erroneous impression' still commonplace that

> the cultivation of the intellect unfits for manual labour, and the fear that education may destroy the present relations between master and servant, and substitute no better. That instead of a plodding, hard-working peasantry ... we shall have an effeminate class of persons, averse to rough work, conceited and insubordinate.
>
> Or again, that the peasantry, when educated, will become ambitious, cease to be content with their condition and aim at the rank of tenant farmers.[49]

In terms of their access to schooling, rural boys did indeed suffer a double burden, with both their class and gender erecting barriers to education. For girls, however, the situation was very different. With little regular work available for them or for their mothers, girls were free to go to school. As many of the schools did not charge fees, they could afford to go to school[50] and, because many rural girls became domestic servants, there was a positive incentive for them to go to school, not least because this gave a contact with local ladies through which a first 'place' commonly was organised. Unfortunately for the girls, however, the districts where circumstances favoured their school attendance were the very districts where farmer hostility, limited resources and rural poverty meant that the establishment of a provided or a private school was less likely; a fact which explains why national statistics were not swelled by large numbers of rural girls in attendance at school.

The situation in the towns and larger villages of the region was different yet again. The social structure of such communities meant that support for schooling was more likely to be forthcoming,[51] there was less demand for boy labour than in the agricultural districts and the prospect of eligible situations gave an incentive to boys' schooling. For girls, the pull of paid employment for themselves or their mothers was most sharply felt in the towns, while, domestic service excepted, the limited employment opportunities available to women offered little inducement to forgo a girl's earnings or her assistance at home in favour of schooling. In short, in contrast to the situation of numbers of rural girls, in districts where circumstances were favourable to the school attendance of boys, there were likely to be school places available to them. And where circumstances were conducive to the provision of schooling, they were inimical to girls' school attendance – factors which must mediate interpretations of national statistics of girls' school enrolment and qualify conclusions regarding gender prejudice.

Girls were even more acutely disadvantaged in the industrial districts of Lancashire, for reasons both of limited provision and of limited demand for girls' schooling. Thus, though the National Society targeted industrial Lancashire as being in particular need of the reforming influence of education and gave exceptional financial and moral support to local initiatives,[52] the supply of school places remained grossly inadequate to the size of the rapidly expanding child population of the Lancashire mill towns. Demand also was limited, however, with high levels of child labour and an inability to pay school fees or to provide decent clothing leading to low levels of school enrolment – and sometimes school failure. And it was as much a pragmatic recognition of where the best returns on scarce resources could be obtained that led to the provision of fewer places for girls than boys, with limited demand being met by limited supply. Thus in Liverpool, for example, an original decision to provide school places for an equal number of boys and girls in the Corporation schools was reversed in 1824 following a surveyor's report that schools for girls 'are never so numerously attended as the boys' schools', and places in the girls' school were reduced by 100.[53] Doubly handicapped by their domestic usefulness in areas of high adult female employment, girls often simply were too useful to be spared to go to school, while the prospect of factory employment offered no encouragement to their schooling. As a result, at only around 41.9 per cent of the day school population,[54] the proportion of female day scholars in Lancashire was far lower than that of boys, far lower than the national average and for lower than that of female day-school pupils in Norfolk and Suffolk. There is some evidence to suggest that Lancashire girls had an enthusiasm for schooling that was probably unmatched by boys or girls anywhere in the country,[55] but the circumstances of their daily lives meant that they also experienced an educational deprivation that also was unmatched elsewhere.

Detailed figures showing local, within the county variations in school enrolment are not available for this early period, but comparison of estimated gender differences in school enrolment in predominantly argricultural counties with those with a high level of urban and/or industrial areas across the country as a whole also supports this argument, with girls' attendance in agricultural regions being superior to that of urban and/or industrial regions, generally higher than the national average and even, in Devon and Hereford, being superior to that of boys (Table 3.2).

The national picture of boys' superior access to schooling overall must further be qualified, as the figures also suggest (the weakness in the statistics disallow any stronger emphasis) that girls outnumbered boys in the Infant schools, with an estimated proportion of 51.2 per cent female pupils overall, matched by similar proportions of female pupils on the books of infant schools in Norfolk and Suffolk, and even in Lancashire.[56] Girls also outnumbered boys in the Sunday schools in 1833, with nearly 10,000 more girls on the books,[57] though admittedly a school attendance of only one day per week had severe limitations.

Table 3.2   Estimated enrolment at day school, UK, 1833[58]

	Girls as % of pupils	Boys as % of pupils
Agricultural		
Cambridgeshire	48	52
Devon	58	42
Herefordshire	50.2	49.8
Essex	49	51
Huntingdonshire	49.5	50.5
Industrial/urban		
Nottinghamshire	45	55
Derbyshire	45	55
Warwickshire	45	55
Surrey*	43	57
Kent*	44	56

*including much of London

In summary then, it can be concluded that, though in general terms girls undoubtedly were disadvantaged in their access to day schooling in comparison with boys, there were considerable regional variations in that experience which could, in certain circumstances, operate to give some advantage to girls. And though girls undoubtedly were handicapped by the 'double burden' of class and gender, their experiences of schooling – or a lack of it – seem to have been determined by local conditions of school supply operating in an interactive relationship with gender divisions of labour in the local labour market and within the working-class family rather than any specific attitudes towards girls' schooling, though the existence of prejudice cannot be dismissed.

CONCLUSIONS

There are a number of ironies to be drawn in the conclusions to this chapter, with the theoretical mandates of girls' schooling being so distorted in the processes of implementation that practices almost contradicted policies. For while anxieties about the corruption of social relationships and the degeneration of the 'lower orders' gave an urgent priority to the education of girls as the chief agents of cultural reproduction in the working-class family of the future, the mixture of indifference, prejudice and instrumentalism with which this rationale was received gave considerably less importance to girls' schooling than to boys'. Thus fewer school places were provided for girls, their levels of day-school enrolment were generally lower, particularly in the publicly provided schools, and their attendance was more erratic, with gender divisions of labour in the family and work-place informing both the supply of and demand for school places to the general detriment of girls. There were exceptions; there were greater incentives and fewer barriers to girls' schooling in rural districts of Norfolk and Suffolk but, largely because economic policing was seen to be sufficient for social control and because boy labour was needed for agricultural work, little support for local efforts was forthcoming, leaving many of the agricultural districts with no day school for either girls or boys.

In industrial Lancashire, on the other hand, where the need to 'civilise' girls was seen to be greatest, the merits of formal over familial education were generally outweighed by the immediate advantage of a girl's wages or her domestic assistance at home. A further irony is apparent in the fact that despite the Herculean efforts of the National Society, conditions were such that the level of school provision in the county was nearly the lowest in the country, probably *the* lowest in the industrial areas. Thus in the area of greatest perceived need, where the greatest amount of money and probably effort was expended, the least success was achieved, with the percentage of Lancashire girls on the books of a day school being the lowest in the entire country.

4 Religion, Reading and Really Useful Knowledge

Embedded within the new concept of schooling as a means of mass social reform was the Protestant and Evangelical belief that this was to be effected by the dissemination of Christian belief through the ranks of the lower orders, via the religious education of their children. It was also necessary that each individual should have personal access to the word of God through reading the Bible and so it was also obligatory to teach the children to read. As a result reading and religion became the staple elements of curriculum provision in the day schools of the two education societies and in the Sunday schools of the early nineteenth century. The National Sunday school for girls in Bath, for example, aimed to instruct the girls in 'the first principles of the established religion, and to teach them reading sufficient to enable them to peruse the New Testament',[1] and these objectives seems to have been typical of the great majority of schools at this point, with perhaps some extension of the programme to include writing and possibly some basic arithmetic for more advanced scholars.

Of equal if not greater importance, however, was the organisation and management of schooling, which was to transmit, through the rules and routines of school life, the attitudes and values felt to be appropriate to the child's station in life. Strict rules of punctuality would instil the time–work disciplines of the new economic order, with children being trained in habits of regularity, order and restraint through the structured experiences of schooling and the values embedded in the hidden curriculum of school life. This was most clearly expressed in the monitorial system adopted by the National and British Societies, where every aspect of school life was carefully regulated in an hierarchical system of organisation, with ordered routines and set procedures intended to make the schools operate like a well-oiled machine of instruction. Thus for Joseph Lancaster, founder of the British Society, the first responsibility of the teacher was to impress upon the pupils the importance of obedience and that 'order is Heaven's first law'.[2] Little or no discretion was to be allowed to individual teachers, with a method of training based on initiation into the workings of the model curriculum and with carefully prepared sets of readers, each with its accompanying teachers' notes, prescribing the content and methodology of each lesson in precise detail.

Within these readers the not so hidden curriculum took an explicitly reformist tone, extolling the merits of the social and economic status quo and the duties of individuals within it. Goldstrom has described the messages thus to be conveyed to working-class children:

> Both societies wished the children to learn through their readers about the demarcations between rich and poor, and the mutual dependence of each in an harmonious society. Contentment in the station in life in which God had placed them was an important precept. Also important was that a child should grow up to take his (sic) place as a member of the respectable, devout and hard-working poor, and not allow himself to become one of the contemptible 'undeserving poor'.[3]

The hierarchical and paternal image of society depicted within these readers also encompassed the forms of behaviours and attitudes thought to be appropriate to the two sexes. William Allen of the British Society explained to a Select Committee on Education in 1834 that teaching children about their duties to their superiors also involved their learning 'the relative duties of husbands and wives' as laid down in the Scriptures[4] and, in *The Sunday Scholar's Gift, or a present for a good child* published in 1814, the model of behaviour for little girls was defined in the character of little Hannah. She was a girl

> ... of temper sweet and mild
> No angry passions ere were seen
> In this engaging child.
>
> She very soon could knit and sew
> And help her mother too
> For Hannah would not waste her time
> As idle children do.
>
> Each Sabbath morn she rose betimes
> And dressed her clean and neat
> Nor ever uttered naughty words
> Or loitered in the street.
>
> She knew that God would never love
> Girls that are bold and rude
> And therefore little Hannah prayed
> That God would make her good.[5]

If gender differentiation was implicit rather than explicit in the model curricula of the early nineteenth-century schools in association with the two societies, this was not the case in the charity and industrial schools.

These schools pursued the other main route towards social reform; that of combining the teaching of religion with vocational training.

Many of the charity schools were established in the eighteenth century and provided an education for selected members of the 'deserving poor' that was often more comprehensive and certainly more costly than that provided in the National and British schools. As such, a charity school education was seen as a means of training girls from the higher ranks of the working classes and the daughter of families in reduced circumstances to become 'well conducted and intelligent servants', with a curriculum that combined a 'moral and religious education' with practical instruction in the duties of a servant. The typical routine in such a school would therefore involve a combination of practical instruction in cleaning, cookery, laundry work and needlework, religious teaching (and church attendance) and some basic literacy – a programme that left little time for more academic learning but was said to produce the 'very best and most useful class of domestic servants'.[6] Older girls might have access to a slightly more extended curriculum. The trustees of the Red Maids' School in Bristol, for example, decided in 1798 that it would 'be greatly conducive to their role in life' for senior girls to 'be able to write and (to be) conversant with the first four rules of arithmetic', but with four hours' tuition per week for only 10 to 12 girls, this cannot be said to have widened the school's curriculum to any appreciable extent.[7]

As would be expected, socialisation came high on the list of priorities of the charity schools, with an emphasis on the inculcation of a proper deference and humility that could extend beyond the immediate context of schooling to include the girls' families, their employment and even their choice of husband. The Revd Daniel Wilson, a minister attached to charity schools in the London area, advised the Select Committee on Education of 1816,

> The very first thing we teach the female children especially is to correct the love of dress, and to lead them to aim at that respect every person acquires who behaves well in their station; and to avoid on the other hand the contempt to which they will expose themselves, by aspiring to that which they will never attain, and which only draws upon them the displeasure of others and the anger of God.[8]

Many were boarding schools, to avoid possible contaminating influences on the girls' behaviour, while parents could be told, as they were by St Leonard's Charity School for Girls in 1813, that they should

> be careful to set their children good examples at home of a sober and religious behaviour, humility, contentment, and a ready submission to the duties of the station wherein God shall be pleased to place them.[9]

Placement in service with a suitable family was also seen as an ongoing part of the educative process, with continuing good behaviour being encouraged by rewards in the form of a bible, books with suitably religious or moral themes or sometimes a gift of money or clothes. This benign oversight of a girl's progress in the outside world could also extend to the payment of a marriage portion – but only where her prospective husband was of a 'good character'.

The charity schools were not without their critics. The editor of the *Bristol Observer* saw 'no occasion for assuming that servitude is the natural or most fitting destination of poor females' and urged that girls should be taught a variety of vocational skills, including bookkeeping, to enable them to contribute 'to the future support of a family'.[10] Such criticisms were rare, however, and though costs precluded the extension of charity schooling beyond a small minority of girls, the principle of combining vocational training was viewed with considerable favour. An alternative and cheaper model, the school of industry, thus also became popular in the later eighteenth and early nineteenth centuries, to provide a similar education for the lower ranks of the working classes.

Schools of industry were frequently not identified by their title and it is impossible to quantify the number of them established as such. Impressionist evidence does suggest, however, that such schools were seen to be especially relevant to the educational needs of girls, both in training them in the skills and behaviours required of the good domestic servant – and the future wife and mother – and in providing them with the means to earn a respectable living.[11] Further, this combination of vocational training with religious and moral education was seen to counteract 'a practical objection that has so frequently been urged, viz that education unfits the poor for their respective situations'.[12]

CURRICULUM DEVELOPMENT

Notwithstanding the National and British Societies' approval of this type of vocationally oriented curriculum, vocational preparation did *not* form part of the model curricula of either society at this time; the three Rs of religion, reading and regulation were quite adequate to the reforming purposes of their schools. Nonetheless, 'industrial work' quickly became a regular feature in many of the provided schools, including the model schools of the two societies, particularly for the girls. Indeed, there were so many incentives to include 'industrial work', notably needlework, in the curriculum of girls' schools that when questioned about the benefits to be gained from its introduction, a witness to an 1834 Select Committee assumed the reference must be to boys' schools as 'the girls have invariably united industry with their establishments in the common practices of education'.[13]

But, it must be stressed, this development in the girls' curriculum did not originate in ideologies of women's roles, nor was it imposed on schools as a means of socialising girls into appropriate class and gender behaviours. In the early nineteenth century curriculum implementation developed via an interactive process, with curriculum practices informing curriculum theories in an ongoing developmental progression. And in the reports of the two education societies can be seen the gradual process of evolution whereby what was perceived to be 'good' practice in some schools was recommended as models for others to emulate. And the emphasis here must be on models in the plural, for what was seen to be good practice in relation to girls' schooling increasingly began to differ from perceptions of what was appropriate or practicable for boys' schools.

Rather than ideology, the immediate incentive to the introduction of industrial work into the curricula of National and British schools was economic; the boost it gave to school funds through profits gained from the sale of children's work. Children, both boys and girls, might make wire buttons, straw plait and straw hats, knitted stockings and so forth for sale, or the school might take in sewing or similar work for the children to do. At Rochester National School, for example, it was found that the employment of the girls in needlework was an effective way of supplementing the inadequate salary paid to the schoolmistress that was all the school committee could afford. 'Our funds ... not sufficing to allow the mistress such a salary as we thought she deserved and her necessities required', it was reported,

> the committee have permitted her ... to add £10 per year to her salary ... by employing the girls at certain hours at needlework, on the articles of apparel in common use, and manufactured for sale in the neighbourhood.[14]

Improvements in attendance could also be encouraged by the girls making clothes to be given as prizes, or with some of the profits being used to fund payments to parents in compensation for loss of children's earnings.[15]

The introduction of needlework was seen to be an ideal way to solve problems of under-resourcing in a way that brought all the benefits of vocational training without any of the additional expense and, moreover, it was consistent with concepts of gender roles and gender divisions of labour. Both societies were therefore quick to implement needlework into the curricula of the central 'model' schools,[16] with strong recommendations for schools in association to follow suit. And for the National Society, the ideal curriculum for girls became one in which as much time and attention was given to needlework as to reading and religion and other subjects. 'In a well-managed school for *girls*' (original emphasis), the 1833 Report stated:

> half the day may be given to needlework or knitting, and the other half will suffice for acquiring a knowledge of reading, writing and summing, besides a more familiar acquaintance with religious truths.
>
> This division of time between learning and industry is actually made in the best conducted schools for females.[17]

The effects of this were several and serious, with a cumulative impact on the curriculum for girls and for boys. For, as the National Society reported in 1832, there was little in the way of comparable work available for boys:

> needlework has supplied ... this want as regards the girls, but it yet remains to discover a system which shall provide a general and effectual occupation for the boys.[18]

So, while the girls were busy with needlework, the boys were able to continue with their more academic studies, to achieve higher standards. As the 1833 National Society report continued:

> the boys, however, being rarely provided with any manual occupation, are carried forward to higher degrees of attainment in religious knowledge, as well as ciphering, writing etc.

In addition, the 'superabundance of time' available was encouraging managers to introduce subjects such as history, natural philosophy, English grammar and music for the boys, to avoid 'repetitions of a tedious and uninteresting nature' in the curriculum.[19] The girls' timetable was full, so there simply was no need to introduce new subjects into the curriculum.

Further, if the words of one harassed schoolmistress are to be believed, the quality of teaching in girls' schools may also have been diminished by needlework. For the time and effort taken up by the preparation of materials left, she said, no time for preparation of other work, for training of the monitors (child teaching assistants) or for recreation, while the collection of money and writing of accounts for the clothing fund could take up two hours of school time every Monday morning.[20]

But, it must also be stressed, though the numerical dominance of the National Society made it in effect the market leader of provided schooling, such curriculum ideals were not uniformly translated into practice, with factors of resource constraints also operating to limit the spread of the needlework-dominated curriculum for girls. A failure explicitly to mention needlework in school records may have arisen from the increasingly axiomatic nature of its place in the curriculum for girls, but there were many schools which clearly did *not* teach needlework even as late as the 1840s and 1850s. Half the schools mentioned in the 1845 report of Inspector Allen did not teach needlework, for example, nor many of the schools visited by the Revd F. Watkins in 1847 or those inspected by the Revd M. Mitchell in 1852.[21] Mr Fletcher's report on British schools in the north of England also suggests that needlework was relatively uncommon in co-educational village schools taught by a master 'often without the assistance of a female teacher to instruct the girls in needlework'.[22] And, indeed, it is likely that many village schools were unable to teach needlework for similar reasons, though the voluntary assistance of local ladies may have enabled some to overcome such 'problems'.

CONSUMER DEMAND

The voluntary nature of schooling provision and attendance meant that schools had necessarily to be responsive to popular views on what children should be taught, particularly in urban areas where schools might be in competition for their 'customers'. And here, a growing cross-class convergence can be seen regarding the ideal curriculum for the two sexes, with working-class concepts of gender roles merging with middle-class views towards a consensus of opinion on what girls and boys should be taught and learn.

The influence of consumer demand on provided education can most clearly be seen on curriculum development in the Sunday schools. As Laqueur has argued, parents and children discriminated between schools on the basis of curriculum content and quality of teaching,[23] and though often reluctant to do so, 'the larger supplies of intellectual food' provided by the Nonconformist Sunday schools forced numbers of Church schools 'to make some advances in order to prevent complete desertion'.[24] Numbers of Sunday schools thus expanded the secular curriculum with the introduction of lessons in writing and perhaps arithmetic and, though this was rare, possibly even subjects such as geography, history and science.[25] Similarly, numbers of largely Nonconformist Sunday schools were beginning to emphasise the attractions of a Sunday school education as a route for individual advancement, with some even acting as informal employment agencies for 'steady and attentive boys' seeking situations where they would be likely 'to be well attended and prosper'.[26] Numbers of day schools associated with the British Society were also beginning to 'sell' their services to the local community by emphasising the improved prospects available to their pupils, in complete contrast to the restrictive, class-cultural control rationale put forward by the society's founders.[27] This development must not be exaggerated. Probably only a small minority of parents were inclined positively to evaluate schooling as a route for occupational and social advancement for their sons at this point – and probably none at all with regard to their daughters.

As consumers of the goods and services offered by the private schools, working-class 'customers' had considerable influence over curriculum provision and, given the popularity of private schools for girls, the curriculum of these schools probably represented what most parents thought of as a suitable education for their daughters, in providing the knowledge that would be *really* useful in adult life. And what parents basically wanted from the private schools and what the schools provided was, in the words of a report from the Manchester Statistical Society, a limited amount of religion, the basic three Rs and needlework for girls:

> religious instruction in common day (private) schools is restricted to learning the Church or Assembly's Catechism by rote, and perhaps, reading the Scriptures ... Taken as a whole the utmost of benefit which accrues to the public from this class of schools will include facility in reading and writing and some knowledge of arithmetic; to which must be added in the girls' schools, needlework, with occasionally an acquaintance with the rudiments of grammar, history or geography.[28]

By around the 1820s, therefore, the purposes of educating girls, as expressed in the realities of curriculum provision, were essentially the same in both the provided and the private sectors, with working-class notions of *really* useful knowledge for girls meeting middle-class views on what constituted a good education for females of this class in pragmatic alliance. Middle-class educationists might express a puzzled bafflement of the working-class 'ignorance' that led them to reject the 'softening of the manners, the improvement of the character, the instruction on moral and religious subjects, and all the more valuable objects of education'[29] but, religion and 'morals' apart, there was a general agreement that the basic curriculum for girls should consist of reading, writing (and perhaps some simple arithmetic) and needlework, in preparation for their adult roles as wives and mothers.

The argument can be taken further to suggest that a cross-class consensus was also emerging, albeit implicitly, that the type of schooling suitable for girls was different from that suitable for boys. Thus, though private schools for girls also came in for their share of pejorative criticism, comments on their 'superiority' over comparable schools for boys may be seen to have carried a note of tacit approval – or at least a less active disapproval – than was the case for private schools for boys. In Manchester, for example, the girls' private schools were said to be

> generally in much better condition than the boys' schools, and have a greater appearance of cleanliness, order and regularity. This seems to arise in part from the former being more constantly employed, and the scholars being fewer in number to each teacher.

In Salford, girls' private schools were said to have 'a better order and discipline', with some of the mistresses possessing 'solid qualifications for their office', while private schoolmistresses in Rutland were described as being persons of 'good moral character, of quiet orderly habits' and as decent and respectable women.[30] All this may well have been true. Certainly limited female occupational opportunities would have meant that many able women were attracted into teaching in the absence of alternative ways of earning a living.[31] Criticisms of the private schools in this period, however, were frequently based on their lack of 'efficiency' which, interpreted according to the prevailing educational theory, meant their non-adoption of the regulated mechanistic system of order that marked the regime of good National and British schools, the lack of which was not so serious in girls' schools. The scanty provision of 'moral' training might be deplored but was not the homely, familial ethos of the private school entirely appropriate for girls? What need was there to instil the time and work disciplines of industrial capitalism in those whose work-place was to be the home? Was not the regulatory mechanical organisation of the monitorial system inappropriate, even unnecessary, for the moulding of the naturally softer female character? And was the practice of combining domestic tasks with teaching as was customary in numbers of private schools quite the distraction it was seen to be in the case of boys, reflecting as it did the familial education in domestic skills that so many of the charity and industrial schools sought to emulate for girls? In short, axiomatic beliefs regarding the natural roles and requirements of girls probably contributed towards an evaluation of the private schools for girls as being, if not good, at least less bad than those for boys, with a bridge across the cultural divide between middle-class and working-class views of what constituted a good education being provided by the common, taken for granted assumption that the education of girls should be shaped in accordance with their roles within the working-class family.

EXPERIENCES AND ACHIEVEMENTS

One of the few female autobiographies available from the early nineteenth century[32] describes a uniformity of experiences in schooling that gives strong support to the argument above. Attending in turn two private schools and a provided parish school, Mary Smith's experiences of formal education in the 1820s were limited to a little reading and religion, with a great deal of sewing and knitting. She commented:

> A girl's education at that time consisted principally of needlework of various descriptions, from plain sewing to all kinds of fancy work and embroidery ... Parents were prouder then of their daughters' pieces of needlework than of their schooling.[33]

Her informal education experiences similarly gave greater importance to domestic matters than to intellectual achievements. Her mother 'looked upon reading ... as a species of idleness; very well for Sundays or evenings when baby was asleep and I was not wanted for anything else', though, very unusually, her father insisted that she should learn arithmetic to the high standard of long division and compound addition.[34] Mary Anne Hearne's experiences also taught her that literacy was less important than domesticity. 'Most lessons came from our parents, chiefly, of course, our mother', she recalled, 'she taught us to sweep and clean, sew and knit ... all the household arts' but she was rather disapproving of her daughter's love of reading:

> Dear mother! She did not like me always having a book in my hand or pocket, and would have been better pleased if I had been equally fond of the brush or the needle.

Through the covert cultural messages embedded in the Sunday school literature of the period she also learned that personal ambition was misplaced in a girl. In one of these, she wrote,

> was a series of articles on men who had been poor boys, and risen to be rich and great. Every month I hoped to find the story of some poor, ignorant *girl* who, beginning life as handicapped as I, had yet been able by her own efforts and the blessings of God upon them to live a life of usefulness, if not of greatness. But I believe there was not a woman in the whole series.[35]

The 'hidden curriculum' of family and community life also impinged on schooling, with an erratic school attendance on the part of girls as they took days off to help with domestic chores and child care. The British Society remarked this in 1834, urging the importance of providing a high-quality education for girls because of 'the frequency with which they (girls) are detained at home to assist in domestic concerns, even while professedly in course of attendance',[36] and school records are full of similar complaints. Certainly, Madoc-Jones's study of attendance at Mitcham National school in the 1830s showed a far higher proportion of girls than boys being dismissed from the school for poor attendance, though they were also more likely to return to school after a temporary withdrawal and sometimes enjoyed a longer period of schooling.[37]

But if the educational experiences of family life were overtly gender-specific, those of formal schooling were probably less so for the majority of girls. For, in practice, gender differentiation in curriculum provision frequently was more potential than actual, with local variations in the conditions and experiences of schooling frequently denying the achievement of curriculum 'ideals' and with many girls experiencing the same, albeit very limited curriculum as their male peers. Only in the 'good' provided schools, where resources were sufficient to allow boys and girls to be taught separately, where the payment of decent salaries attracted trained and/or efficient teachers and where 'good' books and other teaching aids could be afforded, were the 'ideals' of the gender-differentiated curriculum likely to be achieved, and these were few and far between in the early nineteenth century. The village schools of Norfolk and Suffolk, where limited funding meant that boys and girls normally were taught together and where poor-quality teaching and few books limited curriculum provision, were probably far more representative of the majority of schools, both publicly provided and private, in this period. Rural girls may have had a superior access to schooling in comparison to local boys and in comparison to Lancashire girls, but qualitative and quantitative limitations on schooling provision severely reduced this relative advantage. Equal they may have been in terms of what they were taught but here, gender equality meant an equality of ignorance.

Taking education experiences as a whole to include the experiences of family and community life and the 'knock-on' effects of these in relation to girls' access to schooling and the informal and formal curricula of schools, it is clear that girls' more academic attainments were limited by their gender as well as their class. This was immediately apparent where curriculum 'ideals' were achieved, as was likely to have been the case in the central schools of the National Society. Evidence of gender differences in standards of achievement in the secular curriculum is limited, but in an 1829 report on the 'Present State and Efficiency' of the schools there is clear evidence of the low levels of girls' attainments – and of their limited attendance. Though older than the boys in comparable classes in the boys' school, a consistently shorter period of school enrolment for girls was linked to lower standards of work. The 44 girls in class one, for example, had an average age of 12 years and 7 months and had achieved a standard that compared fairly favourably with that achieved by class one boys. The average age of class one boys, however, was nearly two years younger and while both boys and girls were reading the Bible and writing on paper, the boys were considerably in advance in arithmetic. Summary totals of the proportions of male and female pupils at different levels of achievement show clearly the lower levels of girls' achievements (see Table 4.1).

A similar survey of the standards achieved by pupils in attendance at the principal schools associated with the Durham National Society in 1831 also showed the relative underachievement of girls, with far fewer girls than boys achieving the highest standards of 'Catechism and Explaining' in reading or of 'ciphering in rules' in arithmetic.[38]

Table 4.1   Gender differences in standards of achievement in the central National schools, 1829[39]

Subject	Boys (%)	Girls (%)
Reading		
Scripture cards	6.6	14.1
Book no. 2	8.3	14.6
Discourse of our		
Saviour and above	77.7	71.2
Writing		
On slates	49.6	61
On paper	50.4	39
Ciphering		
Digits	–	14.2
Simple rules	63.2	46.8
Compound rules*	20.8	39
Rule of 3 and above	3.7	

*Boys were learning all four rules of compound arithmetic, but the girls learned only compound addition and multiplication.

Evidence of sharp differences in literacy levels (though including both schooled and unschooled children and men and women from all social classes), also supports a generally poor evaluation of girls' educational attainments, with only just over 50 per cent of women able to sign their name in 1840 compared to around 67 per cent of men. Differences in literacy levels within and between industrial Lancashire and rural Norfolk and Suffolk, however, also link to many of the points made throughout this chapter in showing differences in the relative educational experiences of boys and girls and men and women in the two regions.

Thus despite an enormous investment in support of elementary education on the part of the National Society, literacy levels in Lancashire were very low, particularly in the cotton towns. In Manchester and Preston, for example, literacy rates were actually lower in 1831–37 than they had been in the mid-eighteenth century, with around half to three-quarters of their respective populations unable to sign their own names. But as Stephens has pointed out, it was the high levels of *female* illiteracy in the industrial areas that were the crucial ingredient in the well below average county literacy levels, and Lancashire men were actually more literate than their Norfolk and Suffolk counterparts in 1839–45 (female illiteracy 67 per cent, male illiteracy 39 per cent in Lancashire; male illiteracy 44 per cent and 46 per cent respectively in Norfolk and Suffolk). Though fortunate in their access to relatively well-paid employment, the women and girls of Lancashire were acutely disadvantaged in their basic educational attainments, with their very limited access to schooling leading to the highest levels of female illiteracy in the whole of England and Wales.[40]

Women were also more likely to be illiterate than men in Norfolk and Suffolk, with 50 per cent of Norfolk women and 52 per cent of Suffolk women being unable to sign their names in the period 1839–45. Nevertheless, it cannot be assumed that this pattern was uniform within each county and that working-class women and girls necessarily were more illiterate than men and boys of the same class. No evidence is available for this earlier period, but it seems plausible to suggest superior levels of female literacy over male in the more rural parts of each county. This was the case in 1851 and indeed, by 1871 levels of female literacy were superior to those of male literacy in every registration district except Ipswich and Norwich.[41] The incentive of domestic service as the occupational destination of girls, together with the existence of many barriers against boys' schooling, is likely to have had the effect of supporting superior female educational attainments, at least as far as the acquisition of basic literacy was concerned.

In general terms, the education of working-class women seems to have been, at best, on a par with that described by a writer to *The Pioneer* in 1833:

The education of the females of the lower classes, in many cases does not extend even as far as a knowledge of their letters, ... in the agregate [sic] to sew and read (and that but very indifferently) is the sum of their acquirements.[42]

Like the two anonymous factory girls interviewed by the Manchester Statistical Society in the 1830s, poor-quality teaching, erratic attendance or any of the many barriers that limited girls' access to a decent education could mean that girls might learn very little even when fortunate enough to be enrolled at a school. At the private school one attended, she explained: 'the mistress used to set the scholars agate [sic] o' peeling potatoes and fetching water 'stead of setting them to read', and the other said: 'I never went to school' so mitch as to keep me i' learning – cannot tell how it wur – think it was neglect.'

But if many girls, particularly in Lancashire, were denied access to schooling, so also were many boys, and if the factory girl who was taught to read by a friend and then 'bout up histories and books as was nice reading'[43] was denied the opportunity further to develop her knowledge and skills, at least she was spared the needlework and the cultural messages of female inferiority that attendance at a 'good' school would have taught. Mary Smith evaluated the impact of girls' schooling as likely to cripple and cramp the souls of Englishwomen 'as the Chinese women's feet by their shoes',[44] and for many girls the experiences of schooling must have been equally negative in their effects.

CONCLUSIONS

The conclusions to Chapter 3 recognised a number of ironies in the realities of girls' access to schooling. A further irony is suggested in this chapter, in that the reformist rationale of the middle classes probably found more common ground with the 'alternative' educational philosophies of the great majority of male working-class radicals, measured in terms of their perceptions of the purposes of female working-class education. For though the new and reformed society that was the dream of the radicals was strikingly different from that of their professed 'superiors', both groups defined female education in terms of women's role in cultural reproduction and with an axiomatic adherence to gender divisions of labour – an adherence that all too often also slipped over into a definition of women and girls' educational needs in limited, domestically oriented terms.

Curriculum provision also was shaped by instrumentalism and pragmatism, with a charity or industrial school education focusing on training girls for domestic service finding wide support amongst the middle classes. Similarly, the addition of needlework to the initial common curriculum of religion, reading and regulation in the National and British day schools was a popular development. As it evolved, therefore, the 'ideal' curriculum in the provided schools for girls became increasingly gender specific, with pragmatism meeting ideology in defining basic literacy skills, religion and needlework as the core curriculum for girls. And, the teaching of 'morals' apart, the nature of working-class consumer demand, as represented in the private schools that many parents favoured for their daughters, thus matched the ideals of provision as defined by the providers of public schooling, in a common understanding of what was really useful knowledge for working-class girls. Some issues remained unresolved – the relative merits of provided over private schooling for girls and the vexed problem of their notoriously erratic attendance – but the appropriateness of the domestically oriented curriculum was generally agreed by the 1820s, with the 'ideals' of girls' schooling being defined by the limits of what was required to prepare girls for domestic service and marriage and motherhood.

Problems of resourcing did prescribe curriculum content, with, in many schools, insufficient money to support the provision of separate schools or classes for boys and girls or the employment of a sewing mistress to teach the girls needlework. In what may even have been a majority of provided schools, therefore, boys and girls were taught the same basic, if limited, curriculum. Nevertheless, there was a widening division between the education provided in the best schools for boys and that provided in the best schools for girls. While the girls were busy sewing, the boys were busy learning, with more time available to them for the acquisition of basic skills and even, in the very best schools, for the teaching and learning of a range of academic schooling. And with an increasing need for the British and National schools to 'sell' their educational goods in a competitive market-place, the explicitly reformist rationale of boys' schooling was beginning to shade into a view of schooling as a ladder to occupational opportunity, particularly in the British schools in the urban and industrial districts.

This was more a development of the 1840s and later, but evaluation of the effectiveness of schooling policies and practices were beginning to suggest new lines of thinking. More radical initiatives were also to be developed in relation to the formal education of girls, with the imposition of compulsory schooling for factory children being one strategy in continuing attempts to educate girls towards an active awareness of their appropriate class and gender roles. But while views regarding boys' schooling remained fluid and open to negotiation, the parameters of what girls should be taught had been established, with new lines of thinking being directed more towards the extension and implementation of the domestic curriculum rather than any reappraisal of the policies and practices of schooling for girls. The basic principles were established; boys and girls were different, their roles in society were different, and they were, therefore, to be educated in different ways.

We simply do not know to what extent the expressed reform and control purposes of provided education were achieved; whether there was a significant increase in the number of working people who read their bibles and adopted the moral precepts of the Scriptures, whether standards of comfort and order improved in working-class homes or even whether domestic servants became more efficient and better behaved. Continuing, even expanding employment of married women in the factories or fields cannot be taken as evidence of a failure of socialisation, for, as has been argued, relatively few families could afford to lose a wife's wages. Indeed, the impact of schooling on the lives of women and girls can hardly be separated from the operation of gender concepts in daily life, for whether couched in terms of a reformist or radical rationale, whether evolving in response to ideology, consumer demand or pragmatic factors of resourcing, whether ideal or less than ideal, the policies and practices of working-class female education were defined by and compatible with class and gender concepts and divisions of labour. For women, the informal education of experiences in community, work-place and family taught the same lessons as those put forward in schools; that their prime role was defined in familial and domestic terms.

The operation of gender divisions of labour may have had different consequences in terms of access to schooling, girls may even have had some advantage over boys, but the fact remains that their education and their schooling was defined in terms of their class and their gender – with major implications for the 'progress' of girls' elementary education later in the century.

5 An Education of Principle: the Later Nineteenth Century

The theme of education as a vehicle for social control continued to be central to educational debates in the 1830s and 1840s, though with a less repressive, more creative concept of the sort of education most likely to create the harmonious social and political relations between the working classes and their social superiors that were seen to be so sorely needed. Against the arguments that educating the working classes had actually increased crime and sedition by enabling working people to read inflammatory literature, educational 'experts' from the ranks of Whig and Radical politicians and professional reformers such as the new factory inspectors put forward theories which saw the goal of mass education as primarily that of changing and reforming the people.[1] If attempts to train the children of working people in habits of obedience had proved unsuccessful – and the development of mass movements such as Chartism demonstrated that they had – then perhaps educating them in a 'corrrect' understanding of the economic and political ordering of society would lead them to abandon the 'perverted' and 'irrational' beliefs that underlay protest. As a contributor to the *Quarterly Journal of Education*, a publication of the Society for the Diffusion of Useful Knowledge, expressed the argument in 1831, an education aimed at teaching children reading, religion and writing

> is incomplete and may, indeed, be perverted to the very worst purposes. The (working people) should, first of all, be made acquainted with the motives which have induced every society emerging from barbarism to establish the rights of property; and the advantages resulting from its establishment, and the necessity of maintaining it inviolate, should be clearly set forth ... the circumstances that give rise to those gradations of rank and fortune that actually exist ought to be explained: it may be shown that they are as natural to society as differences of sex, of strength, of colour ... and that equality ... violently and unjustly brought about could not be maintained for a week.[2]

Implicit within such theories was the understanding that working-class dissidence was based on a profound misunderstanding of the funda-

78

mentally benign operation of capitalist economic organisation. That periodic crises of capital accumulation caused slumps, unemployment and distress, that there were inequalities between social classes, was unfortunate but inevitable. That industrial capitalism necessarily displaced workers with obsolete skills was also inevitable, and though the poverty experienced by groups such as the redundant handloom weavers was to be deplored, it was also educational in its impact, forcing workers to leave the trade and find alternative employments. Many of the 'evils' associated with industrial capitalism were not inevitable, however, but arose from the ignorance and vice of working people. They were 'in great measure the architects of their own fortune'; poverty frequently was a direct consequence of 'idleness, improvidence, and moral deviation' and disaffection was in large part a product of the failure of working people to understand 'that mechanical inventions and discoveries are always supremely advantageous to them'.[3] And if the problem was ignorance, the solution was education. 'The radical remedy for these evils', argued Kay, who, as Kay-Shuttleworth was responsible for state educational policies after 1839, 'is such an education as shall teach the people in what consists their true happiness, and how their interests may be best promoted.'[4]

The legitimation of the economic and political status quo and the imposition of class hegemony was thus the central rationale of the educational theories developed by 'experts' such as Kay-Shuttleworth. The purpose of schooling was the transmission and reproduction of the dominant values of the middle classes, to convince working people of their manifest superiority over their own barbarous cultural traditions and to transform their behaviours into those more akin to those of 'civilised' people. Schools alone could not achieve this transformation; they would operate in conjunction with the 'educative' pressures exerted by primary agencies such as the law, the 'lessons' of the New Poor Law and the indirect education of capitalist economics. Formal schooling was nevertheless vital in ensuring that such lessons were correctly learned, and not misconstrued as pretexts for disaffection.[5] The ends of mass education remained the same, but the more subtle processes of class-cultural transformation had replaced direct attempts at social control as the means to those ends.

The correct education of working-class girls was crucial to this process. As the primary agent of cultural reproduction it was vital that the working-class wife and mother should be properly educated so that she could and would fulfil her Christian duty as a 'moral missionary' within the working-class family. As Factory Inspector Baker put it, great remedial measures are as necessary for the females, as for the males, if not more so, since to them we are indebted for every home comfort, and we may rest assured that where the homes are right the neighbourhoods are right, and where the neighbourhoods are right the country is right; for what is one's country but a great home, made up of an aggregate of little homes, which are dependent upon the domestic qualities and attractions of the women for their happiness and enjoyment?[6]

The 'good' working-class wife and mother was, like her middle-class counterpart, one who did not engage in paid labour but concentrated her energies on the management of home and family. The sheer inappropriateness of the 'new model' family form to the material conditions of existence for the majority of women in industrial Lancashire and rural Norfolk and Suffolk is evident, but rather than ignorance or lack of understanding, what is exhibited here is a consistent application of ideologically derived perceptions and prescriptions. It was the failure of the ignorant and irrational working classes to adopt attitudes of independence and self-help, habits of frugality and industry and conformity to naturally ordained gender 'roles' and behaviours that caused such poverty and misery. Wives were forced to work for wages because their domestic incompetence wasted family resources and drove their husbands to spend their money on drink. Working-class poverty could, therefore, only be eliminated when such behaviours were eliminated and was itself an integral, if painful part of the educative process. The low wages received by working women, for example, were an ultimately benign element of the 'education of circumstances' (a term coined by a contemporary educationist), in teaching women that their natural and proper place was in the home and not in the factory or fields. 'Some persons feel much regret at seeing the wages of females so low,' explained Dr Mitchell of the Factory Enquiry Commission, 'but perhaps such persons are wrong':

> nature effects her own purposes more wisely and effectually than could be done by the wisest of men. The low price of female labour makes it the most profitable as well as the most agreeable occupation for a female to superintend her own domestic establishment, and her low wages do not tempt her to abandon the care of her own children. Nature, therefore, provides that her designs shall not be disappointed.[7]

The 'education of principle' provided in a 'good' school for girls would thus supplement the 'lessons' taught by such experiences, to teach girls that their proper role when married was that of a full-time wife and mother. Paid work was a necessity for the unmarried girl, of course, and in preparing girls for a 'suitable' occupation such as domestic service, the schools would institute a benevolent cycle, wherein circumstance and principle were mutually reinforcing in the preparation of efficient and capable housewives, imbued with the 'civilised' attitudes and values that experiences of schooling and extended contact with a middle-class family would confer. The Revd J. Brewer praised the influence of middle-class housewives on their female servants in 1856 in terms which make their expected 'educative' function clear:

> The female servants in your household, whom you have taken and instructed in their respective duties – whose manners you have softened – who have learned from you how to manage a household – who have caught up from you, insensibly, lessons of vast utility, lessons of order, lessons of economy, lessons of cleanliness, lessons of the management of children, of household comfort and tidiness; these women eventually become the wives of small tradesmen and respectable operatives ... in all the ordinary duties of a wife ... the class drawn from domestic servants have advanced as their mistresses have advanced.[8]

From what might be called the contingent curriculum of the earlier period, where a mixture of practical aspects of school resourcing, taken for granted gender assumptions and attempts to defuse hostility against girls' education had led to needlework being given a central place in the model curriculum for girls' schools, the 'ideal' curriculum for girls now became explicitly linked to the transforming purposes of their education. This is illustrated in an exchange between Lord Ashley and Kay in the Report of the Select Committee on the Education of the Poorer Classes in 1837–38. Lord Ashley began by asking Kay:

> Looking to education as a means of contributing to the comfort and order of society, are you not of the opinion that females of the poorer classes should acquire the various arts of domestic life as much as reading, writing and arithmetic?

'Certainly,' responded Kay,

> I think that the industrial instruction of females, and particularly their instruction in the arts of domestic economy, would contribute very greatly to the happiness of the poorer classes ... My view of a school is, that the objects which may legitimately sought to be attained in proceeding to develop a system of education for the poorer classes, would be improperly limited if the instruction of the females in domestic economy, particularly in frugal cookery, were omitted.[9]

For Reverend Feild of the National Society the physical and moral 'depravity' and the 'obliteration' of the distinguishing virtues of the female character could only be addressed by a combination of religious teaching and training in needlework, 'that most important and essential part of their education',[10] and 'a thorough acquaintance with household duties' became, for the Society, 'the principle requisite in the education of girls'.[11]

The British Society was also in full agreement with such theories. 'The object of your female schools', stated the Annual Report of 1841,

> is simply to qualify girls for the right discharge of these important duties (i. e. mothers, servants, nurses) and the aim and end of all instruction imparted is to make them at once intelligent and industrious, modest and humble, obedient and conscientious.[12]

Inspector Fletcher of the British Society also defined domestic economy as girls' 'sphere of real knowledge', with instruction in 'the economy of food, fire, clothing, health and cleanliness' providing 'the best possible antidote to indolence and vanity' and opportunities for 'more healthful exercise of all faculties of the mind'.[13]

Evaluated against all criteria – spiritual and moral, social and economic; the capabilities and requirements of the female intellect, of the future welfare, comfort and security of girls and of the working-class family, the comforts of the servant-employing classes and the well-being of society – domestic economy was seen to score full marks, representing, in theory at least, the ideal way forward in the education of girls and the regeneration of society. Other subjects would, of course, be included in the curriculum but the importance of domestic education was such that it should inform all aspects of teaching and learning. Thus Inspector Norris described the 'ideal' curriculum for girls as follows:

> A knowledge of the Holy Scriptures, and the power of reading aloud fluently, and of expressing themselves readily and correctly on paper, and a sufficient acquaintance with arithmetic to help them add up bills and keep household accounts, are of course essentials. But next to these ... knowledge of household matters should be given, with practical training if possible, and if *after this* there remains time for more general information, then let geography and history be added. (original emphasis)[14]

Some concern was expressed that an undue emphasis on the practical skills of domestic economy might detract from the moral dimensions of girls' education. The British Society warned against the dangers of neglecting the 'moral and mental discipline' of girls in the following terms:

it not infrequently happens that girls leave school neat sempstresses, well acquainted with household duties but as the same time with minds as uninformed, principles as unsettled, and hearts as vain as if they had never been brought under the influence of any moral or mental disci- pline whatever ... Needlework and household duties are too important to be neglected or despised; but they must not be allowed to interfere with moral and intellectual cultivation. If girls are to be trained with a view to becoming the wives and mothers of industrious and intelligent mechanics, their education must be less of the lip and the finger, and more of the heart.[15]

Nevertheless, for Inspector Norris, even moral education could be effect- ively combined with the practical skills of needlework.

Independently of the practical value of skill of needlework, it would be well worth while for the sake of the effect on the girls' characters to occupy half their time in school in this way. No one can have marked the quiet domestic aspect of one of our better girls' schools when arranged for needlework ... and that most wholesome union ... of industry with repose, of a cheerful relaxation of mind, with the most careful and decorous order, without seeing at once that it is here rather than during the morning lessons that the character of the future woman is formed.[16]

With the exception of the education provided for workhouse boys, there was no suggestion that industrial work should form part of the curriculum of boys' schools. Indeed, the very thought of combining 'professional' training with teaching was dismissed by Inspector Winder as being 'ridiculously out of place' in the context of boys' schools.[17] Instead of through 'industrial work', the cultural transformation of boys was to be achieved through the rules and routines of schooling and through the inclusion of political economy in the curriculum. Kay-Shuttleworth was an early exponent of such teaching. 'The education afforded to the poor must be substantial', he argued in 1833, and should include 'elevating knowledge', 'correct political educa- tion' and the 'ascertained truths of political economy', including the benefits of 'correct' relations between capital and labour.[18] *Easy Lessons in Money Matters* thus became a staple text in National and British schools for boys, with lessons on matters such as 'good habits to cultivate – diligence, fore- thought, temperance, frugality' and 'stern warnings of the dangers to the working man of challenging the economic order'.[19] Biographies of fictional and living people, fables and fairy stories were also used to transmit the mes- sages of political economy, but this did not preclude the inclusion of a wide range of content within boys' reading books. Nor did the centrality of political economy in the boys' curriculum impose constraints on the inclusion of a wide range of other subjects, with history, geography, grammar, natural philosophy (natural sciences) and so forth being seen as useful sources of the 'elevating knowledge' recommended by Kay-Shuttleworth. The 'ideal' curriculum for boys' schools, as recommended by the Committee of Council for Education in the 1840s, thus included a wide range of subjects, including history and geography, money matters and political economy and even subjects such as popular astronomy.

An increasing involvement by the state in the provision of working-class education also gave emphasis to gender differentiation in other ways. Although attempts to establish a state system of schooling continued to founder before the establishment of Board schools in 1870, state involvement grew steadily from the first grant payment in 1833 with, under the guidance of Kay-Shuttleworth, secretary of the Committee of Council from its establishment in 1839 until 1849, a keen commitment to the 'transformation' and reformation of working-class girls.

The introduction of compulsory schooling for factory and pauper children respectively in 1833 and 1834 and the extension of factory schooling into 'half-time' education in 1844, for example, were both informed by a class-cultural rationale which saw the imposition of compulsory schooling as a means of accelerating the transformation of especially 'deficient' working-class women. Many of the evils of industrialisation were thus to be solved, in theory at least, by the domestication of factory girls, while the training of pauper girls in domestic skills would do much to eradicate 'the germ of pauperism from the rising generation' and secure 'in the minds and morals of the people the best protection for the institutions of society'.[20] Leonard Horner, the Inspector responsible for Lancashire factory schools, was quite explicit regarding the purposes of half-time schooling for factory girls. 'As the largest proportion of the children in factories are females,' he (erroneously) stated,

> it is important that their peculiar wants should be attended to in the school arrangements. By the employment of young females all day in factories, they lose the opportunity of learning many domestic acquirements which are very necessary to make them good wives and mothers … it is therefore part of my plan, that there should be a female assistant in the factory school, and that on three days in the week instruction shall be given in needlework. This, together that the opportunity that their restricted hours of factory work will afford of learning something of domestic duties at home in assisting their mothers, will remove to a

great degree that disadvantage which has been found to attend the employment of females in factories.[21]

The persuasive powers of the Inspectors employed by the Committee of Council were also used to spread 'ideals' of girls' schooling as indeed, they were required to do by Kay-Shuttleworth.[22] Inspector Cook, for example, 'always strongly advocate(d) the introduction of all kinds of domestic employment ... with the ordinary work of the schools'. Similarly, Inspector Norris, ever a tireless champion of the cause of domestic education, suggested to schools that they might arrange for girls to 'take part in turn in the household work of the parsonage or the teacher's residence'. Even where such practical training could not be introduced, suggested the Inspectors, domestic training could be combined with the teaching of other subjects. Arithmetic could be taught by adding up shopping bills and calculating the amount of material needed to make articles of clothing; writing could be on topics such as 'how to boil a leg of mutton', 'a parlourmaid's duties', 'washing' and so forth and even chemistry could be taught, or so it was said, through cookery demonstrations performed by the mistress on a portable stove.[23]

Not surprisingly, the state system of teacher training introduced in 1846 also gave a domestic emphasis to the training of female teachers. Unlike their male counterparts, female pupil teachers (apprentice teachers) were expected to assist with the cleaning of the school as part of their continuing 'education' and, indeed, it was observed that school managers 'who have the interests of their female apprentices really at heart' would require them 'to do sometimes all the household work of the school premises' as part of their 48-hour-plus weekly work-load.[24]

Those who went on to further study at training college continued to study domestic subjects, including instruction in 'clothing, food, cooking, laundry, the duties of servants, household expenses of a labouring man and his family, savings banks the nature of interest, and practical rules, personal and domestic, for the preservation of health'. This heavy burden was 'compensated' for by a reduction in the number and level of other subjects studied in comparison with the syllabus for male trainee teachers.[25] The goals of class-cultural transformation were also made very explicit in the training colleges, with the examination questions in domestic economy for 1852, for example, containing such gems as:

What effect has the employment of women in charing, washing or outdoor labour upon their families?
What effect has the employment of girls in straw plaiting or lace making upon their moral habits and the comfort of their homes?[26]

From the later 1830s, therefore, there was a clear divergence between what was thought to be appropriate to the educational needs of the two sexes, with Evangelical and middle-class views on the supposed roles of working-class women defining the purposes and practices of girls' schooling in line with their domestic and 'moral' responsibilities within the private sphere of the home. That for boys should prepare them for the public sphere and for their future roles as honest and industrious artisans. Men and women were naturally different, their roles and responsibilities in life were naturally different and, equally naturally, the focus and content of their schooling should be different.

WORKING-CLASS VIEWS

Demand for education amongst the working classes was not always the sort of demand that educationists such as Kay-Shuttleworth wished to encourage. For much of this demand was for the 'alternative' forms of education which reflected the political, social and material imperatives of that 'defective' working-class culture that the educational establishment was seeking actively to eradicate. Probably relatively little of this indigenous educational demand was overtly political; working-class alternatives to provided education ranged along a continuum which extended from what might be called the political/resistant forms of education supported by the Socialists and Chartists to the social/expedient schooling provided by the private schools. But the fact remains that many working people were hostile or indifferent to the education provided in the public elementary schools because, as in the early nineteenth century, their views of the purposes of education were very different to those held by the educational establishment. Like many middle-class educationists, the Socialist and Chartist leaders of the later 1830s and 1840s held a passionate belief in the power of education to effect social change. Like them they saw education as an integral part of a wider programme for social and political transformation. Where they differed was in their view of education as a key to understanding the causes of exploitation and class inequalities towards the achievement of an egalitarian society, in which the talents and capacities of working people could flourish and their labour receive its just reward. 'Knowledge is Power' proclaimed the *Poor Man's Guardian*, Educate! Educate! Educate! urged the rationalist socialists, but it was *really* useful knowledge that was sought, and emphatically not the capitalist political economy that was promulgated in the provided schools. As an article in the *Northern Star* stated in 1839, 'let the people have their rights, and they will instruct themselves'; education was a matter not of social control but of personal and political liberation. And if relatively few working people would explicitly have articulated such counter-cultural views of education, the words of the Birmingham private school mistress who insisted 'with much warmth' that it was the duty of the parents and not of the schools 'to teach morals' would have been received with considerable favour.[27]

Alternative counter-cultural views on the purposes of education began to fade in the 1840s, however, as political radicalism began to lose its cutting edge. After the defeats and setbacks of 1848 that marked the effective decline of Chartism and as material conditions began to show a distinct though modest improvement, radicalism, confrontation and 'alternative' ideologies shaded into reformism and respectability as working people began to recognise that they too had a stake in the hedge of industrial capitalism. Independence and class pride were not abandoned but were, as Kirk argues, 'harnessed to more reformist and, often, more privatised ends', with working-class respectability being identified with 'an overall acceptance of a social and cultural world whose dominant influence was bourgeois in character'.[28] In sum, individualistic and success-oriented values and aspirations were beginning to take the place of visions of a social and political revolution spearheaded by the working classes. Independent working-class educational initiatives continued to command widespread support, but this sprang from a more individualistic perception of the value of education as a means of self-improvement and fulfilment and as a route to social and occupational advancement.

There thus developed a bridging-point across the cultural divide between 'expert' educational theories and working-class requirements; a common ground where ideologies of self-improvement and national reform became linked in a pragmatic consensus as to what it meant to be a 'civilised' and/or 'respectable' citizen and worker, with a complementary alignment of educational purposes. That bridging-point was provided by an understanding, common across all social classes, that the main purpose of education was to prepare children for 'the main purpose of life', that of getting and earning a living.

Educationists were quick to condemn what they saw as parental 'apathy' towards provided schooling, and their 'ignorant' failure to appreciate its moral and cultural worth. In the 1851 Education Census, for example, Mann commented:

practically, it is to be feared, the length and character of the education given in this country to the young are regulated more by a regard to its material advantage, as connected with their future physical position, than by any wise appreciation of the benefits of knowledge in itself.[29]

The Newcastle Commission also commented, with an evident disapproval:

> Time for school attendance is spared only with a view to its being preparation for work ... In short, (parents) regard schooling, not as a course of discipline, but only as a means of acquiring reading, writing, arithmetic, sewing and knitting, as a preparation for the main business of life – earning a living.[30]

This made sense in the material context of working-class life, where the opportunity costs of schooling (the loss of a child's earnings or help at home, the cost of school fees and of decent clothing and footwear) had to be weighed against the returns of such an investment. For some *boys*, however, the potential rewards of such an investment could be high. Attitudes of deference and docility, strong sinews and habits of industry were still all that was required of much of the labour force, but in the 1840s and 1850s productivity and efficiency were beginning to place a premium on the skills of educated workers. Clerks and bookkeepers were scarce and well paid, the Great Northern and the London and North Western railway companies would not employ boys who could not read and write and there were examples of men in the community who had achieved advancement, even 'spectacular successes' through education.[31] And when prospective employers went into the schools asking 'what boys have you that are bright and sharp?' for appointment as apprentice and clerks,[32] pupils, parents and teachers sat up and took notice. And, particularly in the British schools, notwithstanding long-term purposes of cultural transformation, the need to take account of consumer demand encouraged school managers to stress the value of schooling as a means of acquiring marketable skills.

The Leeds British school for boys, for example, proudly announced the 'very eligible situations with merchants and tradesmen' occupied by former scholars. Spicer Street school in Spitalfields also reported with pride the 'boys who have been enabled ... to rise in the scale of society and to occupy ... stations of influence and usefulness', and many other schools made similar claims. Even half-time factory boys were told that if 'they followed up the instruction they received, they would not need to be workers in a mill ... they would rise to superior position in the world'.[33] And although the educational establishment continued to place the cultural and moral worth of schooling over the material, even members of the Inspectorate began to evaluate the effectiveness of schooling in terms of the occupational successes of former pupils. Inspector Bowyer, for example, heard constantly, he said, of former workhouse boys 'obtaining situations in shops, warehouses, lawyers' offices, solely by means of a good hand and skill in accounts', and

> the extension of commerce, banking, manufacture, gives employment to hosts of skilful pens and calculating heads; innumerable new offices and establishments undreamt of by our ancestors, arise, opening extensive and untrodden fields to intellectual employment. A striking example of this is afforded by electric telegraph and railway companies. The persons employed by the former ... can earn their living entirely by intellectual labour. Education has consequently been their industrial training ... even for the engine driver and porter some amount of education is indispensable.[34]

The argument cannot be taken too far. There is evidence that the benefits of full-time schooling were recognisable and accessible to only the more 'aristocratic' members of the industrial and urban working classes. Certainly the National and other Anglican schools did not embrace the notion of schooling as a route to occupational and social mobility with the same fervour as the British and other schools with Nonconformist religious allegiance. Nevertheless, as Mr Cumin found in the late 1850s, 'the value of education to boys (was) clear', the instrumental reasons for which are amusingly expressed in his account of a meeting he had with a passing workman. 'An Irishman whom I met driving a cart', he said,

> summed up the case in favour of education thus: 'Do you think that reading and writing is of any use to people like yourself?', I inquired. 'To be sure I do, Sir', the man answered with a strong brogue; 'and do you think I would be shoved into every dirty job as I am now? No, Sir! instead of driving this horse I'd be riding him.'[35]

This was not the case for girls. Respectability had, as we have seen, a familial rather than individualistic orientation for women, with a semantic ambiguity embedded in words and phrases such as 'self-respect', 'independence' and 'self-esteem' that defined their meaning in gender-based terms, neatly reversing the criteria against which the respectable behaviour of the two sexes was assessed. Whether in employment or not, the respectable working-class woman made the care of her home and family her first priority, deferring (at least in public) to the superior authority of her husband or father and demonstrating her self respect by the appearance of her person and home, the quality of her needlework, the tastiness of her cooking and the thrifty economy with which she managed her budget. It was taken for granted that she had an obligation to earn her own living before marriage and possibly also to supplement her husband's wages, but this was something merely that women 'did' before or in addition to their main occupation of housewifery, and in no sense was this on a par with men's employment. No employer would be seeking bright and sharp *girls* to appoint as clerks and engineering apprentices and there were no new 'extensive and untrodden fields' for their intellectual employment as there were seen to be for boys. What a girl really needed to learn were the domestic skills to enable her run a comfortable home, perhaps some basic literacy (though this was a dispensable luxury if a girl's wages or services at home were needed) and, if time and money were available, perhaps a little general knowledge. These were precisely the accomplishments of the 'Model Wife', as described in a lecture at Crossley Methodist Church in 1858, who, in addition to a high level of domestic skills, was 'able to write' and had some acquaintance 'with the history of her own country, with a knowledge of geography, and (of) ... those worthies of England, both men and women, who shed a lustre on their country'.[36] And how should a girl best learn the skills and knowledge she needed but working alongside her mother in the home? Even Inspector Norris was of the opinion that 'the mother is really more competent to teach such things than the teacher',[37] so why bother with the trouble and expense of schooling? Indeed, Inspector Norris also suggested that many people saw girls' schooling as being completely unnecessary:

> a very large number of people who are interested in the progress of education think of it only in connection with our national wealth; they mean by education the extension of skill and knowledge as essential elements of productiveness, and with them girls' schooling is a matter of no moment. Another still larger class of persons, who from native illiberality of mind are opposed to all education, though ashamed to confess this generally, do not blush to won it with respect to girls.[38]

That popular opinion actually *did* see some advantages in sending girls to school is illustrated by the results of Mr Cumin's inquiries:

> Various reasons were given to me for educating girls. One man, ... , said, 'I don't know, Sir, whether you would like to have your love letters read or written by strangers.' Another common labourer ... said, 'I have always heard and read that a virtuous and intelligent woman makes the best mother', ... and declared that where the wife was the reverse the husband might be driven to the pothouse. Another man said that he thought the better educated a girl was the more likely she was to

be married; and certainly there is no doubt that schoolmistresses and pupil teachers are much sought after as wives. At all events, ... with girls as with boys it is impossible to rise to any important position without being able to read and write. Without that knowledge a scullery maid cannot become a cook or a housekeeper.[39]

And there we have it in a nutshell. The purposes of girls' schooling were those of getting and keeping a husband and the production of good wives, mothers and servants. Instrumentalism and ideologies were thus conjoined in a definition of girls' education as being primarily concerned with domesticity.

STATE POLICIES

This emphasis on the domestic education of girls became even more explicit in the latter part of the century, as the state took an increasingly direct involvement in the work of schools. The payment by results system introduced in 1862, though originally conceived as a means of reducing state expenditure on education, became an instrument for state regulation of the curriculum, with payments to those 'good' schools in receipt of grants being linked to standards of achievement in officially approved subjects and levels of attendance. Not surprisingly, first needlework, then theoretical domestic economy, then cookery, laundry work and practical housewifery were given the stamp of official approval, with a consequent enormous rise in the number of girls studying these subjects in the board schools established under the 1870 Education Act.

Anna Davin has pointed out that none of the reasons commonly put forward for the passing of this Act – the extension of the franchise in 1867, the need for an educated and skilled labour force and so forth – actually were applicable to girls, and suggested that one might ask why girls were included in the provisions of the Act at all.[40] But of course one does not need to ask – the purpose of educating working-class girls remained that of making them good wives and mothers and, though state policy refuted this as a primary aim of schooling, the production of good domestic servants continued to be seen as an integral part of the educative process.[41] A subtle shift in thinking was evident in this period; state policies of class-cultural control were informed by the assumption that the 'new model' family form of the male breadwinner and wholly dependent wife represented what Helen Bosanquet called in 1906 the 'stable family', and the aim of inculcating 'appropriate' attitudes appears to have hardened explicitly to convey the idea that paid labour after marriage was *not* consistent with a 'respectable' life-style. Similarly, the rationale for the domestic curriculum increasingly began to be expressed in terms of national 'efficiency', with later nineteenth and early twentieth-century fears that poor standards of health and high rates of infant mortality were undermining the nation's economic and military health. Be that as it may, certainly the growing efficiency and uniformity of schooling that was associated with increasing state involvement in elementary education also saw the extension of gender differences in the purposes and nature of the schooling of working-class children. As Turnball has commented, in the later part of the century, 'the belief that the sexes should have separate but complementary adult roles found expression in every aspect of schooling'.[42] From the provision of a basic curriculum of reading, religion and regulation for both boys and girls in the voluntary provided schooling of the early part of the century, a mixture of pragmatism, instrumentalism, patriarchal ideologies and strategies of class-cultural control now defined curriculum policies in strictly gender-based terms.

ACCESS TO SCHOOLING

As in the first three decades of the century, the identification of women as the chief agents of cultural reproduction within the working-class family continued to give a theoretical primacy to the provision of schooling for girls. Again, however, the practices of schooling generally reversed this priority, to give a greater importance to the schooling of boys. Fewer school places were provided for girls in the public elementary schools and far fewer girls than boys were 'on the books' of such schools, with the proportion of female scholars being only around 44 per cent of total enrolment in 1851.[43] Nevertheless, the available statistics also suggest that girls' attendance at day school (public and private) was improving at a steady rate. So, whilst a very tentative estimate for 1833 puts the proportion of female scholars at around 44.6 per cent of the total, more definite figures for 1851 put the girls at around 46 per cent of pupils at public and private day schools, and by 1861 the proportion of girls in the specimen districts investigated by the Newcastle Commission had risen to 48.7 per cent.[44] Whilst, however, this proportional increase was apparent in the provided schools (44 per cent female scholars in 1851, rising to 45.6 per cent in 1861), it was much more noticeable in the private schools (50.6 per cent female scholars in 1851, 54.7 per cent by 1861),[45] suggesting that, if gender concepts now gave more positive support to the idea of girls' schooling, they continued to limit girls' access to better *quality* schooling – a point that will be returned to later in this chapter. There were also very striking regional differences in girls' access to schooling, with the girls of industrial Lancashire again having particularly poor levels of day school attendance, despite increased efforts by the National Society to extend the civilising benefits of education to them and considerable investment of state grants in the region. If the opening up of new employment opportunities and an ethos of self-improvement and respectability was encouraging a positive appreciation of schooling for Lancashire boys – and adult education classes for Lancashire men – there were few incentives to counterbalance views which saw women's domestic work and 'unskilled' labour as requiring anything more than minimal educational achievements at best. The operation of gender divisions of labour in the family and work-place still continued to depress expectations of what was appropriate to female education and to erect barriers against girls' attendance at school.

In 1851, therefore, Lancashire girls made up the minority of scholars on the books of all day schools (43.8 per cent of pupils), they were much less likely than boys to attend a public elementary school (around 42 per cent of pupils), and were even in the minority at the private schools (47.7 per cent), contrary to common experience in other regions.[46] By the time of the Newcastle survey there had been a slight improvement in girls' day school attendance, and though still very heavily outnumbered by boys, girls now represented around 45.7 per cent of pupils.[47] Neither educational priority nor educational progress can be said to have exercised a particularly positive influence on girls' access to day schooling in the region, and if not the most educationally deprived girls in England as they had been in the earlier period, Lancashire girls remained acutely disadvantaged, with only Metropolitan Middlesex and Bedfordshire (the centre of domestic lace-making) having lower proportions of girls at day school.[48] Even the force of compulsion seemed unable to overcome the barriers limiting girls' schooling, and they were also underrepresented in the compulsory factory schools established under the legislation of 1833 and 1844, representing only 43 per cent of pupils in Lancashire factory schools in 1851.[49]

The reason for this was simple. It was that fewer girls than boys were employed in the cotton factories at the ages when schooling was compulsory. In 1833, for example, when the new Factory Act required that two hours per day were to be spent in school by children aged between nine and thirteen, there were more than a thousand fewer girls than boys aged under fourteen in the factories. And from being 6.2 per cent of the workforce in 1835, the proportion of girls aged between nine and thirteen declined to 3.9 per cent in 1862, while that of boys fell from 6.9 per cent to 4.9 per cent.[50] There were a number of reasons for this. The educational clauses of the Factory Act acted as a disincentive to the employment of children, particularly when teenage girls were cheap to employ, and there was no apprenticeship system such as the spinner–piecer system to counterbalance this disadvantage for girls as there was in the case of boys. Most importantly, the high rate of adult female employment in the industrial regions placed a premium on girls' services as domestic workers and in the same way that girls were said to be 'too useful to be spared to go to school',[51] so also they were too useful at home to be spared for the factories. It is likely then that the experiences of the 20 illiterate female factory workers interviewed by the master of the night school they attended in Ancoats in the later 1860s were fairly typical. None of these girls had attended any day school, and as the master wrote to Inspector Fearon,

> Of these 9 said they remained at home until they were eleven years old when they went to the silk mill and worked full time; 4 remained at home to look after the younger children while their mother went to the mill; 5 went to service until 13 years old; and the other two did what little cleaning they could get at neighbours' houses.[52]

Girls were in the majority of pupils at Sunday school, with nearly 14,000 more girls than boys enrolled as pupils in 1851, making up 52 per cent of total pupils.[53] These part-time schools were extremely important in providing a basic, if limited education for both sexes but, as the Manchester Statistical Society concluded in 1838, 'it is mainly among the younger portion of the female population that these excellent institutions are exercising their powerful influence', with an imbalance of female pupils in the Sunday schools of Pendleton of two girls to every one boy.[54]

Night classes were also provided by a number of Sunday schools for the purposes of elementary instruction at a 'rudimentary' level and, again, girls were likely to be in the majority of pupils.[55] The nature and quality of the education available in these Sunday school evening classes was, however, very limited, with a schooling consisting of a few hours per week providing an opportunity to learn only the basic skills of literacy at best. One of the chief hindrances to the progress of their education was said to be the tiredness of factory children and the effort and commitment that must have been needed to attend these classes after a demanding day's work can only be guessed. Evidence of the low standards of achievement of factory children, especially of factory girls, however, is telling. As Stockport Sunday school, for example, children employed in the factories were less likely to reach the higher classes than children from any other occupational group, with factory girls being particularly badly represented in the advanced girls' class. The same picture of lower levels of attainment was true of factory pupils at Birmingham New Meeting Sunday school.[56]

Other evening classes catering for adults 'sufficiently grounded in educational knowledge', as Inspector Winder described them, were, on the other hand, dominated by male members. 'Founded by men, controlled by men, and for the use of men', the entry of women into Mechanics' Institutes was often met with opposition and suspicion by the male membership, with a whole host of formal and informal barriers operating to limit women's access to such classes.[57] The Lancashire and Cheshire Union of Mechanics' Institutes, for example, claimed a 50 per cent membership of 'operatives on weekly wages' in 1864–65, but women of all social classes made up only around 10 per cent of membership in both the 1830s and 1860s.[58] Similarly, it was rare for women to attend classes at Working Men's Colleges, with, for example, only 20 women members recorded for the Sheffield College in 1857 out of a total membership of 100.[59] Thus in addition to their very limited access to day schooling, women living in the industrial districts of the North also had very limited access to the educational resources which enabled numbers of working men to compensate for limited elementary schooling in pursuit of self-improvement.

In contrast, in Norfolk and Suffolk, though a region that was given very low priority in the allocation of national resources and where there was relatively little public anxiety about the apparent deficiencies of working-class women, girls' levels of day school enrolment were considerably superior to those of Lancashire girls. They were even, in a number of instances, superior to those of boys in the region. This was partly a factor of school supply; the Norfolk and Suffolk National Society and local clergy had made strenuous efforts to establish schools in the more inaccessible rural areas but, as in the early part of the century, the key explanation for this somewhat contradictory pattern can be found in the conditions of the local labour market as they affected the lives and futures of both girls and boys.

Changes introduced by the 1834 Poor Law, for example, were detrimental to the school attendance of poor children. At Fakenham in Norfolk it was said:

the first question asked by the Board (of Poor Law Guardians) when a man applies for relief is 'what is the age of your children?' If they are of 9 or 10 they are held capable of earning something.

As the 1843 Report on the Employment of Women and Children in agriculture commented, 'the New Poor Law had a visible effect on education, in making the children used as earners at an early age'.[60] Even when parents were able and willing to send children to school, in many instances they were 'informed that they must give up the child or be dismissed from labour themselves',[61] with the result that even children as young as six were sent to work in the fields. Or at least *boys* were. For the strong gender divisions of labour that limited the agricultural work of women also limited demand for girls to work in the fields and for their services as domestic helpers. Mrs Cole, the wife of a Norfolk farm-worker and mother of 14 children, clearly had a very positive evaluation of education and made enormous efforts to send her eight daughters to school, but even she was unable to overcome the obstacles to her sons' schooling. The 'boys haven't had as much schooling as the girls', she told the Revd J. Frazer, 'because they had to go out to work so young':

> Three of them went out at 6 and took 1s. a week. Her husband's master ... would have paid him off if he hadn't let them go to work. Her eldest son ... has improved himself and can write pretty well now. He wrote home to his parents to beg that his youngest brothers may be kept at school, as he has found the good of a bit of learning. She has another son ... he can neither read nor write, because he has been at work since he was six years old.
>
> The other two boys who are alive are poor scholars; they've been to night school for two or three winters but are too tired with their day's work when they get there to learn much.[62]

Not only was it easier for a girl to be spared to go to school, there were also good reasons for her to do so and, particularly where schooling was free, as around one-third of Suffolk Anglican schools were, the prospect of a job in domestic service encouraged country girls to attend day school. In 1851, therefore, girls represented the *majority* of day school pupils in 17 of 39 registration districts in the two counties, the *majority* of pupils in the Anglican schools which made up the bulk of school provision in the region, and the *majority* of pupils at Norfolk National schools, and there were equal or higher proportions of girls at school in over half the Norfolk and Suffolk districts.[63] In 1861 girls still remained in the majority at the day schools in association with the Anglican Church,[64] and though new opportunities were beginning to encourage a higher day school attendance on the part of country boys, the continuing importance of boy labour still limited their access to day schooling.

The situation in the towns, however, was different yet again, and as in Lancashire, the pushes and pulls of the local labour market gave the advantage to boys in terms of attendance at a public day school, though girls were in the majority at the private schools and in the part-time Sunday schools. That girls in towns such as Yarmouth and Ipswich were less likely than boys to attend a public elementary school was noted by Mr Hare of the Newcastle Commission, and though he noted that 'no peculiar or extraordinary impediment' such as factory work militated against their schooling, he recognised the additional burden that domestic labour presented to girls in these towns.

> Sometimes, like their brothers they are kept away for the sake of what they can earn by occasional employment ... ; but more frequently they are required to help in domestic matters, in seasons of sickness, or when the mother is out at work, or is secluded by a new birth in the family.

Further, as he also commented, 'the poor are more willing to spend money on the education of their sons than of their daughters'.[65]

That the operation of gender divisions of labour rather than ideology was the key determinant on girls' access to schooling is also borne out by national patterns of school enrolment, with the Lancashire pattern of low levels of female day school enrolment being replicated in the north Midlands, the north-west and Yorkshire – all districts where the textile factories placed high demands on female labour – and in areas such as Bedfordshire, where their work in domestic lace-making prevented girls from going to school.[66] Analysis of statistics of school attendance in 1851, however, also shows that the proportion of the female population at school was equal or superior to that of boys in a high number of districts in predominantly agricultural counties, sometimes even the majority, and that, in general, urban districts had lower levels of female school attendance than rural.[67] Girls were also in the majority of scholars at Church day schools in a number of agricultural counties in 1861, including Berkshire, Cambridgeshire, Dorset, Essex, Gloucestershire, Leicestershire, Oxfordshire, Rutland, Sussex and Wiltshire.[68] Thus we see an almost complete reversal of establishment priorities, with the lowest levels of female schooling attendance where the need was seen to be the greatest, and the highest levels of female school attendance in those regions and districts where the urgency of cultural transformation in the interests of social order and harmony was seen to be far less pressing.

That girls were also more likely to be enrolled on the books of poorer quality schools, with only 40.5 per cent of female enrolment in the 'class one' schools classified by the Newcastle Commission, was not always quite the disadvantage it may at first appear. Evaluative criteria of schooling 'quality' were saturated with gender concepts and a 'good' school for girls generally was one where the domestic curriculum took a high profile.

This was what the theory of girls' schooling prescribed, but as with patterns of school attendance, the precepts and policies of educational experts were mediated by a whole variety of factors, often to moderate or deny the aims of the educational establishment. As will be shown in the next chapter, the realities of girls' schooling experiences could be very different indeed from that prescribed by the theories of educationists.

CONCLUSIONS

Though marked by what Johnson has called a 'change in gear' in the 1830s, with an increasing involvement by the state in educational matters and the evolution of a body of 'expert' educational theory, educational policies after the 1850s remained shaped by the same fundamental belief that the purpose of educating girls was to make them 'good' wives and mothers.

A more creative, less repressive concept of reform may have developed, but whether the goals were social control or class-cultural transformation, the idea that women should be educated as 'moral missionaries' in order to transmit dominant values to their future husbands and children remained central. And if the true happiness of the lower classes lay in their acceptance of the benign operation of capitalist economic organisation and the manifest superiority of bourgeois cultural values, so also it lay in their acceptance of the 'natural' roles of men and women within a civilised society. And how best to promote such recognition but through the provision of a good education, framed in accordance with the 'natural' attributes and future responsibilities of men and women? The 'education of principle' provided in a good school would thus operate in conjunction with the 'education of circumstance' experienced by girls and boys in their daily lives, to aid their 'correct' understanding of the social, economic and political ordering of society in the achievement of working-class hegemony. Working men would become honest, industrious and respectable workers, whilst their wives would become thrifty, hard-working and capable housewives and mothers. Fecklessness and vice would be eradicated, the germ of pauperism would be eliminated and all would be well with English society.

As in the earlier period, an effective consensus operated to define really useful knowledge for girls in very limited, domestically oriented terms – with 'expert' influence encouraging the teaching of domestic economy in all good day schools for girls, not just the charity and industrial schools. And as working-class political and social protest muted into the individualistic aspirations of self-improvement in the 1850s, so also working-class views of the purposes of boys' schooling came into pragmatic alignment with the reformist goals of educationists to give substance to the academic education of boys as a route to occupational and social mobility. In the post-1840 period there was, in short, an *increasing* divergence between the purposes and curriculum ideals of boys' and girls' schooling.

In the earlier part of the century, the ideals of curriculum provision were informed by the control purposes of schooling but also by rather more instrumental criteria, with an ongoing developmental process of curriculum dissemination, whereby what was seen to be good practice in some schools was recommended by the National and British Societies as models for other schools to emulate. Theory and practice were thus interlinked, both conceptually and in the processes of curriculum implementation. With the emergence of educational 'experts' and the increasing involvement of the state as a shaping force in educational policy-making, curriculum theory became conceptually separate from curriculum practices, with the work of the schools being informed by the ideals and advice of 'experts' seeking to achieve class-cultural transformation through specific forms of curriculum provision. At least this was the theory. The extent to which expert theories translated into the actual practices of schooling remains to be explored in the next chapter.

6 Schooling for Domesticity? The Later Nineteenth Century

There is a wealth of evidence available for this later period, allowing a much more extended analysis of school practices across the variety of educational provision available to girls and women, but the same questions – What were girls taught? What did they actually learn? – that provided the framework for Chapter 4 again lie at the heart of this chapter. And, though a limited availability of autobiographical material presents continuing difficulties in evaluation of the experiences of schooling from girls' and women's own perspectives, Inspectors' reports (especially their criticisms of what they saw as the deficiencies of girls' schools) and the evidence contained in school log-books[1] do provide some insights into the everyday realities of girls' schooling. Some reference is made to the likely impact of schooling on the behaviour and attitudes of working-class girls, but overall conclusions are deferred to the next chapter, where the various developments in girls' schooling and their causes and consequences are evaluated within the broad context of socio-economic and cultural developments over the whole period. The chapter ends, therefore, with an assessment of the standards of girls' more 'academic' achievements, drawing also on evidence of standards of literacy to point to the very striking differences in male and female attainments within and between rural and urban Norfolk and Suffolk and industrial and rural Lancashire.

CURRICULUM PRACTICES

The prime purpose of the compulsory schooling provided in the workhouse schools was to break the vicious circle of pauperism by the teaching of a 'tripartite' curriculum of industrial, moral and intellectual training designed to instil habits of industry and morality and to equip a workhouse child with the skills he or she needed in adult life. The education of pauper girls was thus to consist of three hours of daily instruction in 'ordinary' school subjects, together with 'such other instruction ... as may fit them for service, and train them to habits of industry'[2] under the guidance of a skilled teacher.

In practice, the provision of schooling was beset with difficulties which drastically undermined the value of even this limited curriculum. There was firstly a widespread prejudice against the provision of anything other than the most basic education ('only a pauper education must be given to workhouse children' was said to be a common belief) and, in Mr Ruddock's district, the inclusion in the curriculum of 'ordinary' subjects such as history and geography was 'so strongly objected to by the Guardians' that few schools taught them. Even where children attended a local school Poor Law Guardians were often reluctant to pay the extra 1d per week for children to learn arithmetic.[3] Such prejudice was particularly directed against girls, with a general hostility to the idea that their more academic learning should extend beyond basic reading. Workhouse Inspector Mr Carlton Tufnell reported in 1850:

> I continually hear objections against giving girls the same amount of education as boys, and even the proposal to teach them geography is frequently treated as too palpably absurd to deserve the trouble of an answer. ... It is not uncommon to meet with respectable persons who seem imbued with the Mohametan idea, that it is quite supererogatory to cultivate the intellectual faculties of females, or they will only go so far as to concede that they may be taught to read their Bibles, but nothing else.[4]

There were also problems of teacher supply which, despite considerable efforts towards improvement, remained probably the most serious deficiency in workhouse schooling. The untrained former dressmakers or servants or adult paupers who were the only people prepared to suffer the low salaries, poor conditions, limited prospects and high demands of workhouse teaching frequently were 'grossly incompetent, cannot write or spell',[5] and were totally inadequate to the task. It is likely then, that most, if not the majority of workhouse schools for girls were on a par with those described by Mr Ruddock in 1849, where 'the girls were not taught ciphering or writing', where the schoolmistress was expected to take care of all the infant children while their mothers worked, and that 'industrial training' consisted of the girls doing the domestic work of the establishment. It was common, he said, for girls to work in the kitchens and to do the cleaning and they were often kept busy 'waiting upon the governor or matron, nursing the infants, knitting, repairs of clothing, sewing, and more rarely, washing and ironing'. Older and 'more robust' girls were, he found,

> usually occupied in the mornings with the household work of their own or the female wards; ... this work not infrequently delays their presence

in the schoolroom until 10 or 11 o'clock, ... and, the afternoon being
usually devoted to mending or knitting, ... (these girls) did not really
obtain more than 7 or 8 hours schooling weekly, instead of the eighteen
ordered by the Poor Law Board.

Boys might be similarly served, being kept busy 'cleaning shoes, knives
and yards, long after and during morning school hours'. Frequently,
however, difficulties in finding 'suitable' work for them meant that the
industrial and vocational element was missing from their schooling. In
more than half the workhouse schools in Mr Bowyer's district in mid-
century, boys spent all their school time on their 'ordinary' lessons.[6]
Some workhouse schools were efficient, and the variety of provision
and quality in workhouse schooling makes it difficult to evaluate its
overall worth to boys and girls. Some girls, as in the Cosford union school
in Suffolk, might become 'remarkably skilful' needlewomen, able to do
'the most beautiful fancy work' that Mr Bowyer had ever seen, while the
girls at Plomesgate school learned the very useful skills of dairy work.[7] Mr
Carlton Tufnell was quite scathing, however, about the standards achieved
by girls in the more academic aspects of their schooling, with an awareness of the implications of the limited education they received for their
future prospects.

> the children get taught needlework, but nothing else. They are perhaps
> placed in servants' situations on first leaving the workhouse, but their
> ultimate destination is to swell already overcrowded ranks of needle-
> women, and to reduce by competition the wages of this unfortunate
> class to the lowest liveable point ... It is a frequent remark, in
> London, that the situation of haberdashers' assistant, apparently so
> fitted to women, is almost entirely monopolised by men. But the occu-
> pants of such situations have to make, in the daily conduct of busi-
> ness, the most rapid calculations of the process of articles sold, and
> not one girl in fifty, ... would be able to make such calculations with
> the necessary accuracy and dispatch ... This educational defect at
> once cuts them off from several occupations which would seem well
> adapted to females.[8]

Mr Bowyer claimed that girls' progress in more academic subjects was on
a par with that of boys, but the table of comparative achievements he drew
up for 1848–49 indicates that the girls' standards of achievement were
lower than those of boys, that differentials between relative achievements
were becoming greater and that, whether by cause or effect, the girls' curriculum was narrower than that of the boys (see Table 6.1).

Table 6.1 Gender differences in standards of achievement in workhouse schools, 1848–49 (%)[9]

Subject	Boys		Girls	
	1849	*1848*	*1849*	*1848*
Reading	48.2	33.4	39.4	25.5
Scriptures				
Book of general information	40.3	21.8	25.8	15.4
Writing on paper from copies	49.9	46.8	33.8	33.0
Ditto on slates from dictation and memory	28.7	9.0	19.8	5.2
Arithmetic				
Addition	15.8	10.7	11.6	10.9
Simple rules	19.6	19.5	17.1	15.3
Compound rules	19.4	17.8	10.3	8.4
Proportion and practice	5.9	4.8	1.6	0.8
Other subjects				
Geography	23.3	12.0	12.4	6.4
Grammar	11.3	3.6	4.5	1.4
History	4.7	3.6	1.3	1.1

In every curriculum area mentioned here girls were outperformed by boys, most particularly at the higher levels of achievement and in only two instances, simple and compound arithmetic, were they showing any signs at all of catching up with the boys' standards. The fact remains, however, that class and gender perceptions of the sort of schooling suitable for a pauper girl meant that whether she received a good education or a poor-quality one, academic learning was, by definition, less important than training in domestic skills.

Domestic skills training, similarly, was seen to be the *sine qua non* of the compulsory schooling provided for girls working in the textile factories, but again, a whole variety of factors operated to pervert expert theories. Log-book entries from a girls' school described by the Inspector as being 'one of the best schools in Leeds' illustrate many of the problems that undermined the quality of the half-time schooling these girls received.

The number of factory children fluctuates; sometimes 40 at others less than 20. Several children are leaving this week for various reasons – some for change merely; others for work, others again to support a poor neighbour who has begun a dame school close by. Another family moving – few really stay a whole year.

The half timers were very slovenly. Sent three home dirty. Two of them have been visited and found very poor and distressed from want of food.

(half timers) make rough work in the school and do not seem to carry away much knowledge. Very few of them can read when they come to school.

Complained to the overseer ... of the irregular attendance of the half timers.

Find the half timers coming late again. Parents careless about them.[10]

And so the list of difficulties could be continued, with children even missing school altogether for weeks on end if not working for any reason. Even if regular in attendance, few girls would have enjoyed a broad curriculum or have learned very much. Mr Winder reported to the Newcastle Commission:

the time ... during which a half-timer is under effective instruction is very short indeed: short as it is, however, in the case of girls a large portion is abstracted for teaching sewing ... a mill girl may, during her afternoon turn, lasting a week or month as the case may be, have not more than an hour a day for intellectual instruction. Indeed, in not a few private, and some public schools, needlework takes up the whole afternoon and the girls may be left a whole month without even having a reading lesson.[11]

The girls' parents do not seem to have objected to this and, if the experience of one teacher of factory girls is anything to go by, were not above manipulating the attendance of their daughters to make sure this happened. The teacher complained:

It is most difficult to make half-timers take the same interest in their lessons... This is particularly the case with those whose mothers work in the same factory and are anxious to have their needlework done by the girls when at school. Such mothers have contrived that the girls should come almost always at the hours when needlework is done so that the girls, though great dunces, rarely have a reading or writing lesson.[12]

Great dunces indeed they often were. Of 196 factory girls entering 'a most meritorious' girls' school in Bradford, nearly half were unable to read more than the alphabet and words of one syllable, though more than 40 of them were aged 12 and over. At another school none in a class of mill girls aged between eight and 13 were able to read at all. As Inspector Winder explained,

> Everywhere the lower classes were crammed with them (half-timers), passing the later period of their school time under the lowest grade of instruction, drudging hopelessly among children many years younger than themselves, and finally leaving the school unable to read a simple narrative with understanding, writing a most miserable scrawl, and incompetent to do more than a simple addition or subtraction sum in arithmetic.[13]

Half-time factory girls did, however, largely escape lessons in domestic economy. For reasons which will be considered further below, very few public elementary schools actually taught practical housewifery skills before the later nineteenth century, and it was really only in the Charity and industrial schools that these particular 'ideals' of girls' schooling were even approximately achieved before the 1870s and 1880s. At the Jubilee Charity school in Manchester, typical of many elsewhere, the girls were taught housework, kitchen work, laundry work and needlework and very little else. With a weekly timetable crammed to capacity with 'vocational' work, with Church attendance and religious studies taking up almost the whole of Sunday, and with the importance of needlework as a source of income for the school requiring that 'a large proportion of time ... be devoted to its practice', there was little time left for any more academic studies. 'The time available for ordinary school lessons', remarked the Management Committee,

> is necessarily short in an industrial establishment like the present, and therefore regulations should be made, whereby the children engaged in housework should not entirely lose the advantage of their ordinary lessons, when they happen to be detained out of school during the lesson period. They ought at least to read, and to go through the lessons prepared out of school on the preceding evening.

The Management Committee was clearly very caring of the welfare of the girls, recommending the encouragement of 'cheerful singing' and opportunities for long walks and 'callisthenic exercises' to maintain their health and spirits. Effort and achievement was also encouraged, with girls being promoted to the first class only if they had 'distinguished themselves in two, at least, out of the three sections of employment, viz., school studies, domestic studies and needlework', and with 'special encouragement and opportunity' being given to girls who showed promise in cookery. The girls may have shown 'considerable proficiency' in reading, knowledge of the Scriptures, arithmetic, dictation, etc., as reported in the *Manchester Guardian* in July 1869,[14] but this was incidental to the main purpose of their schooling, with everything directed towards the production of skilful, obedient and hard-working superior servants for the middle classes.

Industrial schools catered for girls of lower socio-economic background but there was little to differentiate curriculum content between the two grades of school. At the Royal School of Girls at Windsor, sponsored by Queen Victoria, girls again spent most of their time learning domestic skills in preparation for service and marriage and motherhood.

> It being understood to be her Majesty's wish that the girls should be so trained in the school as to fit them for service and to enable them to discharge in after life the duties of wives and mothers, to the usual instruction in religious and secular knowledge a good deal of teaching in domestic economy is added. Besides making their own clothes and those of the boys, they do ... all the housework of the schools – the cleaning, cooking, washing, and baking ... on one day in the week the lessons of the girls are in domestic economy; on another their industrial work consists of cooking cottage dinners.

It was claimed that the large portion of time devoted to industrial work did not depress the girls' attainments in other areas, but, notwithstanding possible assumptions that girls simply were not capable of high levels of attainment, it is difficult to see how this could have been the case with only half the day being given to lessons (including theoretical lessons in domestic economy) and half to housework.[15]

Few public elementary schools, however, had sufficient financial resources to implement the domestic curriculum. Inspector Norris, a tireless advocate of practical domestic training for girls, tried hard to persuade school Managers that this need not be an expensive innovation:

> There is frequently a notion on the part of school that an industrial department would involve them in much additional expense ... the simpler and cheaper the apparatus the better will be the training because the girls are less likely to be spoiled for such accommodation as they will probably find when they go out into service, and are much more likely to learn to be inventive and self reliant.[16]

Probably of equal importance was the fact that parents objected to their daughters being taught practical housewifery in school. The father who complained to the mistress of Ewell girls' school that he paid the school pence for his daughter to learn rather than to dust the school was not alone in his views.[17] Parents 'insist that they send their children to school in order to get the kind of knowledge that they cannot themselves teach them', said Inspector Cumin – a viewpoint that even Inspector Norris found reasonable. 'In many cases', he said,

> there is much that is reasonable in what the parents urge. The daughters' clothes wear out much sooner if they are employed in industrial work; more time is occupied than can be spared from home duties; the mother really is more competent to teach such things than the teacher.[18]

In practice, therefore, despite the perceived importance of domestic economy as girls' 'real sphere of knowledge', despite a heavy investment in the training of female teachers in domestic economy and suggestions from the Inspectorate that theoretical work in domestic economy might be combined with other curriculum areas, the subject remained peripheral in the curriculum of most elementary schools for girls before the later nineteenth century, with only just under 6 per cent of female pupils learning 'industrial occupations' in the Newcastle survey.[19]

In the 1850s and 1860s, therefore, it was needlework rather than domestic economy which was the mainstay of the domestic curriculum with, by the time of the Newcastle survey, an enormous increase in the teaching of sewing in private as well as public elementary school. Though nearly half the girls in the mining district inspected by Mr Jenkins still were not taught sewing, around three-quarters of girls attending day school were now so occupied for part of their time at school.[20] Improved resources, with increasing grant payments to inspected schools and the relative cheapness and availability of female teachers may well have been contributory here, in enabling more schools to employ a mistress to teach the sewing, but needlework was also very popular with parents. A Mrs Townsend accused the mistress of Norbiton National School of 'taking money under false pretences', saying that she sent her children to school to learn to read and write and to do arithmetic and that 'any mother with common sense could teach her child needlework',[21] but most parents seem to have concurred with the educational establishment in evaluating needlework as a useful skill. And if it was fancy work such as embroidery and crochet they wanted their daughters to learn, then numbers of schools were prepared to accommodate themselves to parental demand, despite the disapproval of Inspectors. Bradford Parochial School thus taught embroidery to the older girls and though this was said to be 'outrageous to many ears!' it was also said to be effective in encouraging extended school attendance. Similarly, St Andrew's school in Derbyshire permitted fancy work on two afternoons a week,[22] and no doubt many other schools did likewise.

The direct influence of the Committee of Council for Education – and the power of its purse – was probably of greater significance in the increased provision of needlework in this period. Thus in 1846 practical inducements added to the persuasive powers of the Inspectorate when needlework was made a requirement for female pupil teachers. Indeed, after 1862, grant payments demanded the inclusion of needlework in the girls' curriculum and schools in receipt of state support had to teach plain sewing to the girls whether they wished to or not. In the case of at least one school, that of Rochdale Parochial, this had serious, if unintended consequences as, rather than the massive reorganisation of the timetable that the inclusion of sewing would have required, the Managers decided that grant payments could more efficiently be secured by excluding girls from the school altogether.[23]

The power of the purse was also a major factor in the massive expansion of the domestic curriculum in the 1870s and 1880s, with grant payments from the Education Department linked directly to the teaching of domestic economy from 1874, cookery from 1882 and laundry work from 1889. As a result, the number of girls studying domestic economy in public elementary Board schools rose sharply from 844 to 59,812 between 1874 and 1882 and to 134,930 in 1895–96. By this date, 2,729 girls were also learning cookery and 11,720 were being taught laundry work.[24] That this development was accompanied by teacher scepticism about the value of such teaching and continuing parental hostility may have been a matter of some concern, but the aim of transforming working-class girls into thrifty and efficient housewives (and servants) meant that such objections generally were ignored.[25]

STANDARDS OF ATTAINMENT

The implications of the time spent on such subjects were far-reaching and serious. It was not simply that it pointed girls towards domestic pursuits and values, but also that it diverted time and attention away from other subjects of study. As Inspector Fletcher found in 1847, in grant-aided British schools for girls,

> it may be said that the instruction of the majority of the children is not so much in reading, writing and arithmetic; as in reading, writing and needlework. All efficient instruction in the branches which yet remain to be noticed is restricted to a minority ... who attain to a position in the monitor's classes, or in the upper sections of a simultaneous school.[26]

That girls' access to a broad curriculum was more limited than that of boys' was clearly shown in the results of the Newcastle Commission's enquiries in the later 1850s (see Table 6.2). As Mr Jenkins commented,

A comparison of the male and female columns shows that the differences in their respective centesimal proportions increases in favour of the males as we progress from the rudimentary to the more advanced branches of schooling instruction – proving that, from whatever cause, the education of girls is not carried out to the same extent as that of male scholars.[27]

Indeed, the only subject areas where the proportion of female pupils was greater than that of boys was in reading, religious studies, industrial work and, of course, needlework – which represents an apt summary of what was felt to be important in the education of girls of this class.

The more rudimentary level of girls' studies was not solely attributable to the presence of needlework and domestic subjects in the girls' curriculum but was also a factor of the common assumption that 'intellectual pursuits and intellectual power are by no means so necessary' for females.[28] The lady manager of one school told Inspector Kennedy in 1854 that, in

Table 6.2 Gender differences in curriculum in the later 1850s[29] in public schools in the UK

	Boys	*Girls*
Proportion of pupils (%) studying:		
Reading	94.9	95.4
Writing	79.2	76.8
Arithmetic	71.6	66.9
Needlework		75.8
Other industrial work	2.4	5.6
Geography	42.4	35.4
Grammar	29.8	25.8
History	22.6	15.6
Mechanics	1.1	
Algebra	1.5	
Euclid	1.4	
Elements of physical science	4.5	1.3
Music	10.4	6.1
Drawing	16.2	4.0

her opinion, 'sewing was all that girls needed to learn' and, as he commented, 'the fact of their being unable to read, or write, or spell, or do a sum tolerably, evidently caused her no concern'.[30] Not only was an academic education unnecessary, it could also be positively harmful. According to Inspector Moncreiff, it was a common belief that 'a high standard of general instruction' worked against the 'sound moral and industrial training of girls' and that 'it is better and safer for girls to be confined to a very narrow circle of knowledge'.[31] Indeed, 'over'-educating girls by teaching them subjects such as geography and grammar was felt to give them an unwelcome disinclination against domestic service – and what practical use was such learning to girls? Would geography help a housemaid to scour a floor?[32] The many prejudices against providing girls with anything other than a very limited education at best were summarised in an appendix to Mr Cumin's report to the Newcastle Commission. According to the Revd G. W. Proctor,

> Already we hear complaints from all parts of the country of the difficulty of procuring domestic servants, and of their unwillingness to do many of the details of household work ... Respectable Christian mothers of humble life who would have their daughters live a modest, virtuous, useful life of industry, complain to me that the present system of female education is placing many new and unlooked for difficulties in their way. All this is greatly decreasing the number of women who are fitted to make a home for a handicraftsman or a labourer comfortable and happy as his wife and the mother of his children. In my experience I have found it makes young girls impatient of and dissatisfied with home restraints and home circumstances, more attractive to the seducer of higher social position, and more susceptible of the influence of his refinement of manner and of tastes, and so, more easily his victim.[33]

The example of arithmetic, the quintessentially 'male' subject, illustrates how assumptions about natural abilities and what constituted *really* useful knowledge for working-class girls could create a vicious circle of low expectations, limited teaching and low achievements. The Revd Feild of the National Society found that in many instances, and particularly in girls' schools, 'arithmetic was merely an amusement, of no practical use'; a state of affairs arising from the view that

> if it be said that a knowledge of arithmetic is of little importance to poor children, and especially to girls, surely, then, time need not be wasted on it.[34]

Indeed, in some schools time was *not* 'wasted' on it. In the girls' school of Industry at Eye in Suffolk in the 1840s, for example, girls were not permitted to learn arithmetic, and of the girls examined by the Inspector, none could manage even a simple addition sum.[35] And in the schools visited by Inspector Noel in 1841, one teacher explained 'that she thought girls should not learn beyond compound addition in arithmetic and she taught them no further'. Another accounted for the fact that none of the girls learned arithmetic by stating that in her opinion it was unnecessary for them.[36]

Female pupil teachers were, however, permitted a lower standard of attainment in this area, female teachers in training were not taught to the same level as their male counterparts and, as Mr Carlton Tufnell recognised, the standard of arithmetic in girls' schools often suffered from a vicious spiral wherein, because their teachers knew little, 'their pupils know less'.[37] Inspector Marshall made the same point, though in noting that there were 'remarkable exceptions' where girls were well taught, he went on to say:

> I can by no means admit that female teachers are necessarily inferior to males in teaching this subject. There are no doubt, many of the former who have made up their minds that this supposed inferiority is in the nature of things, and to be accepted as inevitable. To such faint hearted teachers I would suggest, that if they teach arithmetic imperfectly, and with feeble results, it is not because the science of numbers presents any special or insurmountable difficulty to female students but because they were badly taught in their own school days and have not yet attempted to remove this original defect.[38]

But there was little incentive for female teachers to overcome their 'torpor', as he described it, not least because few parents seem to have been concerned about their daughter's progress in this area. 'Arithmetic does not seem to be at all in demand', commented Inspector Fitch, 'mothers do not care for it, or put any questions concerning it',[39] and the schoolmistress in Wakefield who changed the timetable so that arithmetic came before instead of after needlework in the hope that 'the parents will perhaps allow their children to stay until dismissal in consequence of the needlework coming last'[40] was in no doubt as to their order of curriculum priorities. The absence of arithmetic from the girls' curriculum altogether was viewed as 'a marked deficiency', but low standards of attainment seem to have been accepted as a fact of life – or a lesser evil than low standards in needlework. Though Inspector Alderson, for example, found arithmetic in girls' schools to be unsatisfactory in character and limited in extent, only 'special circumstances' would, in his opinion, merit a reduction in the time given to needlework in order to raise standards in other subject areas. All that was required of girls was a sound and 'humble' level of arithmetical knowledge.

> It has been rather the exception to find them aiming at more than the compound rules. That in this branch of instruction they should display an inferior capacity to that of the generality of boys *is to be expected* (my emphasis); but their knowledge of it, however humble, should at least be sound and correct.[41]

When direct comparisons of the standards achieved by boys and girls can be made, the poor performance of girls is evident. Inspectors Allen, Cook and Moseley compiled detailed tables of attainment for their respective districts in 1847, to show that whereas, on average, 13.5 per cent of boys were studying compound arithmetic, only 8 per cent of girls were so doing and while just over 5 per cent of boys had reached the level of 'proportion and practice', only 0.5 per cent of girls had done so. Similarly, 0.6 per cent of boys were learning fractions, but no girls at all were doing so.[42] Although Inspector Cook spoke with gratification of improving standards in arithmetic in the public day schools between the 1840s and later 1850s ('it was then very unusual to find a girls' school in which the first class could make out an easy washing bill'[43]), the findings of the Newcastle Commission showed that clear differences in the standards achieved by boys and girls still remained. Even where girls were able to achieve the same standards, axiomatic assumptions often operated to deny any ability on their part. Inspector Johnstone was much struck by the fact that though handicapped by what he saw as an inherent incapacity and the time devoted to needlework, girls were actually showing that they could be successful in learning. His observations led him to believe that no substantial differences existed between the work of boys and girls:

> As might be expected from their greater care and neatness, the girls both read and write in a slight degree better than the boys, and as might also be expected from the want of reasoning power, they do their arithmetic worse, though by no means so much worse as the ordinary contrast between boys' and girls' schools leads us to expect. The thought then naturally occurs that if girls who ordinarily devote the half of their day to needlework can produce results which are equal to the boys, they must more than equal them in natural ability, since they produce the same work in half the time.

This proposition found little favour with the teachers, and Mr Johnstone was surprised to find that teachers ascribe the equality not to greater quickness on the part of the girls, but to the comparative uselessness of the afternoon's work to the boys. These, while the girls are all at their needlework, are occupied with extra lessons, that are but amplifications of the morning ones, and present no novelty or interest.[44]

That the 'hidden curriculum' of many schools militated against girls' academic achievement is also evident from the flexibility they showed in accommodating school organisation to the domestic demands of girls' home lives. Thus Mount Pleasant School in Liverpool sought to reduce the disruption to school routines caused by irregular attendance not by seeking to encourage more regular attendance but by sanctioning time off.

In consequence of the inconvenience arising in the school from girls absenting themselves without adequate reasons, a resolution was passed that the mothers be requested to fix a morning or afternoon in the week on which their daughter stays at home.[45]

Even pupil teachers might be permitted to have time off to assist with domestic work at home and it is very likely that many schools turned a blind eye to girls' absences as a fact of life, as Anna Davin has suggested was the case in the Board Schools of the post-1870 period.[46] Schools were also likely to be sympathetic towards the need for girls to take care of younger siblings and sometimes were willing to admit young infants into the girls' school to encourage the attendance of their older sisters. Indeed, one visitor to a Liverpool school in 1842 found ten little children at school with their sisters, though none of these infants were enrolled at the school. The presence of infants may have seen to be 'a mere encumbrance' in a boys' school, but this was frequently seen to be beneficial to girls, both in supporting attendance and providing useful opportunities to learn the skills of child care.[47]

But if time spent on needlework, erratic attendance, indifference and prejudice and a self-perpetuating cycle of ignorance set an apparently fixed ceiling on girls' levels of achievement in arithmetic – and all the 'higher' areas of the curriculum, as Mr Jenkins noted – this was as it should be. While *attendance* at school could be the means of obtaining a first post in domestic service and a *little* education was desirable as evidence of training in 'civilised' social and moral habits and of some ability in needlework,[48] anything more was unnecessary – and potentially dangerous in encouraging girls away from the path of domestic righteousness. As the Revd J. Pocklington of the Salford Ragged and Industrial schools explained:

In employing servants we did not ask whether they could read, write or cipher for the sake alone of these acquirements – but simply as a means of understanding whether the servant could be regarded as moral, trustworthy and industrious.

Yet, though the word has an ironic ring, this was what popular opinion – and the educational establishment – saw as the 'ideal' of girls' education. Though the Inspectors might deplore the limited attention given to domestic economy in the generality of schools and poor standards of teaching and learning, the purposes of girls' schooling manifestly were *not* the cultivation of girls' intellectual abilities. Even in the best schools for girls the level of academic study was expected to be lower than that the best boys' schools, with female teachers being trained accordingly. And as schools improved, as more trained teachers were employed, as more schools qualified for grant aid and became subject to Inspection, the more girls were handicapped and the more unlikely it was that their schooling experiences would be on a par with those of boys.

THE 'DEFICIENCIES' OF SCHOOLING

Fortunately, then, as now, theoretical imperatives did not always translate into the realities of schooling in a smooth and uninterrupted process of imposition. Such 'ideals' were mediated, transformed and even perverted and subverted by the immediate economic and social context of the schools, by the attitudes and responses of teachers and parents, and also of the pupils themselves. And the information gleaned from 'reading between the lines' of official documents and the picture of school life contained in many log-books suggests that, even in the best schools, the education provided often fell far short of the ideals of the educational establishment.

The development of the state system of teacher training after 1846, for example, seems to have had some unanticipated, and unwelcome, consequences. Carefully selected girls of some ability and the right moral calibre and respectable background[49] would learn the professional skills of their trade through a five-year apprenticeship to a teacher in a 'good' inspected school, to be followed, in some instances,[50] by a further period of college training. This was expected to produce a plentiful supply of female teachers ready and able to transmit the 'correct' moral, social and Christian principles to their pupils and, of course, to provide an efficient education in domestic economy.

One consequence of the pupil–teacher scheme was to open up new opportunities for social and occupational mobility for able and ambitious girls from the working classes. As the journal *The Pupil Teacher* enthused,

> Many a country girl will now, by becoming a pupil teacher, be first in her family, for many generations, to be accounted of a higher grade than that of peasants and domestic servants.[51]

Even allowing for some exaggeration in the above remarks, the scheme did open up a professional career to girls which placed some premium on academic achievement and provided 'at the public expense', a more extended education than that normally available to girls of this class. Thus notwithstanding requirements for careful screening and the heavy emphasis on inculcation of appropriate class and gender attitudes, female pupil teachers and schoolmistresses not infrequently refused passively to accept the role ascribed to them. Further, they could and did give active support to the more academic achievements of girls. There were many criticisms of schoolmistresses for the sin of 'false pride', for example, which meant that they failed to convey the correct moral and social values to their female pupils and, equally seriously, led them to devalue the domestic curriculum. Inspector Cook complained that they often spoke 'slightingly' of the needlework and, in her evidence to the Newcastle Commission, a Miss Hope complained of deficiencies in female teachers' needlework skills and their attitudes towards this most essential subject. They were, she said,

> unable to cut out the most common garment, and without an idea how to prepare and arrange (needle)work for the class, or how to teach children to do the plainest and coarsest work with even common neatness. They have plainly owned that they could not make the children work, and seemed to think that it was unreasonable to expect they should do so. I have asked what they would think of a teacher who said she could not make her scholars spell. It would undoubtedly prove her to be totally unfit for her office, and no less so does the incapacity they think it no shame to avow.[52]

Nor could female pupil teachers always be relied upon to present the desired model of female docility and decorum; chatting to the male pupil teachers (even behaving 'indecently' with them in public), carrying on clandestine correspondence with men, wearing 'hoops' to achieve the fashionable crinoline style and even refusing to do the domestic work of the school on the grounds that it was 'not fit work for pupil teachers'.[53] And though Miss Hope's criticisms must be taken with an appropriate scepticism, there was a concern – and it seems to have been a justified concern – that the attitudes of their teachers were causing girls to place a lesser importance on domestic skills than on intellectual pursuits. As the Newcastle Report commented,

> The apprentices and mistresses exercise a great influence on the public opinion of the school. If they attach the notion of indignity to the scrubbing-brush, blacklead-brush, washing tub and stew pan, they soon, perhaps in some cases unconsciously, impart it to the girls ... and so bring up a race of girls of humble life, who prefer scribbling to scrubbing, or reading Walter Scott, Byron, James, Harrison Ainsworth, translations of Eugene Sue, and the London Journal, to reading their Bible or cookery book. *I have seen this effect produced.* (my emphasis)[54]

The National Society similarly expressed concerns that the real objectives of the girls' education were being neglected. 'It is to be hoped', the Society warned in 1862,

> that no desire to make girls little Newtons, little Captain Cooks, little Livingstones, Little Mozarts and Handels, and little Sir Joshua Reynoldses, will ever take us too low for keeping in sight the object of teaching them to make and mend shirts, to make and mend pinafores, and darn stockings and socks. If it does then from that day the Society will go back.[55]

Even the Inspectorate were sometimes guilty of overestimating the importance to girls of book learning, complained Inspector Norris.[56]

Many of these female teachers must have been valuable role models for their female pupils, particularly in the rural areas where, despite disadvantages such as lower female salaries, social isolation and additional duties such as playing the piano in church, the lot of the schoolmistress compared very favourably to that of the average farm labourer's wife. This point is supported by evidence of higher attainments on the part of girls when taught by a woman rather than a man, particularly when they were taught in mixed classes.[57] Marion Johnson found this to be the case in Derbyshire village schools and in the schools inspected by Inspector Allen, for example, girls outperformed boys in all the three Rs when taught by a woman. Indeed, attendance at a mixed school (and most rural schools were co-educational) does appear to have been generally supportive of girls' attainments whether they were taught by a man or woman, with a tendency, noted and disapproved by the Inspectors, to discourage the domestic studies of girls in favour of other subjects.[58] Girls attending the admittedly exceptional school at Hitcham, for example, were taught botany by a retired Cambridge professor.[59] A number of the girls attending

Little Bramford school in Suffolk in the 1860s were taught by the able and energetic Miss Hicks to a very sound standard of basic education, with four girls achieving standard six (no boys did so), and seven girls (and four boys) reaching standard five.[60] At least three Hitcham girls were able to use their education as a route for occupational mobility.[61] Two of these, both the daughters of agricultural labourers, became pupil teachers in the 1860s, with one, Sarah Sipson, going on to attend the Diocesan training college in Norwich to become a certificated teacher. The other, Amy Grimwood, went on to become a letter-carrier (post woman) and the third girl, Mary Ann Baker, became an untrained teacher, a job that must be considered an improvement on the domestic service that was the lot of her sister Elizabeth, in indicating that her education gave Mary Ann some choice regarding her occupational future.

Practical day-to-day considerations could also erode barriers against equal achievement. The schoolmistresses in Derby, Leeds and Trowbridge who neglected the needlework in order to bring the girls up to examination standard in arithmetic probably represented a not uncommon response to the pressures of the 'payment by results' system of grant aid introduced in the early 1860s.[62] And despite the payment of grants to support the teaching of domestic subjects in the later part of the century, the heavy costs of implementing such teaching meant that, particularly in rural areas, many girls did not receive the training in housework that the Education Department deemed so essential.[63]

It is also very difficult to believe in the efficacy of the overt and covert moral pressures the schools were supposed to convey and their ability to inculcate approved models of feminine behaviour when one reads log-book entries detailing what actually happened in classrooms. Nothing brings the realities of schooling experience more vividly to life (and the inadvisability of assuming the deed for the word) when one reads of the antics of pupils such as the girls at school in Kingston upon Thames in the 1860s. The teacher described several incidents of misbehaviour:

Emma Stevens came to school with hoops and took occasion to make them conspicuous, swaying them against my leg. I said Emma, you know the rule about hoops. She swung out of the room calling out that she would not take them off and she would never come again. She came again in them at 2 o'clock. … I said Emma, you have not taken off the hoops, you know the rules as well as I do. She made grimaces and walked out of the playground.

Emma Bayton brought her own (needle)work to school and said as she paid two pence per week she was not obliged to help with school work.

Eliza Bennet very disobedient, idle and insolent. She called to other children to sit idle and not to knit.

There was also the incident when the girls refused to curtsey on entering the school, 'muttering that they should come in as they liked, they did not make curtsies going into Sunday school and they would not make them here'.[64] There was also the Suffolk girl who became so bored with the repetitious nature of the needlework that, as she recounted in her autobiography, 'I threw it on her (the Headteacher's) desk, jumped the seat, through the door, jumped the playground wall and was away home.'[65] One might continue with many similar instances, and probably far more except that teachers must have exercised discretion in always recording the truth of what went on in their classrooms, but the point is made; girls did not necessarily adopt the approved models of behaviour simply because this is what was taught to them in the schools.

There were, also, a number of schools where girls appear to have been well taught even by present day standards. These would have included the 'admirable' schools in Nottingham, St Leonard's and Wolverhampton which so impressed Inspector Marshall with the standard of their arithmetic, and King Edward's school in Birmingham, where one-fifth of the pupils were the daughters of working men. Inspector Fitch described this school in the following terms:

> I know no other schools which so refute the popular fallacy as to the incapacity of girls for the advanced study of arithmetic, and the inappropriateness for them of many of the intellectual exercises generally confined to the best boys' schools. The teaching of needlework is not neglected, but fortunately neither the governesses or the parents seem to think that the mental improvement of girls should be sacrificed to that art.[66]

The condemnation of ambitious expectations for girls on the part of the National Society also suggests the existence of schools where girls enjoyed access to a broad curriculum, as does Inspector Marshall's strong disapproval of the outcomes of girls' schooling. As he reported in 1858:

> You may meet a girl coming out of school, aye, and her instructress too, who may be able to state the height of every mountain in Europe, and the specific gravity of every mineral, and yet be unable to boil a leg of mutton, or hem a pocket handkerchief; able to pass a first class exam, but not able to perform the duties of a domestic servant or a domestic wife.

Schools where girls were well taught against present day criteria were, however, exceptional and it would be foolish to conclude that the majority of working-class girls normally attended schools such as these. Problems of under-resourcing continued to undermine the quality of country schools in Suffolk and Norfolk, for example, with the majority of schools teaching only the most basic curriculum of the three Rs. Thus, though an equality of educational opportunity between boys and girls in the generality of village schools is evident, even a superiority of opportunity for girls in some schools, it was an equality that stemmed from the inability of the schools generally to provide a 'good' education, as defined by the gender-specific criteria of the period. In a 'good' town school educational 'quality' was synonymous with gender differentiation and inequality and it is likely that those girls who were fortunate enough to attend a day school had very limited educational experiences and attainments. This can be illustrated by a comparison of the British schools in Ipswich where, despite a professed priority given to the education of girls, the narrow curriculum of the girls' school and the poor quality of the teaching meant that more than half the girls achieved only standards one or two in 1864–65, while the boys' school was probably on a par with the best in the country. At the opening of the schools in 1848 much was made of the greater importance of female education, though fewer school places were provided for girls – and even fewer attended the school (150 places, 59 pupils in 1848) – though the boys' school had its full complement of 300 pupils. Visits were made to places as far distant as Bradford and Jersey to assess the suitability of candidates for the post of master to the boys' school, but not for the mistress of the girls' school, while her known incompetence did not lead to her dismissal but only to a reduction in her salary. The boys were taught history, geography, linear and model drawing, natural history, elements of natural science, music and grammar in addition to the basic three Rs. The girls' school taught 'as much of this course as may be deemed suitable, together with ... plain and useful needlework and knitting'.[67] Like the girls of industrial Lancashire, the girls of urban Norfolk and Suffolk were grossly disadvantaged by their class and their gender, with their chances of experiencing a decent standard of academic education being so small as to be almost non-existent.

That girls' access to schooling and educational achievements were linked to occupational opportunities and prospects in the local labour market is also supported by evidence of literacy standards. For similarities and differences in the schooling experiences of girls within and across the two regions are pointed up very clearly by evidence of changes in male and female literacy levels in this period. In Norfolk and Suffolk, for example, though male illiteracy remained well above national average in the period 1839 to 1885, there were striking improvements in female literacy, rising from an average of 50 per cent in Norfolk and 48 per cent in Suffolk in 1839–45 to 76 per cent in Norfolk and 78 per cent in Suffolk in 1870, and 91 per cent in both counties in 1885. Though women were more illiterate than men in 1839–45, the situation had reversed by 1855 and by 1858 Suffolk and Norfolk women had literacy levels above the national average. Disadvantaged they may have been in terms of their occupational choices, but the women of Norfolk and Suffolk clearly enjoyed educational advantages not available to their male peers.

Standards of literacy also improved in Lancashire, though here the striking fact is the continuing very high levels of female illiteracy. Only 33 per cent of Lancashire women could sign their names in 1839–45, compared with 61 per cent of men, with a level of female illiteracy higher than that in any other county in England and Wales before the 1850s and with only Monmouth having higher levels even as late as 1885 (see Table 6.3).

Superior levels of female literacy were not, however, maintained in the urban districts of Norfolk and Suffolk, while the sharp differences between male and female literacy levels were softened considerably in the more rural, less industrialised districts of Lancashire. In the county towns of Norwich and Ipswich, for example, female illiteracy remained higher than that of male illiteracy in 1871, while in the Lancashire districts of Fylde, Ormskirk, Lancaster, Ulverstone and Lunesdale differences between male and female literacy levels were 5 per cent or less.[68]

Table 6.3 Regional and gender differences in levels of illiteracy in Lancashire, Norfolk and Suffolk, 1839–85[69] – proportions of illiterate brides and grooms (%)

| | Lancashire | | Norfolk | | Suffolk | |
	Brides	Grooms	Brides	Grooms	Brides	Grooms
1839–45	67	39	50	44	46	52
1850	64	37	44	41	48	47
1855	59	33	39	41	41	42
1860	54	29	30	35	30	38
1865	46	24	27	32	28	34
1870	39	21	24	30	22	31
1875	34	18	20	25	19	26
1880	27	14	14	21	16	22
1885	18	10	11	17	11	19

The employment of women and girls in the textile factories of industrial Lancashire may have enabled them to earn relatively high wages, but the costs were high, not least in the educational deprivation experienced by women.

CONCLUSIONS

The chapter has continued themes introduced earlier, with evidence of girls' superior access to schooling in the rural areas of Norfolk and Suffolk over that of Lancashire girls giving further support to the proposition that the operation of gender divisions of labour in the local labour market was the prime determinant of working-class girls' school attendance.

The schools they attended were of a variety of types; public elementary day schools, private schools, Sunday schools and evening classes and other part-time classes, charity and industrial schools and the compulsory schooling provided for children in the workhouses and textile factories. But, notwithstanding differences in degrees of emphasis, all pursued the same curriculum goals, with the teaching and learning of reading and writing (and possibly arithmetic), religion and domestic skills being seen as the basic learning requirements of working-class girls. What might be described as the contingent curriculum of the earlier period, where needlework was a practical and useful fund-raising expedient, had been replaced by a curriculum model where the inculcation of domestic skills and home-centred attitudes were imbued with a moral purpose, with the values of respectability intertwining with the goals of class-cultural transformation to define the production of 'good' wives and mothers as the *sine qua non* of working-class female education.

In the charity schools and industrial schools the domestic curriculum reached full flower, and these schools came closest to matching the ideals of curriculum implementation. Limited resources and parental hostility placed severe constraints on the teaching of practical domestic skills in the public elementary day schools before the 1880s, however, despite the efforts of the Inspectorate and the development of teacher training specifically designed to improve the 'quality' of girls' schooling in regard to the teaching of domestic economy. The power of the Treasury purse nevertheless proved to be an effective persuader, and as grant payments were linked firstly to the teaching of needlework and later in the century to the teaching of domestic economy, cookery and laundry work so these became increasingly prominent in the curriculum of girls' schools.

Increased provision of needlework had serious implications, in restricting the time available to more academic studies for more and more girls. Perhaps equally influential on the limited curriculum taught in girls' schools was the common assumption that more academic studies were irrelevant for the majority of girls of this class, with only those who were intending to become teachers really needing to study subjects such as history and geography in any sort of depth, if at all. The teaching that most parents seem to have wanted for their daughters may have differed from the ideals of educationists in that arithmetic was not seen to be important and fancy needlework was preferred to plain, but most seem to have agreed that 'over'-education was not only unnecessary, it was downright dangerous. 'Good' wives and mothers or even domestic servants manifestly must not prefer reading novels to cookery books or attach the notion of indignity to domestic labour.

It is clear, however, that though intended to be heavily imbued with patriarchal meanings, the hidden curriculum of girls' schooling could also operate to invert curriculum priorities in favour of more intellectual achievement, particularly when girls were taught in mixed classes by a mistress. Thus there were some girls, albeit probably only a small minority, who were able to enjoy a broadly-based academic education, and there were also some who were able to use their education as a route to occupational mobility. In the context of a system of schooling specifically designed to foster gender differentiation, however, equality of opportunity and experience generally was the product of an inability to provide more than the most basic and limited education. Whether their schooling was 'good' or 'poor', whether evaluated against contemporary criteria or that of present day, a very limited education of basic literacy and needlework was probably what the majority of educated girls received.

7 What a Woman Knows[1]: the Significance of Education in the Lives of Working-class Women

This study began with the observation that the formal education of working-class girls has been much neglected in historical research, with the 'established truths' of the history of education presenting a picture of elementary schooling undifferentiated by gender during the period 1800–70, and with boys and girls having very similar experiences of schooling. More recently, feminist historians and writers have presented a contrary view, to argue that issues of gender were an integral shaping factor in the provision and practices of elementary schooling throughout this period and that girls of this class were educationally disadvantaged by their class and by their gender. Indeed, this particular version of the history of female education had become sufficiently widespread by 1991 for a review article to take as axiomatic the 'well-known' fact of 'the injustice which denied women and girls the right to learn' during the nineteenth century.[2]

The many details of girls' schooling and of the broader educational experiences of women and girls given here do confirm, in broad terms, the revisionist view of girls' schooling. Issues of gender *were* integral to the purposes and practices of schooling, at least in general terms. Girls *were* doubly disadvantaged by their class and their gender in relation to their access to schooling and the nature of the education available to them and, on the whole, their education was quantitatively and qualitatively more limited than that of working-class boys. But there is also evidence to support the former view, with a similarity of experiences between boys and girls and an absence of overt gender differentiation being sufficiently widespread to lend some substance to this particular 'established truth'. While it may be said that the purposes of schooling were defined in gender as well as class-based terms, this did not necessarily imply overt gender differentiation in the practices of schools. Nor were girls always disadvantaged relative to boys in their experiences of schooling, for boys equally could be handicapped by class and gender concepts, with divisions of labour operating to define formal schooling as irrelevant to their needs and generating active hostility against boys' schooling.

The evidence that has been presented here has shown significant variations in the nature and degree of gender differentiation in education; over time and place, in provision and use, and between educational theories and schooling practices. And no singular, straightforward or static shaping element can be identified in the education of working-class girls, but a mixture of elements which took different forms and emphases within different socio-economic and occupational groups, with a complex interactive relationship between ideological, cultural, social and economic forces operating at a variety of levels to inform a variety of experiences over time and place. Thus, though the simple model of a 'double burden' of class and gender operating to limit the formal education of women and girls has some initial explanatory usefulness, it has obvious inadequacies as an interpretive framework for understanding shifts and variations in the purposes and practices of schooling over this period. For the ideological, social and cultural imperatives which defined the schooling of girls as being a prime instrument in the cause of social reform could be supported *and* contradicted by the operation of patriarchal ideologies embedded in the socio-economic organisation of community life. And while the rationale of education for the lower orders derived from social and cultural ideologies, the practices of schooling corresponded rather more to the economic requirements and structures of local production – which might or might not be in harmony with dominant belief systems. Nor were economic structures and requirements, nor even social and cultural ideologies singular or static. Patriarchy is not an historical constant, nor is it expressed in a singular concept of what it means to be feminine. Individual experiences of patriarchy were mediated by the balance between and intensity of its social structures[3] and the notion of what it meant to be a 'good' nineteenth-century working-class wife and mother was also subject to considerable variation over place, time and circumstance.

Here lies the crux of the matter. As Lown has argued, 'in both ideology and practice there were constantly shifting meeting points and contradictions between patriarchal and capitalist interests' throughout the period[4] as gender and class relationships were reassessed and renegotiated towards the re-establishment of an equilibrium between economic and familial relationships disturbed by the growth of industrial capitalism. Similarly, as an agency of cultural transmission operating in the socio-economic context of capitalism and the cultural context of patriarchy, the development of elementary education was characterised by shifts and contradictions in a continuing process of development and change, assessment and reassessment.

INDUSTRIAL CAPITALISM, CLASS STRUGGLE AND PATRIARCHY IN NINETEENTH-CENTURY LANCASHIRE

Gender and class are not continermous systems; they each have their own separate dynamic. Nor is patriarchy a by-product of capitalism, as some Marxist feminist analyses have suggested.[5] Nevertheless, the development of nineteenth-century patriarchy cannot historically be separated from the development of a class-based society within industrial capitalism, nor can it be separated from approaches to class-cultural control during the period. Tensions between patriarchy and capitalism were provoked by the exploitation of women's labour leading to changes in the balance between and intensity of the social structures of patriarchy and, therefore, also to changes in its form and degree.

Though utilising the practices of patriarchy in their exploitation of gender divisions of labour in the early stages of industrialisation, the organisation of production in cotton textile manufacture attacked established concepts of working-class masculinity and femininity and the customary organisation of family labour. This in turn provoked resistance and protest on the part of working people; a reaction which was acutely feared in the virtual absence of traditional authority and control structures in the new urban and industrial communities. New approaches to social control were therefore sought to contain class alienation and resistance, including the development of mass schooling.

The concept of elementary schooling that was developed in the early nineteenth century took as axiomatic the gender assumptions of the period, with the order that was to be restored to the industrial districts via the instillation of 'habits of obedience' being one which encompassed conformity to expectations of gender as well as class behaviours. As the wives and mothers of the future, it was particularly important that girls should be 'properly' educated to ensure that the influence they exercised over their menfolk was directed towards the support of the socio-economic status quo, but there was no explicit identification of the processes of schooling as a means of inculcating or transforming gender identities at this point. Indeed, though conflict between working-class views of what was appropriate to gender divisions and the organisation of production was a prime source of class antagonisms, there was no explicit identification of a need to *transform* indigenous gender concepts in any way.

The upside-down world of the factory districts denied the theoretical imperatives of bourgeois reformers, however, and where the first rule of life was that of survival girls were far too useful economically and domestically to be spared to go to school. Further, by tradition the purpose of education was to prepare boys and girls for their adult responsibilities and, as those of women were seen to be determined by their 'natural' responsibilities within the family, so the education of girls should be familial. Thus, though there was considerable common ground between different social groups in relation to the function of girls' education in the first three decades of the century, with the production of 'good' wives and mothers being a prime aim of education for many middle-class reformers and working-class radicals alike, there were considerable class-cultural differences as to how, specifically, a 'good' wife and mother of this class might be expected to behave and also with regard to the role of schooling in the transmission of 'appropriate' skills and behaviours.

This was to change in the 1830s. A wave of moral panic labelled the 'factory girl' as deficient and depraved and a major cause of the ignorance, insalubrity and intemperance that was seen to underpin social and political disaffection. At the same time a more creative concept of elementary education as an instrument of class-cultural transformation came gradually to replace the crude social control model of the early nineteenth century, to give a greater emphasis to the achievement of an harmonious interaction between the 'education of circumstance' experienced by Lancashire women in their daily lives and the cultural messages conveyed by the 'education of principle' carried on in a good public elementary school. Class-cultural hegemony rather than 'obedience under control' was to provide the lasting solution to social and political ills, and, as the prime agents of cultural reproduction within the working-class family, the broader educational experiences of the women of the industrial communities should operate firmly to teach them the values and behaviours more appropriate to their God-given responsibilities as wives and mothers. And if they refused voluntarily to accept these responsibilities to the detriment of the social order, then they must be compelled to do so. Hence the imposition of 'protective' controls on women's employment in the factories and of compulsory schooling for factory girls.

By the 1830s and 1840s, however, the goals of bourgeois reformers were received with some sympathy by working-class groups and even by some industrialists, with the interests of patriarchy, of capital and of organised labour finding common ground with regard to perceptions of what was appropriate to the lives and work of working-class women in the industrial regions. This was not a one-way process of transmission, with

workers and industrialists conceding to the cultural values of the bourgeoisie. The pursuit of hegemony is an active process, involving struggle
and conflict and developments in working-class views of what was appropriate to gender 'roles' were integral to the processes of class struggle. In
what Lown has called 'the rationalisation of patriarchal relationships',[6]
traditional strategies to safeguard the patriarchal and economic interests of
male workers adapted to changing circumstances. Organised labour thus
utilised the patriarchal domestic ideologies of the middle classes to give a
moral impetus to their claims for improved conditions of employment, and
to argue the undesirability of women's factory work and the importance of
breadwinner wage levels for male workers. Through lengthy and sometimes bitterly fought processes of conflict and accommodation a position
was reached wherein the interests of capital and of the male work-force
were accommodated via the restructuring of the factory labour force in
forms compatible with patriarchal values. For skilled workers this meant
the payment of breadwinner wages sufficient to keep a wife at home in her
'proper' place and the achievement of employer/employee relations characterised by paternalism rather than conflict. For all workers it meant the
reassertion of the secondary place of women within the labour market and
of their primary responsibilities within the home and the family. As the
values of respectability came to replace political radicalism and as
reformism replaced revolutionary fervour, so also traditional patriarchy
became adapted to the new order of industrial capitalism. From being a
major source of social and political unrest in the early part of the century
when the erosion of 'natural' gender divisions were seen to threaten the
material and cultural bases of patriarchy, in the post-1850 period the
reaffirmation of the divisions of labour and values of patriarchy became a
major force for stabilisation. Both class struggle and the achievement of
class-cultural hegemony thus took a gendered form in the industrial districts, with the endorsement of patriarchal principles representing the cornerstone of the alliance that was struck between capital, the male labour
force and the state.

Working-class women in the industrial districts also appear to have concurred with the 'ideal' of private patriarchy represented by the new model
family form of the wholly domestic wife economically dependent on a
male breadwinner. Whether or not this was the result of free and active
choice is impossible to judge. A self-perpetuating relationship between the
different structures of patriarchy operated to constrain choice and to persuade women that marriage and housewifery was a more attractive option
than a life of poorly-paid drudgery in the factories. Small wonder then that
many Lancashire women were 'choosing' full-time domesticity as the best

of life's limited choices from the 1840s – if, that is, their circumstances permitted. For many thousands of women, however, life offered no such choice.

That such women continued to shoulder the heavy burden of ill-paid employment and domestic labour was not seen to be problematic. Indeed, the withdrawal of married women and mothers from factory work would very quickly have exposed the sheer incompatibility of bourgeois domestic ideologies to the family economies of most working people and the essential contribution of women's paid work to manufacturing profit margins. But with male domination supported by women's segregation into specific areas of 'women's work' and the payment of 'supplementary' wages to them, and with social stability *and* economic profitability supported by the coexistence of public with private patriarchy, such employment could safely be ignored. Indeed, the presentation within bourgeois public rhetoric of the 'new model' family as both the ideal and the norm served to obscure the very existence of women's paid work (and the economic exploitation it represented), by cloaking the material conditions that made such work a continuing necessity. If married women and mothers chose to continue in unsuitable employment, that was a result of their own 'deviant' choices or of individual or family inadequacies.

CLASS ALIENATION AND PATRIARCHY IN RURAL NORFOLK AND SUFFOLK

The relationship between capital and patriarchy was not inevitably one of conflict in the early part of the century. Little economic benefit was seen to be offered by the widespread employment of women in cereal production and the organisation and recruitment of labour in capitalist farming presented little challenge to patriarchal relations. Yet, though traditional gender divisions of labour in the family and work-place were maintained, problems of rural poverty and the erosion and abrogation of bonds of social obligation between the labouring classes and their employers generated considerable social tension. In this instance, however, there simply was no need to create 'moral panics' about the apparent collapse of family life and the supposed deficiencies of working-class women to support social cohesion. Nor was there any incentive to call upon secondary strategies such as schooling for the purposes of social control. The immediate economic power of the farmers and their control over the system of poor relief were seen to be sufficient to maintain the status quo, with little possibility of overt resistance on the part of the labourers. Indeed, to have labelled the paid employment of rural women as a 'deviant' practice would have been against the economic interests of the farming, middle and ruling classes of rural society, for in the context of high poor rates, the 'good' wife and mother of the agricultural districts of the east of England was one who contributed as much as she possibly could to the family purse. The influence of bourgeois domestic ideologies can be seen in the expressed perplexities of Commissioners investigating local conditions, but the notion that rural women 'ought' to adopt a wholly domestic life-style or to be educated towards a proper appreciation of their practical and moral family responsibilities generally was alien to the rural communities of Norfolk and Suffolk before the 1860s. It was only when economic conditions improved that Norfolk and Suffolk women began to renounce field labour, and this increasing home-centredness seems to have been more a factor of the understandable desire to escape the ill-paid, physically demanding work in all weathers that women's agricultural work represented than a product of domestic ideologies. And with no perceived need for additional strategies to subdue working-class recalcitrance, with economic penalties rather than social benefits the result of any moves to define the paid work of women as unacceptable, and with no advantage to employers or to male labour in any exploitation of gender divisions of labour, issues of gender remained peripheral to class struggle and to strategies of social control in rural Norfolk and Suffolk.

Nevertheless, the examples of Norfolk and Suffolk illustrate, albeit in negative form, the significance of gender in the achievement of class-cultural hegemony. In Lancashire the need to subdue the working classes was seen to be acute and the 'civilising' of working-class women into their appropriate gender 'roles' was central to the processes of reform. Issues of gender were also central to the cross-class consensus that underpinned the social and economic harmony of the era of 'reformism and respectability' in later nineteenth-century Lancashire. In Norfolk and Suffolk an apparent (if forced) acquiescence on the part of working men and women in the social and economic status quo removed the need for such reforms. Where coercion was sufficient to subdue class struggle there simply was no need to seek a hegemonic alliance with working people. Nor were there, in the situation of an overabundance of cheap and compliant labour, grounds for negotiation between capital and labour. Bitter grievance and class antagonism might be lying just below this surface veneer of respect. The agricultural labour force might be equally as ignorant as their industrial counterparts as to the necessarily benign operation of capitalism and the women of rural England might be seen to be as deficient in their domestic capabilities as their Lancashire sisters. In the absence of any serious challenge to the social order, however, such ignorance could safely be left undisturbed, without any need for moral panic or investment in softer forms of social control. With a sense of their 'honourable' labour as men reaffirmed by the operation of a patriarchal consensus in the work-place and the community, Lancashire working men had won a 'stake in the hedge' of industrial society that was noticeably absent in the rural districts of eastern England. The bridge that patriarchy had provided across the chasm of class divisions was absent in Norfolk and Suffolk and continuing class antagonisms rather than class-cultural hegemony was the result.

SCHOOLING AND EDUCATION

The power of dominant interests is not inviolate and consent must actively be pursued and won if hegemony is to be achieved and maintained. Further, though one version of social reality may become dominant within social and economic structures, beliefs, values and customary ways of life a range of alternatives still remains, some of which, as we have seen, may be more compatible with the material circumstances of people's lives or their individual aspirations. Tensions within the different structures of patriarchy provoked changes and adjustments within and between these structures which intensified male domination over women – but these changes also offered the possibility of the diminution of patriarchy. Even in nineteenth-century England there were those who argued that neither the safeguarding of the social order, nor economic efficiency, nor even the well-being of male workers were dependent on the oppression of women. There were also those who challenged gender inequalities, with the middle-class women of the Langham Place group, for example, actively working for access to higher education for women and for the widening of their occupational opportunities, and they and others actively sought the reduction of patriarchal oppression in a whole number of areas from around mid-century.[7] Male hegemony was not complete, nor did women universally and passively accept their subordination within patriarchy.

The processes by which dominant ideologies are reproduced are thus central to the maintenance of patriarchal hegemony; the educative experiences of family, work-place and community life and the processes of cultural reproduction, including schooling.

The 'education of principle' to be taught in all 'good' schools encompassed both the content and the culture of schooling. The inculcation of class and gender codes was the prime function of schooling and the processes of schooling – the content of the curriculum, the daily ordering of the school and the values thus conveyed – were seen to be the means of inculcating and shaping the formation of class and gender identities. The existence of tensions and contradictions between bourgeois ideologies of class and gender and working-class cultures and experiences was recognised, but the successful inculcation of bourgeois mores via the education of principle taught in good schools would resolve such tensions, by ensuring that the 'education of circumstance' conveyed by daily experience would be 'correctly' understood. Provided schooling would thus construct a close and reciprocal harmony between the principles of schooling and the circumstances of working-class existence through the assimilation of bourgeois class and gender codes by working-class children, to achieve a close and reciprocal harmony between bourgeois socio-economic and cultural values and those of the working classes.

This was the theory but, as the preceding chapters have shown, such ideals often failed fully to translate into the realities of schooling. Firstly, economic constraints and the failure of teachers always to adhere to the principles and practices of 'good' schooling as defined by educationists meant that the processes of schooling were flawed in their implementation. Secondly, the purposes of schooling were contested.

A key factor here was that, as voluntary institutions for most of the period, the majority of schools had effectively to market their services, both to attract financial support from the more middle-class members of the community and to induce the working classes to attend the schools. And, if they gave any support to schooling at all, what consumers of all social classes wanted from the schools was that they should provide working-class children with *really* useful knowledge. That is, in the popular view, the main function of schooling was to meet the needs of the labour market and to prepare pupils for the main business of life, that of getting and earning a living. Other, more personal benefits were recognised. Literacy was useful for girls in protecting the privacy of lovers' correspondence, for example, but popular views as to the value and purposes of schooling corresponded with gender divisions of labour in the local labour market intersecting with gender divisions of labour within working-class family life. There were, therefore, often considerable tensions between the attitudes and circumstances of the 'consumers' of education and the socialisation purposes of the educational establishment.

With limited support for the provision of schooling as an instrument of social control or cultural transformation in the rural east of England, for example, the degree of local support for schooling largely corresponded to the requirements and organisation of agricultural production. Hence a general hostility to the formal education of boys and an unwillingness to give financial support to schooling that led to severe problems of under resourcing. But hence also the relative advantages enjoyed by girls in the region, with a lesser demand for their labour in the immediate situation linked to an occupational destination where school attendance could be advantageous. And with limited resources severely constraining the implementation of 'good' (i.e. gender-differentiated) schooling girls were also able to enjoy a more equal, if limited, experience of schooling. And if class-cultural imperatives provided the motive force for the heavy investment of National Society and state funding in the provision of schooling in industrial Lancashire, immediate local support and demand similarly corresponded to the requirements and organisation of the local labour market. Some working-class radicals may have shared the view that education was the means towards an improved society (albeit an alternative one to that envisaged by bourgeois reformers), but popular views were rather more instrumental. If schooling had any purpose at all beyond that of looking after children when their parents were at work, it was to provide children with useful and marketable skills and, as in Norfolk and Suffolk, the organisation of the local labour market was more important a determinant on school provision and attendance than the expressed priorities of the educational establishment. In this instance, however, this was to the severe detriment of girls' schooling. Schooling had to be seen to provide positive advantages outweighing its opportunity costs – school fees and the loss of a child's wages or their help at home, the expense of a clean pinafore and so forth – and if factory work placed no premium on a girl's literacy skills or more academic learning, why bother to send her to school?

Tensions between the views and circumstances of the working classes and the purposes and practices of schooling were not, however, either inevitable or irreconcilable. The goals of cultural transmission remained central to the 'ideal' precepts and practices of provided schooling throughout the period, but as the organisation of factory labour adapted to reconcile the interests of capitalism and of patriarchy, and as bourgeois notions of what it meant to be a good citizen came effectively to merge with working-class models of what it meant to be a respectable husband, father and worker, so the urgency of cultural transformation as the chief rationale of schooling declined in importance. And as market forces encouraged the provision and use of 'rational' schooling, cross-class evaluations of what constituted useful learning and quality education came effectively, if pragmatically, to share the same criteria. A core curriculum of basic skills and *really* useful knowledge was the cornerstone of this pragmatic alliance, representing as it did the common ground where reformist ideals and instrumental attitudes could coexist in harmonious reciprocity. This was the case in the larger urban and industrial centres, where the British schools in particular operated to provide the 'bright and sharp' clerks and apprentices needed by the local economy and the ladder to superior occupational opportunities that some parents sought for their sons. Similarly, the limited education provided by the country schools of Norfolk and Suffolk matched the occupational destination of domestic service for rural girls. Within the context of a variety of schooling provision and a variety of individual circumstances and attitudes, harmonious relations were therefore possible where the nature and content of schooling matched the cultural and material conditions of working-class life. Where, however, there was a mismatch, the relationship was one of resistance and tension, with the example of factory girls' experiences in industrial Lancashire demonstrating the failure of the schools to 'sell' their services when these conflicted with local conditions and expectations. Even under compulsion, girls and their parents successfully were able to subvert the intentions of educationists, though unfortunately this also had the effect of confirming the subordinate status of Lancashire women, in making them amongst the most illiterate and ill-educated people in England and Wales.

A harmonisation of parental expectations and schooling aims and provision was not, on the whole, to the advantage of girls, although the conclusions above might suggest otherwise. As reformism removed the urgency of schooling girls for the purposes of cultural reproduction and working-class women became more 'respectable' and 'civilised', even the theoretical importance given to the schooling of girls became less cogent. For while reformist ideals had given support to girls' claims to education, albeit at a largely theoretical level, instrumental attitudes derived from the organisation and requirements of the labour market only very rarely did. And even where they did, as was the case for rural girls in Norfolk and Suffolk, the operation of patriarchal values and gender divisions of labour placed considerable limitations on the nature of the education thought suitable for girls. While a *little* learning was useful and desirable, the criteria against which girls' schooling were evaluated were derived from gender-based assumptions about the innate capabilities of women, the skills and behaviours required of 'good' (i.e. home-centred) wives and mothers and of domestic servants, and the practical and moral dangers of 'over'-educating working-class girls.

This was – and is – the essential paradox of patriarchy and it is one which pervaded the whole development of working-class girls' education throughout this period. For, notwithstanding assertions about the worthiness of the female 'role', women's assumed responsibility for child care and housework and their association with reproduction (biological and cultural) rather than production, meant that their work within the family was accorded little value. Their primary role within the family also defined their work in economic production as being, *ipso facto*, secondary; of lesser importance to that of men, to be 'fitted in' around the demands of family and home and 'worth' less economically and culturally than that of men. Equal, even superior to men in moral and theoretical terms, working-class women, like their middle-class sisters, were also supposed to be (and sometimes were) economically dependent upon and subordinate to men. Across all social groups, therefore, women were defined as being 'relative creatures' of lesser value and status than men, and requiring only a limited education of a nature and quality relative to their 'natural' and God-given role within the family.

Though subject to a variety of interpretations and reinterpretations throughout the period, the concept of the 'good' wife and mother as being one primarily concerned with domesticity and child care in line with her 'natural' biological, intellectual and moral attributes provided the bottom line to all aspects of girls' educational experiences, and it was not one which gave support to any idea that high standards of intellectual achievement were necessary or appropriate for girls. Indeed, within the climate of reformism and respectability that marked the second half of the century, even the educational establishment may have reverted to some extent to the pre-industrial and traditional view that a familial training in domestic skills represented an adequate education for girls of this class. Certainly, the view that the mother was the best person to teach a girl her domestic duties and responsibilities was widespread across all social groups; a viewpoint which even Inspector Norris, ever a tireless advocate of the importance of the 'correct' education of girls, was willing to concede had some merit.

Whether shaped by ideology or instrumentalism there was no intention to 'disadvantage' girls educationally. The term is a subjective one, embedded within a wealth of cultural understandings and the notion that limitations on the intellectual knowledge and skills to be gained from formal education constituted a 'disadvantage' to working-class girls would have been foreign to educationists and parents alike. Indeed, the intention was to confer advantage – both to girls and to society as a whole – by educating girls towards a proper appreciation of where their 'true' interests lay; that is, in the home. Really useful knowledge, therefore, whether acquired in the home or school, encompassed both the immediately practical – basic literacy, needlework, domestic skills – and an understanding of the common cultural code of class/gender behaviours. Consensus took some time to achieve, but emerging in the 1820s and established by the 1840s intra-class and cross-class understandings of what was expected of working-class women and the purposes and nature of girls' schooling had become compatible with patriarchal values and practices and the concerns of capitalism.

Individual experiences may have varied, with the private patriarchy that in theory, if not in practice, was the lot of all women coexisting with the more public forms of oppression experienced by the many thousands of women who continued to engage in paid labour. But working together in close and harmonious reciprocity, the education of circumstance experienced by working-class girls was compatible with the education of principle provided, in theory at least, in the public elementary schools.

This is not to suggest that the realities of girls' schooling necessarily reproduced the principles of 'good' female education, nor that girls inevitably took on board the lessons they were supposed to learn. Issues of resource provision and erratic attendance apart, there is evidence that the patriarchal cultural messages conveyed by even good schools for girls could be rejected by their pupils. Even teachers, carefully selected and trained to inculcate the 'correct' moral and cultural code, could invert the patriarchal hierarchy of domestic over intellectual attainment to give a premium to the more academic learning of girls – as the complaints of Inspectors testify.

Indeed, both the location and chronology of changes in the lives (and possibly also of the attitudes) of working-class women suggest that formal schooling played a minimal part in the process. For while Lancashire women were beginning to withdraw from an active and public involvement in 'male' concerns such a trade unionism and political activism and were even, if their circumstances permitted, withdrawing from public paid employment from the 1840s, their access to formal schooling was so limited as to deny any major influence on the part of the schools as agencies of socialisation. Conversely, the 'educated' girls of Norfolk and Suffolk, though conforming to traditional gender expectations of what was suitable paid labour for women, do not seem to have adopted home-centred views until around the 1860s.

None the less, the *education* of working-class girls must be counted as a successful enterprise measured against the aims of educationists and reformers. For, taking education to include the educative influence of family and community life and of the labour market as well as schooling, evidence of changes in women's lives in both regions indicate that they were educated successfully to conform to expectations of their class and gender roles. The education societies and the Inspectorate may have condemned the failures and inadequacies of girls' schools and a failure generally to appreciate the real spiritual and moral purposes of their schooling, while others may have deplored the 'over education' that was supposedly tempting girls from the paths of domestic righteousness, but one is tempted to ask, in the context of the purposes of schooling girls, whether formal schooling was needed at all? Was it not, given the all pervading strength of the patriarchal social structures of the socio-economic and cultural circumstances of working-class life, almost a total irrelevancy for girls?

In the reality, the real impact of schooling was a negative one, in denying working-class girls an opportunity to challenge the values and practices of patriarchy. Just as the onset of mechanised production had offered the potential for more equitable relations between the sexes in undermining the material bases of patriarchy, so schooling might have offered girls opportunities to develop the knowledge and skills that would have helped them to fight gender inequalities. Both options, however, were equally unacceptable in a cultural climate that defined the principles of patriarchy as fundamental to concepts of masculinity and as a major mediator of social and political stability. Equally, the provision of a broad range of marketable skills to girls and women and the fostering of attitudes of assertiveness and independence was unacceptable where the exploitation of women's 'cheap' labour was seen to be an essential element of economic profitability. Female pupils and teachers may actively have contested the gender messages promulgated by provided schooling. Formal schooling may have been of relatively minor importance in actively forming gender identities. A failure to provide 'good' schooling may have meant that some girls had equal or even superior experiences of schooling to that of boys. Some girls may have been fortunate enough to be supported by family and teachers in their more academic achievements and rural women may even have been more literate than their male peers. But very few girls or adult women had access to more academic studies beyond the level of general knowledge. Indeed, the concept of 'quality' schooling, like that of educational 'progress', was inseparable from gender differentiation, with an acceptance of lower academic standards for girls as entirely natural and appropriate. By design and by default, through success and through failure, the education of working-class girls operated to support and legitimate the values and practices of patriarchy and the interests of capitalist economic organisation. Disqualified from many occupations by limited knowledge and skills, generally able only to earn the wages 'of the poorest poor'[8] and with only teaching offering any chance of a halfway decent standard of living to an independent woman, who can wonder that many saw full-time domesticity as the best possible option in a hostile and difficult world?

As the school reading book quoted in the title of this chapter had it, 'what a woman knows (was) comparatively of little importance to what a woman is', and schooled or unschooled, the force of the education of circumstance was such generally to encourage adherence to the behaviours, if not the ideologies, of patriarchy. But as a final summary of the determining influences on the schooling and education of working-class girls, a reversal of the statement is evens more apt. For ideologies regarding 'what a woman is' were of profound importance in determining 'what a woman knows'. Women and men were different, their abilities and destinations were different, and, therefore, for the general well-being of society, their schooling also should be different.

8 From the Past to the Present

There would seem to be little similarity between the lives, work and education of nineteenth-century working-class girls and women and their late twentieth-century counterparts. The patriarchal ideological climate which located women in the home as their natural sphere and educated them accordingly has been replaced by one where gender equality is taken as axiomatic. British women now have equal rights in employment, in education and in marriage that are enshrined in law and public consciousness. Viewed from a liberal feminist perspective such developments are part of a cumulative process of progression whereby gender inequalities gradually are being eliminated. Women fought and won battles for the vote, for education and for access to positions of influence, and seized the advantages offered by expanding work opportunities to gain some degree of economic independence. Those following after have built on these advances to open up further opportunities for others – and so the process will continue.[1] If gender equality has not yet been achieved, we are well on the way towards its achievement.

I am less sanguine. There has been an enormous expansion in British women's paid employment since the end of the Second World War, for example, yet women remain concentrated in lower grades and different areas of work from men. Female wage levels also are only around three quarters of male wage levels. Quantitative change has been unmatched by qualitative change, with only a very slight decline in women's segregation into low-paying occupations and industries and part-time work.[2] Probably as a consequence of lower earnings, more women than men have second jobs (almost 590,000 women in 1993, over 100,000 more than men), and it comes as no surprise that, as reported in *Social Trends*, 'women have less free time than men because they spend more time looking after the children, cleaning, cooking and shopping'. Women in full-time work typically spend 45.5 hours per week on cooking, shopping, housework and child care compared with the 26.2 hours typically spent by men in full-time work, and have an average 14 hours' less leisure. Even part-time women workers have less leisure than men in full-time work.[3] Further, though there are public statements of state support for equality of occupational opportunities for women, with much trumpeting of schemes such as 'Opportunity 2000' which purports to encourage business actively to support openings for women,[4] the operation of free-market economics and the removal of minimum wage legislation leaves British women even more vulnerable to exploitation as the traditional source of cheap labour. The erosion of many welfare-state provisions also are having a disproportionate impact on women, since they customarily provide much of the so-called 'community' care of the sick and old that is replacing public provision, and are more dependent on the housing and other benefits that have been cut back by the British government. There is also evidence to suggest a cultural backlash against the very concept of gender equality with, for example, the successes of girls in the 1994 school examinations being greeted by questions such as 'have the girls had it too good for too long?'[5] I would argue, therefore, that though there have been changes in both the degree and forms of its operation, patriarchy remains fundamental to British society of the later twentieth century. I also suggest that the public expression of gender equality is dissimulative, operating to deny the continuing existence of inequalities, and that the current economic, political, and educational climate is inimical to the advancement of genuine equality between the sexes.

Madeline Arnot has commented that an historical analysis is needed to identify the causes and processes of the construction of gender concepts in order to sort out the specificity of our particular version of gender classification and to seek the source of that classification.[6] The pessimistic evaluation outlined above stems from the historical research detailed in the previous chapters and the model of analysis and interpretation that has arisen from it. The focus of this final chapter is thus to apply that model to an analysis of present developments and experiences and to suggest possible future strategies towards the achievement of more equitable gender relations.[7]

FROM PRIVATE TO PUBLIC PATRIARCHY[8]

The greatest change in gender relations since the nineteenth century has been a shift from 'private' to 'public' patriarchy as the dominant form. From the 'private' form of the mid-nineteenth century, where the exclusion of women from public life meant that the dominant site of oppression was the private world of the home, the 'public' form of patriarchy of the later twentieth century operates largely through strategies of gender segregation and female subordination in the work-place and in other areas of public life.

There has also been some attenuation in the degree of patriarchy across all its key structures. British women have equal rights of political citizenship, of legal rights within employment and marriage, including some degree of protection against marital violence, and have access to economic independence through paid work and through state welfare payments. There has also been a lessening of double standards of sexual morality, and of overt discrimination in cultural institutions such as schooling and the media. Nevertheless, if the full-blown private patriarchy of Victorian Britain is comparatively rare today, British society is still a patriarchal society. It is, in Bradley's terms, 'androcentric' and centred around male definitions, male priorities, male requirements and male employment and career patterns.[9]

Different experiences relating to social-class and ethnic differences also still remain in both the form and degree of patriarchy. Those of Muslim women of Bangladeshi family origin, for example, come closer to the private form of the nineteenth century. These women's experiences of family life, schooling and paid work are thus likely to differ quite considerably from those of a white middle-class Englishwoman, though all groups may share common experiences as women.

Two main influences have been significant in these changes. Firstly, challenges arising from the inability of patriarchal hegemony to gain universal acceptance have been successful in extending women's rights across a number of spheres. Secondly, tensions between the labour needs of advanced capitalism and domestic ideologies have opened up employment opportunities for women. That is, tensions between the different structures of patriarchy have given rise to challenges to and changes in the operation of patriarchy.

Detailed analysis of what Walby calls 'first-wave' feminism lies beyond the scope of this study as, though it may be dated from the 1850s, it was predominantly a middle-class movement, though working-class women were active in unionism and the suffrage movement from the later nineteenth century.[10] The impetus for many of these early feminist campaigns sprang from specific problems in the social relations between men and women; the poverty of 'surplus' single women and the importance of education in enabling women to be economically self-sufficient, the vulnerability of women whose husbands abused their patriarchal rights, the exercise of double standards of sexual morality and so forth. Indeed, much of later nineteenth- and early twentieth-century feminism was characterised by conservative views about the family, with an assertion of the value of women's domestic and family responsibilities rather than attempts to win equal rights for women within the labour market.[11]

First-wave feminism was, however, an important spur to change. The winning of political rights, of legal rights within marriage and of rights of access to higher education and entry to professions previously closed to women constituted a major turning-point by giving women access, albeit in limited form, to some degree of political citizenship. Thus women's possession of the vote meant, for example, that the role of the state in endorsing patriarchal control was constrained. From active support for 'protective' legislation regulating and restricting women's paid work, the state moved to a more ambivalent stance in the inter-war period, with the passing of the Sex Disqualification (Removal) Act of 1919 which provided for the removal of bans on women's employment. The state also refused to enact legislation to exclude women from paid work during the 1930s depression despite considerable pressure to do so, but also pursued unemployment policies which discriminated against women and took a *laissez-faire* approach to the spread of the marriage bar which excluded married women from many areas of paid work.[12]

Buoyant demand for labour during and after the Second World War, however, led many employers to abandon marriage bars. And with *laissez-faire* state policies also operating to deny the controls over women's labour that many unions sought, women were relatively well placed to take advantage of new employment opportunities in the post-war period. A number of 'knock-on' effects followed from this expansion of women's paid work, with an undermining of private, domestic patriarchy linked to women's access to some degree of economic independence, and with their presence in significant numbers in the work-force (and an involvement in union politics) contributing to an increasing recognition of women's interests on the part of the labour movement. Political pressure from women unionists and from 'second-wave' feminism after the later 1960s was also influential on state policies, with an endorsement of the principle of gender equality in employment and a range of services (albeit with little vigour and under considerable pressure from the European Community) through legislation such as the Sex Discrimination Act of 1975, the implementation of the Equal Pay Act in the same year, and subsequent modifications in the 1980s.[13]

There is, however, an apparent paradox in the situation in the later 1990s. In the context of economic recession, high levels of male unemployment and the crisis of hegemony signalled by high crime rates and the presence of a disaffected 'underclass', a resurgence of domestic ideologies might be expected as a panacea for social and economic ills. Patriarchal pressures on women to leave paid employment and to concentrate their energies on child-rearing and domesticity might, therefore, be expected as providing a simple solution to such problems. Indeed, there has been some suggestion of this in calls for married women to leave paid employment,[14] the castigation of single 'welfare mothers' and, in Britain, government attempts to reaffirm social and cultural hegemony through a nostalgic (and erroneous) evocation of an apparent 'golden age' some time around the 1950s, when the perceived universality of the stable two-parent family and shared adherence to 'family' values underpinned the well-being of the social order. Rather than falling, however, the number of employed women actually increased in the 1980s. Does this mean that patriarchal solutions to economic and social problems are now seen to be unacceptable? That social relations and the organisation of labour based on principles of gender equality are replacing male hegemony as the cornerstone of social harmony and economic efficiency?

It might correctly be argued that, as in the nineteenth century, the material conditions of later twentieth-century life disallow the withdrawal of women from paid labour. It is also the case that sectors of 'women's work' have been less affected by recession,[15] and there is a perceived shortage of skilled labour which cannot be met by the male work-force. The historical analysis put forward here, however, suggests that this apparent paradox can be explained by a recognition that tensions between the labour requirements of advanced capitalism and the state are being resolved by a re-definition of the 'ideal roles' of women. Rather than 'equality', we are seeing a reversion to the traditional expectation that women have a dual wage-earning and familial role, with the precise formulation and balance of those roles being informed by socio-economic and ethnic differences. Ideologies of gender equality thus serve to mask the continuing existence of two paradigms of family organisation – one based on an ostensible equality in gender divisions of labour in the work-place and the home, the other on gender-differentiated divisions of labour – towards the accommodation of conflicts between the perceived needs of the economic and of the social order. The economic requirements of late twentieth-century capitalism are/would be met by the 'casual' and 'flexible' employment of largely working-class and many black women in low-paid and part-time work, while the full-time employment of largely middle-class, predominantly white women does/will meet labour needs in traditional areas of 'women's work' such as teaching, whilst also providing 'reserve' labour in areas of skills shortage. And, given the cause and effect relationship between women's paid labour and familial roles, the employment of the majority of women in low paid and part-time work does/would reinforce their primary role within the family whilst conversely, their primary responsibility for the family does/would reinforce their economic dependence within marriage (a dependence that is reinforced by the cutting of state benefits), thus giving some protection to family stability – and to the social stability of the nation. As the historical record has shown, however, patriarchal hegemony is neither inviolate nor universally accepted, and such 'ideals' are susceptible to challenge. The processes by which dominant ideologies are reproduced are thus central to the maintenance of patriarchal hegemony, the educative experiences of family, work-place and community life and the processes of cultural reproduction, including schooling. The particular schooling experiences of girls *and of boys* are thus integral both to the reinforcement and to the challenging of patriarchy.

SCHOOLING, EDUCATION AND THE REPRODUCTION OF CLASS AND GENDER

The Education Reform Act of 1988 defines the purpose of education in the UK as the preparation of pupils for 'the opportunities, responsibilities and experiences of adult life'. 'Embedded within this', in the words of Her Majesty's Inspectors of schools (HMI), 'is the assumption of equal opportunities for male and female pupils'[16] with access to a common curriculum being seen to provide opportunities for girls to achieve on a par with boys in their schooling and, it is assumed, also in their adult lives.

Certainly, the absence of overt differentiation in the curriculum of schools goes some way towards the achievement of formal equality, in the removal of the strong class and gender differentials evident in the curricula of schools in the nineteenth and early twentieth centuries. Unlike their nineteenth-century counterparts all girls, in theory at least, now have equal opportunities with boys to gain educational qualifications that, again in theory, will open all occupations to them on an equal basis. Educational life chances are determined by ability, irrespective of gender, socio-economic or ethnic differences.

One might wish that a commitment to equality of educational opportunity for all pupils whatever their sex or socio-economic or ethnic origins had been made explicit. The concern of central government with the *quality* of schooling, however, does not extend to an explicit concern for *equality* and, indeed, policies promoting egalitarianism are seen to be inimical to educational quality, as representing competing objectives. As Kenneth Baker, the Secretary of State for Education declared in the run-up to the 1988 Act, 'the days of egalitarianism are over'.[17] Educational equality is thus seen to lie in the provision of a quality education for all pupils, with a singular concept of 'quality' as being an absolute standard, of equal applicability and access to all pupils, irrespective of their sex, class or ethnic origins.

'Quality' learning, as defined by the statutory National Curriculum is, however, one where 'male' subjects such as mathematics and science, where boys traditionally have out-performed girls and where teachers are predominantly male, have high status, while 'female' subjects such as home economics have low status. Home economics (food technology) is not even seen to be a subject in its own right, but is subsumed into the technology curriculum, where it exists as a very poor relation to 'hard' technology. Though the National Curriculum clearly provides opportunities for girls in giving equal prominence to their achievements in subjects such as mathematics, science and technology, its subject hierarchies may also confirm girls' sense of themselves as second-class citizens in devaluing 'female' areas of interest and expertise.[18]

Further, a common curriculum may be a necessary condition for gender equality but it does not ensure it. Equality of opportunity for girls was a 'common and well-meant assumption' in the mixed schools visited by HMI in 1990–91, for example, but the Inspectors found that the processes of schooling often operated to undermine these aims. Boys' domination of classrooms remained unrecognised and unchecked and governing bodies and senior teaching posts were similarly male dominated. Self-fulfilling assumptions about boys' and girls' capabilities also constrained curriculum experiences and future career choices, dependent behaviour on the part of girls was unchallenged, gender differences in achievements were left unmonitored and although some staff and departments had a 'sensitive awareness of girls' needs and achievements', little overall 'could be identified as positive action to raise the expectations and widen the horizons of girls'. As might be expected, though boys' schools had paid some attention to equal opportunities issues, this was not a central concern and HMI found no co-ordinated attempts to develop boys' knowledge and understanding of areas such as prejudice, discrimination and the changing roles of men and women in society.[19] There was also little evidence of technology being broadened to include home economics in boys' schools. In short, many of the practices of mixed and boys' schools operated to reinforce rather than challenge stereotypical gender assumptions and behaviours. As in the nineteenth century, the processes of schooling often run counter to the intentions of educationists.

Yet is there a problem here? Despite the many barriers to their achievements, the standards of girls' attainments have risen steadily and continue to rise. A long-term study of the achievements of English boys and girls born in the first week of March 1946, for example, reported in 1964 that though girls achieved higher standards than boys up to the age of 11, the position then reversed with boys overtaking and outperforming girls from the beginning of their secondary school careers.[20] Today, girls are outperforming boys in public examinations at 16 and at 18 and though some differences in the patterns of attainment still remain, the educational achievements of girls have advanced considerably since the 1960s. Between 1988 and 1990, for example, 54.6 per cent of 16-year-old girls achieved grades A to C in GCSE examinations compared with 41.5 per cent of boys, and though boys outperformed girls in subjects like mathematics (34.6 per cent of girls achieved grades A to C and 38.9 per cent of boys), the girls are catching up. Indeed, while the gap between male and female achievements is diminishing in subjects such as biology, chemistry, economics and mathematics where boys tend to do better, that between male and female achievements in subjects where girls are more successful (for example, English literature, history, geography and French) is increasing.[21] If, as it would seem, girls are learning to succeed through schooling, why should we continue to be concerned about gender inequalities in education?

Riley has suggested that a continuing focus on gender is important because girls still suffer unequal educational experiences and this certainly is the case. There is also a continuing tendency for the post-school education of young women to be at a lower level than that of young men, with a higher proportion of women than men entering sub-degree-level courses in Colleges of Further Education, and a higher proportion of men than women enrolled on undergraduate and postgraduate courses in universities and Colleges of Higher Education (HE). The situation is changing, however, and from a proportion of only 42 per cent of the university and HE populations in 1985/6, women represented 47 per cent of undergraduate and postgraduate students in 1991/2.[22]

Riley also argues that, because girls still lag behind in areas like mathematics and sciences, they are excluded from many high-paying careers,[23] and certainly girls' relative under-achievement at degree level would exclude them from many occupational opportunities. But if there is a direct causal relationship between girls' educational achievements and gender differences and inequalities in the labour market as Riley implies, why are girls with high aspirations and high achievements still reluctant to enter non-traditional occupations?[24]

This can be understood in terms of the education of circumstance experienced by girls (and by boys) in the later twentieth century; the material and cultural conditions which operate to inform them of their 'appropriate' class and gender roles within public patriarchy, and which the continuing existence of gender differentiation in schools does little to challenge. Indeed, for the majority of pupils there is an harmonious match between their gender-differentiated experiences of schooling and the gender-differentiated experiences of family and community life that are mutually reinforcing. Girls learn, as HMI put it, that 'a range of roles is undertaken by women and their quality of life depends on the ability to balance and accommodate the demands of these various roles'. Boys, on the other hand, learn that paid work is the main business of life. Thus while the schooling and broader educational experiences of boys teach strong distinctions between the public and private, home and work, male and female spheres, the experiences of girls teach them to blur such distinctions, while both sexes learn to accept such differences as being 'natural'.[25]

This is not to suggest that girls – or boys – are passive recipients of such messages. As has been argued, girls could resist even the strong and explicit gender messages conveyed in nineteenth-century elementary schools. Riley's research on the schooling experiences of black British girls of Afro-Caribbean family origin, though small scale, also shows that girls are able actively to resist gender models put forward by the schools, when these conflict with those transmitted within the family. The family experiences of these girls are such that they are likely to take as axiomatic the importance of economic independence,[26] with positive female role models and with strong family encouragement for girls to do well at school, to gain qualifications and get good jobs. A majority (27 of 42) black British girls interviewed by Riley described their experiences in three different schools as being predominantly negative, with varying experiences of gender differentiation, of covert racism and of depressed teacher expectations based on the assumption that all black pupils came from working-class backgrounds. But while it might be expected that these combined barriers would depress their achievements relative to black boys and to white girls as representing additional burdens on black girls, Riley found the school achievements of black girls generally to be superior to those of black boys and, in the case of Afro-Caribbean girls of non-Jamaican family origin, also superior to those of white girls. Driver and Fuller similarly have argued that black British girls are academically successful relative to their male peers and to white pupils. Fuller attributes this to a strong sense of self-worth amongst black girls and and a clear view that academic success would enable them to take control of their own lives and this would appear to be linked to the ability of black girls to challenge male domination and to reject notions of female economic dependence that Riley recognised.[27] It may be that the importance of the family as a basis of resistance to racism[28] strengthens the influence of positive gender messages that are conveyed by the families of black girls, but their example gives further support to the significance of the education of circumstance as a primary educative force. It also gives support to the argument that the degree of match between these broader educative circumstances and the purposes and processes of schooling is a major mediator of girls' schooling experiences.

Put simply, if somewhat crudely, I would argue that the positive gender models put forward by many of the girls' schools inspected by HMI are likely to be in harmony with the cultural and material conditions of the lives of largely middle-class girls, to encourage and support the achievement of high academic attainments and high ambitions for future careers. This was the case in an independent selective schools for girls inspected by HMI, where common expectations of success in a wide range of adult roles and occupations was shared by pupils, parents and teachers, leading to high aspirations on the part of girls. Conversely, the gender-differentiated models conveyed by many of the mixed schools are likely to be consistent with the broader educative experiences of largely working-class girls, effectively to give a primacy to family concerns in girls' expectations of their future lives. The intersections of class, gender and ethnicity are, of course, infinitely more complex and subtle than this crude analysis suggests, but the concept of match also allows for the possibility of resistance and challenge. Thus, a positive 'education of circumstance' will encourage able and ambitious girls and those with a strong sense of self-worth from whatever socio-economic or ethnic background to reject gender-depressed expectations. This is, it is suggested, a prime cause of the higher standards increasingly achieved by girls, in that an attenuation in the degree of patriarchal oppression since the 1960s represents a more positive education of circumstance. Unfortunately, the experiences of some girls also will lead them actively or passively to reject positive messages of high ambition and achievement as being in-appropriate to the cultural and material conditions of their lives. Challenge can also be negative in its effects, operating to confirm depressed class and gender expectations.[29]

Despite explicit rejection of the pursuit of equality as being central to the work of schools, government funding has supported initiatives such as 'Women into Science and Engineering', actively to encourage girls to follow non-traditional careers. Subject programmes within the National Curriculum may also address gender issues. This is most strongly expressed in relation to the cross-curricular theme of 'Economic and Industrial Understanding' where, it is urged,

All pupils regardless of culture, gender or social background, should have access to a curriculum which promotes economic and industrial understanding. Schools should be aware of pupils' attitudes and assumptions which relate to this area of the curriculum, for example, gender stereotypes about technology as a subject and engineering as a career. Programmes for economic and industrial understanding should explore and combat such stereotypes.[30]

No such argument is expressed for subject areas such as home economics. And is it merely coincidence that a focus on the achievement of gender 'equality' is found in subject areas of direct relevance to the economy, where a perceived shortage of skilled labour is seen to depress economic profitability and progress?

I suggest that rather than the promotion of gender equality, the function of schooling is that of preparing girls for a dual economic and familial role in line with the perceived needs of the economy and the well-being of the social order, with the precise formulation of that role being mediated by socio-economic, ethnic and ability differences. In teaching girls that their adult roles as women must 'balance and accommodate' the demands of paid work and family life the schools are thus meeting the needs of the advanced capitalist state for skilled workers, cheap and 'flexible' workers and domestic workers. Economic efficiency and social stability is thus supported by the continuation of patriarchal hegemony which takes gender differentiation and gender inequalities as axiomatic and 'natural', though disguised by an ideology of gender 'equality'.

FUTURE PROSPECTS IN SCHOOLING?

The present situation in education in England and Wales gives little grounds for optimism. The implementation of the Education Reform Act of 1988 has added considerably to the workload of teachers, and the extent to which they will have the time or energy to 'understand and work with the varied but firmly held attitudes and values of parents', or to provide the individual guidance that HMI deemed essential in extending the aspirations and performance of girls is questionable.[31] Further, as Riley suggests, government strategies to improve the quality of education are likely to be detrimental to the career prospects of women in education, in encouraging styles of management where senior appointments 'increasingly (are) being seen as "men's business"'.[32] And with an ever-increasing emphasis on immediate and 'practical' classroom competences in initial teacher education and with government policies supporting largely school-based training, it is unlikely that newly-qualified teachers will be equipped effectively to challenge rather than to reinforce gender inequalities.

Nevertheless, some grounds for discretion[33] still remain. The boys' school cited by HMI which gave serious attention to food studies may have been motivated by long-standing traditions of preparing boys for careers in the navy, including catering,[34] but this option is available for all boys and mixed schools under the National Curriculum. And it is here, I suggest, that the formal 'equality' of the National Curriculum is most flawed, in the 'masculinisation' of the schooling of girls, with little corresponding 'feminisation' of the schooling of boys. It is also here that schools may do much towards the achievement of greater gender equality, that is, *through the education of boys*.

HMI make many recommendations relating to the policies and practices of schools, with an awareness that the reproduction and/or 'transformation' of social and cultural ideologies of gender through schooling may be flawed and contested. Implicit in these recommendations also is a recognition of the significance of the 'education of circumstance' as a primary educative force. This is shown in the recognition of the need to encourage girls actively to resist stereotypical views, of the need for schools to work actively with parents and employers, and of the importance of schools developing boys' knowledge and understanding of prejudice, discrimination and the roles of men and women in society.

Somewhat ironically then, concerns about the education of boys that have been prompted by their under-achievement in school examinations relative to girls are, I suggest, well founded. But, rather than improvements in the quality of boys' more academic achievements, what is needed is the increased 'feminisation' of the education of boys; the inclusion of subjects such as home economics and personal and social education to blur distinctions between the public and private, family and work, male and female, and to help boys also to 'envisage adult roles which may involve work, caring and family responsibility'.[35] While girls must be educated in the skills and attitudes to achieve an academic equality with boys and to enable them to challenge inequalities in adult life, the education of boys in the skills and attitudes to address their equal responsibilities within the family are of equivalent if not greater importance. If schooling is to be a positive influence towards the achievement of greater equality between the sexes, it must thus recognise and challenge the reproductive androcentric messages that all too often are conveyed by family, community, and work-place values and practices. As Riley has argued, equality and quality can be complementary objectives[36] and, it is suggested, a quality education for boys and for girls is one that challenges the inequalities that deny opportunities for both sexes to experience the opportunities, responsibilities and experiences of adult life in the family, the work-place and the wider world on an equal basis.

Notes

Introduction

1. Inspector Norris, B.P.P., 1856, XLVII, p. 386.
2. Burstyn, J., 'Women's Education during the Nineteenth Century: a review of the literature', *History of Education*, 5, 1, 1976, 18. Publications in this area have included, for example, Bryant, M., *The Unexpected Revolution*, London, 1979; Delamont, S. and Duffin, L., *The Nineteenth-Century Woman: her cultural and physical world*, London, 1978; Dyhouse, C., *Girls Growing Up in Late Victorian and Early Edwardian England*, London, 1981; Hunt, F., (ed.), *Lessons for Life: the schooling of girls and women 1850–1950*, Oxford, 1987; Purvis, J., *Hard Lessons: the lives and education of working-class women in nineteenth-century England*, Cambridge, 1990.
3. This term is used for ease of reference, though it is recognised that such classifications refer mainly to occupational differences amongst men and that a class-based society was not fully formed until around the 1830s and 1840s.
4. Gomersall, M., 'The Elementary Education of Females in England 1800–1870, with particular reference to the lives and work of girls and women in industrial Lancashire and rural Norfolk and Suffolk', unpublished Ph.D. thesis, Institute of Education, University of London, 1991; Gomersall, M., 'Ideals and Realities: the education of working-class girls, 1800–1870', *History of Education*, 17, 1, 1988; Gomersall, M., 'Women's Work and Education in Lancashire, 1800–1870: a response to Keith Flett', *History of Education*, 18, 2, 1989; Gomersall, M., 'Challenges and Changes? The education of Lancashire factory women in the later nineteenth century', *History of Education*, 24, 2, 1995; Gomersall, M., 'Education for Domesticity? A nineteenth-century perspective on the education of girls', *Gender and Education*, 6, 3, 1994. Purvis, *op. cit.*
5. Delamont and Marks, for example, argued that the content and experiences of schooling were very similar for girls and boys in this period. Delamont, S., and Duffin, L., *The Nineteenth-Century Woman: her cultural and physical world*, London, 1978, p. 164. Marks, P. 'Femininity in the Classroom: an account of changing attitudes', in Mitchell, J. and Oakley, A. (eds.), *The Rights and Wrongs of Women*, Harmondsworth, 1976, p. 10. Beddoes, on the other hand, called such 'accepted truths' 'absurd, even nonsensical' in schools where vocational training was given. Beddoes, D., *Discovering Women's History: a practical manual*, London, 1983, p. 52. Digby and Searby also argue this revisionist view: Digby, A., and Searby, P., *Children, Schools and Society in Nineteenth-Century England*, Basingstoke, 1981, p. 46. In all of these cases, however, very little evidence is presented to support such views, particularly for the pre-1870 period.
6. Purvis, J., 'The Double Burden of Class and Gender in the Schooling of Working-class Girls in Nineteenth-century England, 1800–1870', in Barton, L., and Walker, S., *Schools, Teachers and Teaching*, Lewes, 1981, pp. 97–116.

7. Silver, H., 'Aspects of Neglect: the strange case of Victorian popular education', in *Education as History*, London, 1983, p. 21.
8. Rose, S., *Limited Livelihoods: gender and class in nineteenth-century England*, London, 1992, p. 13.
9. Lown, J., 'Not so much a factory, more a form of patriarchy: gender and class during industrialisation', in Gamarnikow, E., *et al.* (eds.) *Gender, Class and Work*, London, 1983, 29.
10. Purvis, *Hard Lessons*, p. 21.
11. Lown, *op. cit.*, p. 29; Purvis, *Hard Lessons*, p. 18. The four main theoretical perspectives are Marxist feminism, radical feminism, liberal feminism and socialist feminism (dual systems theory). These are discussed in Purvis, *Hard Lessons*, p. 18 and note 42, p. 238 and in the introduction to Walby, S., *Theorizing Patriarchy*, Oxford, 1992, pp. 1–24.
12. The main criticisms are that the concept necessarily is ahistoric, essentialist and universalist though, as Walby argues, such criticisms are relevant only to a few of the cruder earlier analyses. Walby, *op. cit.*, p. 2. Black feminist writers argue that there are significant differences in family forms between ethnic groups and that the family is less a source of oppression than it is for white women. Hooks (1984), for example, suggests that for Afro-American women the family is a basis of resistance to white racism, and also that the comparison between domestic labour and paid work is less favourable to waged work for such women because racism means that they get the worst jobs. Cited in Walby, p. 76.
13. Walby, *op. cit.*, pp. 20–1.
14. Walby differentiates between 'degrees' and 'forms' of patriarchy. 'Degrees of patriarchy' refers to the intensity of oppression on a specified dimension, for example, the wages gap between men and women. 'Forms of patriarchy' means the overall form of patriarchy (for example public or private patriarchy) as defined by the specific relations between the different structures of patriarchy. Walby, *op. cit.*, p. 174.
15. Marx, K., *Capital*, Vol. 1, 1867, New York, 1967 edn, pp. 489–90.
16. See, for example, Thompson, E. P., *The Making of the English Working Class*, Harmondsworth, 1968, p. 10; Anderson, M., *Approaches to the History of the Western Family*, Basingstoke, 1980, p. 78.
17. Quoted in Pinchbeck, *Women Workers and the Industrial Revolution 1780–1850*, London, 1930, 1981 edn, pp. 1–2.
18. Alexander, S., 'Women, Class and Sexual Differences in the 1830s and 1840s: some reflections on the writing of a feminist history', *History Workshop*, 17, Spring 1984, 137.
19. Anderson, *op. cit.*, p. 78.
20. Lown, J., *Women and Industrialisation: gender at work in nineteenth-century England*, Cambridge, 1990, p. 214.
21. Bryant, M., Review of Purvis, *Hard Lessons*, *History of Education Quarterly*, 31, 1, 1991, 137.
22. Walby, *op. cit.*, p. 187.
23. Clarke, A., *A Working Life of Women in the Seventeenth Century*, London, 1919, 1968; Pinchbeck, *op. cit.;* Alexander, S., 'Women's Work in Nineteenth-Century London: a study of the years 1820–1850', in Mitchell

and Oakley, *op. cit.*, 59–112; Berg, M., *The Age of Manufactures: indus-try, innovation and work in Britain, 1700–1820*, London, 1985; Lown, *op. cit.*; Rose, S., *Limited Livelihoods*; Snell, K. D. M., *Annals of the Labouring Poor: social change and agrarian England 1660–1900*, Cambridge, 1985.

1 Patriarchy Challenged? Women and Work in Nineteenth-century Industrial Lancashire

1. Pinchbeck, *Women Workers and the Industrial Revolution 1780–1850*, 1930, 1981 edn, p. 148.
2. B.P.P., 1833 XX, D1, 79.
3. B.P.P. 1843 XXVII, 19.
4. Engels, F., *The Condition of the Working Class in England*, 1892, 1969 edn, 171, 173.
5. Lord Ashley is better known as the Earl of Shaftesbury, the title he inherited on the death of his father in 1851. He was the parliamentary spokesman for the factory reform movement and, as a devout Evangelical Christian, was much concerned with the undermining of women's moral and spiritual role within the family that factory work represented to him.
6. Friefield, M., 'Technological Change and the "Self-Acting" Mule: a study of skill and the sexual division of labour', *Social History*, 11, 3, 1986, 334–5.
7. Quoted by Smelser, N., *Social Change and the Industrial Revolution*, Chicago, 1959, p. 232.
8. Friefield, *op. cit.*, pp. 335–6.
9. *Ibid.*
10. Smelser, *op. cit.*, p. 241. Anderson, M., 'Smelser Revisited: sociological history and the working-class family', *Social History*, 3, 1, Oct., 1976.
11. Quoted by Taylor, B., *Eve and the New Jerusalem*, London, 1983, p. 114.
12. *Ibid.*, 114–15.
13. Perkin, H., *The Origins of Modern English Society*, London, 1969, 1972 edn, 218–52.
14. B.P.P., 1834, XIX, 33–9.
15. The proportion of adult women employed in the cotton factories rose from around 41 per cent of female factory labour in 1835 to 42 per cent in 1841, a total of just under 66,000 adult women. 1841 census in Pinchbeck, *op. cit.*, p. 318.
16. Hewitt, M., *Wives and Mothers in Victorian Industry*, 1958, p. 12.
17. *Hansard*, 15 March 1844.
18. Quoted by Smelser, *op. cit.*, p. 301.
19. Barrett, M., and McIntosh, M., 'The Family Wage', in Whitelegg *et al.* (eds.), *The Changing Experience of Women*, Oxford, 1982, p. 74; Hartmann, H., 'The Unhappy Marriage of Marxism and Feminism: towards a more progressive union' in Dale *et al.*, *Education and the State volume II: Politics, Patriarchy and Practice*, Lewes, 1981, p. 201.

20. Quoted by John, A., *By the Sweat of Their Brow: women workers at Victorian coal mines*, Beckenham, 1980, p. 57.
21. *Preston Chronicle*, 12/11/1853, 3; *Bolton Chronicle and South Lancashire Advertiser*, 10/12/1853, 8. The speeches of Ann and Margaret Fletcher are the only evidence I have found of support for the male breadwinner wage among weavers at this time, though they were more common later. See, for example, Rose, S. O., *Limited Livelihoods: gender and class in nineteenth-century England*, London, 1992, pp. 154–84.
22. Quoted in Hollis, P., *Women in Public: the women's movement 1850–1900*, London, 1979, p. 76.
23. Schwarzkopf, J., *Women in the Chartist Movement*, London, 1991, p. 38.
24. Chartist views on the issue of female suffrage are discussed in Schwarzkopf, *op. cit.*, Chapter 2, pp. 35–77.
25. B.P.P. 1840, XXIV, 44.
26. The arguments of the main contributors to the debate on the reasons for these developments are summarised in Kirk, N., *The Growth of Working-Class Reformism in Mid-Victorian Britain*, Beckenham, 1985, pp. 1–31.
27. Hewitt, *op. cit.*, p. 12.
28. Hartmann, *op. cit.*, p. 202.
29. The Manchester Labour Society in Kirk, *op. cit.*; Factory Inspector Leonard Horner, 1858, quoted in *ibid.*, pp. 247, 270. Dutton, H. I. and King, J. E., 'The Limits of Paternalism: the cotton tyrants of north Lancashire, 1836–1854', *Social History*, 7, 1, 1982, 63–4.
30. Kirk, *op. cit.*, p. 105.
31. Joyce, P., *Work, Society and Politics: the culture of the factory in later Victorian England*, London, 1980, 1982 edn.
32. Kirk, *op. cit.*, p. 93.
33. Joyce, *op. cit.*, p. 109.
34. Liddington, J., and Norris, J., *One Hand Tied Behind Us: the rise of the women's suffrage movement*, 1978, pp. 58–9.
35. There is a very suggestive geographical correlation which seems to link paternalism with spinning, with the majority of the paternalist employers identified by Joyce being located in the spinning districts in south Lancashire. Joyce, *op. cit.*, 60, 158–201.
36. Quoted in Liddington and Norris, *op. cit.*, p. 272 n. 33. Also see Rose, *op. cit.*, for evidence of continuing discrimination later in the century.
37. Rose, *op. cit.*, p. 175.
38. Joyce, *op. cit.*, p. 113.
39. Barrett and McIntosh, in Whitelegg *et al.*, *op. cit.*, p. 73.
40. State interests were served by both 'new' and 'traditional' patriarchy, not least in devolving many of the problems experienced by working-class families on the 'deficiencies' of the working-class wife and mother. When combined with the tenets of political economy, patriarchal ideologies could also absolve the state from any responsibility for working-class poverty. Men were at liberty to sell their labour at any price they chose, and if they chose to sell it at a price which disallowed the adequate maintenance of a wife and family that too was their choice. Women and children 'ought' to be supported by husbands and fathers, not by the state.

41. Mill, J., *Essay on Government*, 1821, in Taylor, *op. cit.*, p. 293 n. 48, p. 131 n. 103.
42. Taylor, *op. cit.*, p. 33.
43. *Ibid.*, p. 96.
44. Taylor, *op. cit.*, p. 80; Rendall, J., Introduction to Rendall, J., (ed.), *Equal or Different: Women's Politics 1800–1914*, Oxford, 1987, p. 5.
45. Quoted by Pinchbeck, *op. cit.*
46. Schwarzkopf, *op. cit.*, p. 4.
47. Thompson, D., 'Women and Nineteenth-Century Radical Politics: a lost dimension', in Mitchell, J., and Oakley, A. (eds.), *The Rights and Wrongs of Women*, Harmondsworth, 1976, p. 137. Schwarzkopf similarly argues 'decisive shifts in working-class women's sexual behaviour' and 'apparently high rates' of marital violence in the period around 1830 to the 1850s. Schwarzkopf, *op. cit.*, pp. 32–3.
48. Liddington and Norris, *op. cit.*, p. 61.
49. Barlee, E., *A Visit to Lancashire in December 1862*, in Hewitt, *op. cit.*, p. 67.
50. Joyce, *op. cit.*, 113.
51. Burnett, J., *Destiny Obscure*, London, 1983, p. 218.
52. Taylor, *op. cit.*, p. 112.
53. Roberts, E., *Women's Work 1840–1940*, Basingstoke, 1988, p. 48.
54. Kirk, *op. cit.*, p. 146.
55. Reports of the Factory Inspectors, B.P.P. 1849 XXII, 144.
56. Merryweather, Mary, *Experiences of Factory Life*, London, third edn, 1862, p. 19.
57. *The Pioneer*, 22/3/1834.
58. See, for example, B.P.P. 1833, XX, D1, 39.
59. Kirk, *op. cit.*, pp. 216, 28.
60. See, for example, B.P.P. 1842, XIV, f131.
61. This draws on Kirk's discussion of Lancashire respectability. Kirk, *op. cit.*, pp. 112–13.
62. Joyce, *op. cit.*

2 Women's Work in Agricultural Production

1. Hobsbawm, E., and Rudé, G., *Captain Swing*, 1968, p. 83.
2. P. P., 1843, XII, 220.
3. Middleton, C., 'Women's Labour and the Transition to Pre-industrial Capitalism', in Charles, L., and Duffin, L., *Women and Work in Pre-Industrial England*, Beckenham, 1985, pp. 181–206; Roberts, M., 'Sickles and Scythes: men's work and women's work at harvest time', *History Workshop*, 7, Spring 1979, 3–28.
4. Snell, K. D. M., *Annals of the Labouring Poor: social change in agrarian England 1660–1990*, Cambridge, 1985, 1987 edn, pp. 22, 49–50, 65.
5. Quoted by Pinchbeck, *Women Workers and the Industrial Revolution 1780–1850*, 1930, 1981 edn, p. 59.
6. P. P. 1834 XXVIII, 359–61A in Pinchbeck, *op. cit.*, p. 76.

7. Snell, *op. cit.*, p. 60.
8. Poor Law Commission 1834, quoted by Hobsbawm and Rudé, *op. cit.*, p. 45.
9. Pinchbeck, *op. cit.*, p. 80.
10. Thompson, F., *Lark Rise to Candleford*, 1976, edn, pp. 155, 166.
11. Jeffries, R., *The Toilers of the Field*, 1892, quoted by Snell, *op. cit.*, p. 327.
12. Glyde, John, *Suffolk in the Nineteenth Century: Physical, Moral, Social, Religious and Industrial*, London, 1851, p. 59.
13. Glyde, John, *The Moral, Social, and Religious Condition of Ipswich*, Ipswich and London, 1850, p. 70.
14. Richards, E., 'Women in the British Economy since about 1700: an interpretation', *History*, LIX, 1974, 348.
15. See, for example, Higgs's calculations of servants' wages in the nineteenth century which suggests, taking board and lodgings into account, that general servants' earnings were on a par with those of women working in the cotton industry, whilst those of cooks were superior. Higgs, E., 'Domestic Service and Household Production' in John, A. (ed.), *Unequal Opportunities: women's employment in England 1800–1918*, Oxford, 1986, p. 138.
16. Snell, *op. cit.*, pp. 348, 210–17.
17. Quoted in *ibid.*, p. 349 n. 77.
18. Poor Law Report, P. P. 1834, XXXVIII, 127.
19. Pinchbeck, *op. cit.*, p. 83.
20. See p. 23.
21. Hobsbawm and Rudé, *op. cit.*, p. 83.
22. Report on the Poor Laws, B.P.P., 1834 XXIX, 297a.
23. B.P.P. 1834, XXVIII, 683a.
24. Poor Law reports, for example, comment on increases in women's agricultural work in this period. Census returns are very unreliable regarding women's paid work and show much lower numbers than these revised estimates. Higgs, E., 'Women, Occupations and Work in the Nineteenth-Century Censuses', *History Workshop*, Spring 1987, 74–5. Also see Miller, C., 'The Hidden Workforce': female fieldworkers in Gloucestershire 1870–1901', *Southern History*, 6, 1984, 139–55.
25. Higgs, *op. cit.* Drawing on the evidence of the 1843 Commission of Enquiry into the work of women and children in agriculture, Pinchbeck estimated that women and children represented around one-third to one-sixth of the male agricultural labour force in the district between Ipswich and Woodbridge, and that around half the working-class women of the Woodbridge district were employed in field-work. Around Lavenham, however, there was little agricultural work for women, while in the Mildenhall district women's work ranged from nothing at all in the winter months to employment on a variety of tasks over the rest of the year. Pinchbeck, *op. cit.*, pp. 93–4; B.P.P., 1843, XII, 227.
26. B.P.P. 1843 XII, 224.
27. *Ibid.*, 280.
28. 1837–38 Select Committee on the New Poor Law, quoted by Snell, *op. cit.*, p. 122.
29. Digby, A., *Pauper Palaces*, London, 1981, pp. 224–5.
30. Quoted by Snell, *op. cit.*, p. 122.

31. Foster estimated that at least 70 per cent of family earnings were spent on food and basic shop goods, with the diet of the average family being vastly inferior to that provided in the supposedly 'less eligible' workhouse. Cited in Jones, D., *Crime, Protest, Community and Police in Nineteenth-Century Britain*, London, 1982, p. 37.
32. Quoted in *ibid.*, p. 52.
33. B.P.P. 1843 XII, 243.
34. *Ibid.*, 143.
35. See Joyce, P., *Work, Society and Politics: the culture of the factory in later Victorian England*, London, 1980, 1982 edn., pp. 134–55.
36. B.P.P. 1843 XII, 25–6.
37. *Ibid.*, 27.
38. *Ibid.*, 225–6.
39. Glyde, *Suffolk*, p. 55.
40. Author's calculations, based on 1861 census returns.
41. B.P.P. 1867–68 XVII, 17.
42. B.P.P. 1868–69 XIII, 54.
43. B.P.P. 1867–68 XVII, 16–17, 80.
44. There is no evidence of Suffolk and Norfolk women being forced to work in the fields as happened, for example, in Dorset. Pinchbeck, *op. cit.*, p. 110. Suffolk was the centre of agricultural machine manufacture and it is likely that increased use of machinery reduced demand for female labour in the region.
45. Stephens, W. B., *Education, Literacy and Society, 1830–1870: the geography of diversity in provincial England*, Manchester, 1987, p. 319.
46. Jones, *op. cit.*, pp. 60, 61.

3 Schooling for Social Control? The Early Nineteenth Century

1. Stephens, W. B., *Education, Literacy and Society 1830–1870: the geography of diversity in provincial England*, Manchester, 1987, p. 2.
2. Sanderson, M., 'Social Change and Elementary Education in Industrial Lancashire 1780–1840', *Northern History*, University of Leeds, vol. 3, 1968, 136; Thompson, E. P., *The Making of the English Working Class*, Harmondsworth, 1968, p. 321. Also see Johnson, R., 'Really Useful Knowledge: radical education and working-class culture 1790–1845', in Dale *et al.*, *Education and the State volume II: Politics, Patriarchy and Practice*, Lewes, 1981, pp. 12–13.
3. Sanderson, M., 'Literacy and Social Mobility in the Industrial Revolution in England', *Past and Present*, 56, 1972; Sanderson, M., 'Social Change', p. 136.
4. In Hadleigh in Suffolk, for example, of three endowments for the education of 'children' in the early nineteenth century, only one was used to finance girls' schooling. B.P.P., 1819 IX. 2, 891; B.P.P. 1829 VII, 607–11.
5. 59 per cent of male weavers marrying in Manchester between 1754 and 1764 could sign their names, but only 11 per cent of their brides could do

so. Laqueur, T. W., 'Debate: literacy and social mobility in the Industrial Revolution in England', *Past and Present*, 64, August 1974, 96–7.

6. Sanderson, 'Social Change', 14–15.
7. *Ibid.*, 16.
8. Letter to James Martin MP quoted in Perkin, H., *The Origins of Modern Society*, London, 1969, 1972 edn., p. 195.
9. Hannah More, in a letter to the Bishop of Bath and Wells, 1801, in Digby, A., and Searby, P., *Children, Schools and Society in Nineteenth-Century England*, Basingstoke, 1981, p. 75.
10. Annual Report of the National Society, 1818, 252.
11. Annual Report of the National Society, 1825, 13.
12. Annual Report of the British Society, 1820, 121; 1818, 55.
13. Annual Report of the Stockport Sunday School, 1810–11, 6.
14. Annual Report of the British Society, 1815, 109.
15. Annual Report of the British Society, 1833, 7.
16. *Mechanics Magazine*, October 1823, quoted by Simon, B., *Studies in the History of Education 1780–1870*, London, 1960, p. 215.
17. Johnson, R., 'Notes on the Schooling of the English Working Class', in Dale, R., *et al.*, *Schooling and Capitalism*, London, 1976, p. 49.
18. William Thompson, quoted by Simon, *op. cit.*, p. 208.
19. *The Co-operative Magazine*, 1826, quoted by Taylor, B., *Eve and the New Jerusalem*, 1983, p. 233.
20. Quoted by Simon, *op. cit.*, p. 214 n. 2.
21. Quoted in Laqueur, T. W., *Religion and Respectability: Sunday schools and working-class culture*, New Haven, 1976, p. 90.
22. *The Pioneer*, 8/2/1834; 26/10/1833.
23. Taylor, *op. cit.*, p. 233.
24. *The Pioneer*, 26/10/1833 and 8/2/1834; Taylor, *op. cit.*, p. 341 n. 50.
25. *The Pioneer*, 8/2/34; *New Moral World* 18/10/1838 in Taylor, *op. cit.*, p. 232.
26. *Ibid*, p. 234.
27. Quoted in Purvis, *Hard Lessons: the lives and education of working-class women in nineteenth-century England*, Cambridge, 1989, p. 101.
28. Quoted by Taylor, *op. cit.*, p. 234.
29. Johnson, 'Really Useful Knowledge', pp. 86–7, 94.
30. Simon, *op. cit.*, p. 193.
31. Purvis, *op. cit.*, p. 101.
32. Taylor, *op. cit.*, p. 229
33. Johnson, 'Really Useful Knowledge', p. 82.
34. Thompson, E. P., *The Making of the English Working Class*, Harmondsworth, 1968, p. 183; Johnson, 'Really Useful Knowledge', p. 96.
35. Annual Report of the National Society, 1832, 51.
36. Annual Report of the National Society, 1829, 13. Author's calculations.
37. Annual Report of the British Society, 1826, 33.
38. Calculated from Stephens, *op. cit.*, p. 352.
39. Girls represented 50.6 per cent of private school pupils in the 1851 Education Census. B.P.P. 1852–3 XC, 4–5, cxlvi–cxlvii.

40. Author's calculations, based on the summary national returns in B.P.P. 1835 XLIII, 1208.

41. Purvis, J., 'The Double Burden of Class and Gender in the Schooling of Working-class Girls in Nineteenth-century England, 1800–1870', in Barton, L., and Walkes, S., *Schools, Teachers and Teaching*, Lewes, 1981, p. 108.

42. The education of girls was seen to be the business of females and responsibility for the everyday running of girls' schools (though not for major management decisions or financial management) was generally delegated to a Ladies' Committee. This committee then submitted reports to the male Management Committee. See, for example, 'Rules for Schools in Association with the British Society', B.P.P. 1816, IV. 2, 121. The likely effects of this would have been to limit the male management committees' knowledge of the operation of the girls' schools and to reinforce their interest in those schools with which they have a direct involvement, that is, the schools for boys. Annual reports sent to the parent society in London would almost invariably have been written by men, though some reports of Ladies' Committees are included.

43. Quoted by Purvis, *Hard Lessons*, p. 76.

44. Bryant, M., review of Purvis, 'Hard Lessons', *History of Education Quarterly*, 31, 1, 1991, 136–7.

45. Stephens, *op. cit.*, pp. 252, 12–13.

46. Author's calculations from the educational returns for 1818, B.P.P. 1819, XI. 2, vol. 2, 877–915.

47. Calculated from the 1833 Returns, B.P.P. 1835 XLII, 652 (Norfolk); XLIII, 932 (Suffolk).

48. Letter written in response to a general enquiry from the Archdeacon in 1814. The Anglican clergy of Norfolk outlined the numerous obstacles they encountered in their efforts to establish schools in these letters. NDS/275, Norfolk County Record Office, Norwich.

49. B.P.P. 1845 XXXV, 102.

50. Over half the school population of Norfolk and Suffolk attended school without payment in 1820. Marsden, W. E., *Unequal Educational Provision in England and Wales- the Nineteenth-Century Roots*, London, 1987, p. 46.

51. Stephens, *op. cit.*, p. 37. Also see Stephens, W. B., *Regional Variations in Education During the Industrial Revolution: The Task of the Local Historian*, Leeds, 1973, p. 4.

52. Sanderson, M. 'The National and British School Societies in Lancashire: the roots of Anglican supremacy', in Cook, T. (ed.), *Local Studies and the History of Education*, London, 1972, 12–13.

53. Minutes of the School Committee in Murphy, J., 'The Rise of Public Elementary Education in Lancashire', *Transactions of the Historic Society of Lancashire and Cheshire*, 1966, p. 128.

54. B.P.P. 1835 XLI, 473.

55. Following Marsden, gender differences in the proportions of child populations at Sunday school were estimated to show an estimated 91 per cent of the female child population of Lancashire on the books of a Sunday school, compared with 87 per cent of Lancashire boys and 61 per cent and 49 per cent of Suffolk and Norfolk girls respectively. Gomersall, M., 'The

Elementary Education of Females in England 1800–1870, with particular reference to the lives and work of girls and women in industrial Lancashire and rural Norfolk and Suffolk', unpublished Ph.D. thesis, University of London, 1991, 262.

56. It must also be remembered that children were not necessarily classified according to their age, and it would be quite possible for an older girl to be registered as an 'infant' if this was appropriate to her level of attainment. Calculated from summary table for England and Wales, B.P.P. 1835 XLIII, 1208. Figures for Lancashire show an estimated proportion of 51.1 per cent and 51.2 per cent of girls on the books of infant and day-and-infant schools. B.P.P. 1835, 473.

57. Again a proportional breakdown of the 'not specified' category has been calculated. B.P.P. 1835, XLIII, 1208.

58. Author's calculations from summaries of returns in B.P.P. 1835 XLI, 64, 214, 298, 380.

4 Religion, Reading and Really Useful Knowledge

1. Minute Book for the Bath National Sunday School and School of Industry, 1806, 5.

2. Norfolk and Norwich National Society Minute Book, February 1806, 5.

3. Goldstrom, J. M., 'The Content of Education and the Socialisation of the Working-Class Child 1830–1860', in McCann, P. (ed.), *Popular Education and Socialisation in the Nineteenth Century*, London 1977, p. 98.

4. B.P.P. 1834 IX, 72.

5. Quoted by Laqueur, T. W., *Religion and Respectability: Sunday schools and working-class culture*, New Haven, 1976, p. 215.

6. Rules of the Jubilee School for Girls, Manchester 1810, in Reports of the Committee 1856–70, 3, 13, 22.

7. Vanes, J., *Apparelled in Red: the history of the Red Maids' School*, Bristol, 1984, pp. 42, 65.

8. B.P.P. 1816, IV. 4, 282.

9. Minute Book, St Leonard's Girls' School, Shoreditch, London, 5/5/1813.

10. Vanes, *op. cit.*, pp. 70–1.

11. Annual Report of the National Society, 1832, 119.

12. Annual Report of the British Society, 1815, 60.

13. B.P.P. 1834 X, 211.

14. Annual Report of the National Society, 1817, 193.

15. Annual Report of the National Society, 1818, 193.

16. Annual Report of the British Society, 1827, note to p. 57; Annual Report of the National Society, 1818, 14.

17. Annual Report of the National Society, 1833, 53.

18. Annual Report of the National Society, 1832, 119.

19. *Ibid.*

20. Reports of Weymouth House Girls' school, Bath, 1836, 2.

21. B.P.P. 1845 XXXV, 31–2 (Allen); B.P.P. 1847 XLV, 185–8 (Watkins); B.P.P. 1852–53, LXXX, 297 (Mitchell).

22. B.P.P. 1847 XLV, 289.
23. Laqueur, *op. cit.*, p. 151.
24. Laqueur, *op. cit.*, p. 149.
25. *Ibid.*, 103–4; Report of the Manchester Statistical Society (afterwards M.S.S.) Education in Salford, 1836, 35; Education in Liverpool, 1835–36, vii.
26. B.P.P. 1816, IV, 79. Also see Laqueur, *op. cit.*, pp. 174–5.
27. Also see Frith, S. 'Socialisation and Rational Schooling: elementary education in Leeds before 1870' in McCann, *op. cit.*, pp. 76–7.
28. Report of the M.S.S. Education in Birmingham, 1840, 35.
29. M.S.S. Education in Manchester, 1835, 22.
30. M.S.S. Education in Manchester, 1835, 10; Salford, 1836, 11; Rutland, 1839, 9.
31. Only 38 of the 340 teachers of private schools in Finsbury in the early 1840s were said to be teachers from choice. Those in Birmingham were said to find their work 'tiresome and unpleasant' but were forced to do it by 'harsh necessity'. Report of the Education Committee of Finsbury, *Journal of the Royal Statistical Society of London*, vols. 3 and 6, 1840 and 1843 (Birmingham), vol. 6, 1843 (Finsbury).
32. Vincent located only six autobiographies written by women in the early nineteenth century. Vincent, D., *Bread, Knowledge and Freedom: a study of nineteenth-century working-class autobiography*, London, 1982, p. 8.
33. Smith, Mary, *The Autobiography of Mary Smith, Schoolmistress and Nonconformist: a fragment of a life*, London, 1892, pp. 17, 24, 30.
34. *Ibid.*, p. 24.
35. Quoted by Gorham G., *The Victorian Girl and the Feminine Ideal*, London, 1982, pp. 143–6.
36. Annual Report of the British Society, 1834, 8.
37. 7.5 per cent of girls and 1 per cent of boys were dismissed for poor attendance (or bad behaviour). Girls stayed at school an average 7.9 months longer than boys and 25 per cent were enrolled for more than five years compared with only 14 per cent of boys. This was encouraged by girls' occupational destination as domestic servants. Madoc-Jones, B., 'Patterns of Attendance and their Social Significance: Mitcham National School 1830–1839', in McCann, *op. cit.*, pp. 35–6, 45–50.
38. Annual Report of the National Society, 1831, 30.
39. Author's calculations. Annual Report of the National Society, 1829, 25.
40. Stephens, W. B., *Education, Literacy and Society, 1830–1870: the geography of diversity in provincial England*, Manchester, 1987, pp. 7, 93, 322–3.
41. *Ibid.*, pp. 94, 332.
42. In Taylor, B., *Eve and the New Jerusalem*, London, 1983, p. 232.
43. M.S.S., Education in Pendleton, 1839, 10, 16.
44. Smith, *op. cit.*, p. 32.

5 An Education of Principle

1. This section draws on the work of Richard Johnson: 'Educational Policy and Social Control in Early Victorian England', *Past and Present*, 49, 1970;

'Notes on the Schooling of the English Working Class', in Dale, R., *et al.*, *Schooling and Capitalism*, London, 1976; 'Really Useful Knowledge: radical education and working-class culture 1790–1845', in Dale, R., *et al.*, *Education and the State: Vol. II: Politics, Patriarchy and Practice*, London, 1981; 'Educating the Educators: 'experts' and the state 1833–1839', in Donajgrodzki, A. P., *Social Control in Nineteenth-Century Britain*, London, 1977.

2. Quoted by Hurt, J., *Education in Evolution: church, state, society and popular education*, London, 1971, pp. 24–5.

3. Kay-Shuttleworth, J., 'The Moral and Physical Condition of the Working Class in Manchester in 1832', in *Four Periods of Public Education*, London, 1862, p. 64.

4. *Ibid.*, p. 74.

5. Johnson, 'Notes', pp. 87, 89.

6. B.P.P. 1860 XXXIV, 458–9.

7. B.P.P. 1834, XIX, 39.

8. Brewer, 'Workhouse Visiting', 298–300, quoted by Purvis, J., in *Hard Lessons: the lives and education of working-class women in nineteenth-century England*, Cambridge, 1989, pp. 67–8.

9. B.P.P. 1837–38 VII, 23.

10. Annual Report of the National Society, 1841, 151, 156.

11. Annual Report of the National Society, 1847, 30.

12. Annual Report of the British Society, 1841, 7.

13. B.P.P. 1847 XLV, 303.

14. B.P.P. 1856 XLVII, 385.

15. Annual Report of the British Society, 1833, 13.

16. B.P.P. 1856 XLVII, 384.

17. Report of the Newcastle Commission on Education, B.P.P. 1861 XXI. 2, 95–6.

18. *Ibid.*

19. Goldstrom, J. M., 'The Content of Education and the Socialisation of the Working-Class Child 1830–1860', in McCann, P. (ed.), *Popular Education and Socialisation in the Nineteenth Century*, London, 1977, p. 102.

20. Kay-Shuttleworth in B.P.P. 1838 XXVIII, B3, 140.

21. B.P.P. 1834 XLIII, 13.

22. He instructed the Inspectors always to enquire whether the girls were receiving instruction in household management. B.P.P. 1840 XL, 13.

23. B.P.P. 1847–48 L, 8; 1852–53 LXXX, 21; 1854–55 XLII, 482; 1857–58 XLV, 253.

24. Evidence of G. W. Proctor to the Newcastle Commission, B.P.P. 1861 XXI. 3, 134.

25. Newcastle Commission, B.P.P. 1861 XXI.1., 123–4.

26. B.P.P. 1852–53 LXXIX, 469.

27. B.P.P. 1843 XVIII, 168–9.

28. Kirk, N., *The Growth of Working-Class Reformism in Mid-Victorian Britain*, Beckenham, 1985, pp. 145, 222.

29. B.P.P. 1852–53 XC, xli.

30. B.P.P. 1861, XXI. 1, 350–1.

31. Kirk, *op. cit.*, p. 225. Tylecote also cites examples of working-class men achieving social and occupational mobility through education. Tylecote, M.,

The Mechanics' Institutes of Lancashire and Yorkshire before 1851, Manchester, 1957, p. 262.

32. Mr Ransome of the agricultural machinery company of that name in Ipswich in Suffolk was in the habit of doing this. Annual Report of the Ipswich British and Foreign School Society, 1848.

33. Annual Reports of the British Society, 1826, 48; 1828; 36; 1831, 78; 1832, 55–6; 1838, 81; 1842, 77, 90; 1843, 80; 1845, 11; *Oldham Chronicle*, 7/4/1860.

34. B.P.P. 1850, 58–9.

35. Newcastle Commission, B.P.P. 1861, XXI. 2, 247.

36. Quoted in Kirk, *op. cit.*, p. 218.

37. B.P.P. 1856, XLVII, 386.

38. B.P.P. 1856 XLVII, 386.

39. Newcastle Commission, *op. cit.*

40. Davin A., '"Mind that You Do As You Are Told": reading books for Board school girls', *Feminist Review*, 3, 1979, 89.

41. Dyhouse, *Girls Growing up in Late Victorian and Edwardian England*, London, 1981, p. 83.

42. Turnball, A., 'Learning Her Womanly Work: the elementary school curriculum, 1870–1914', in Hunt, F. (ed.), *Lessons for Life: the schooling of girls and women, 1850–1950*, Oxford, 1987, p. 98.

43. B.P.P. 1852–53 XC, xxvii, 4.

44. Author's calculations, based on the figures given in B.P.P. 1835, XLIII, 1208; B.P.P. 1852–53, XC4–5; B.P.P. 1861, XXI. i, 79.

45. Author's calculations from *ibid.*

46. Author's calculations from B.P.P. 1852–53, XC, 7.

47. B.P.P. 1861, XXI. 2, 596.

48. Author's calculations from B.P.P. 1852–53, XC, 4–7.

49. *Ibid.*, cxlvii.

50. B.P.P. 1834, XIX, 139; Kirk, *op. cit.*, p. 34.

51. M.S.S., Education in Pendleton, 1838, 6 n. 10.

52. B.P.P. 1870, LIV, 145. Silk factories were not covered by the 1833 and 1844 Factory Acts.

53. B.P.P. 1852–3, XC, 7.

54. M.S.S. *op. cit.*, 3.

55. I have calculated around 1,490 boys and 2,700 girls on the books of night classes run in association with the Sunday schools of Manchester, Salford, Pendleton and Bury in the 1830s. Author's calculations from Reports of the Manchester Statistical Society.

56. Laqueur, T. W., *Religion and Respectability: Sunday Schools and Working-class Culture*, New Haven, 1976, pp. 120, 122.

57. Purvis, *op. cit.*, pp. 100–2.

58. Kay-Shuttleworth, U. J., 'On the East Lancashire Union of Institutions having Evening Schools, on its Bearing on the Question of the Education of the Labouring Classes', *Transactions of the National Association for the Promotion of Social Science*, 1866, 18. Purvis has estimated a proportion of 8.2 per cent female membership of the Mechanics' Institutes of the north-western counties, including Lancashire and Cheshire, in 1851. *Ibid.*, 107.

59. *Ibid.,* 166–7, 171, 182.
60. B.P.P. 1843, XII, 347, 238.
61. B.P.P. 1847–48, L, 27. Also see B.P.P. 1854–55, XLII, 392; 1857, XXIII, 467; 1861, XXI.2, 148–9.
62. B.P.P. 1867–68 XVII, 192.
63. Author's calculations from figures in B.P.P. 1852–53 XC, 106–114. cxlix (Norfolk), clii (Suffolk).
64. B.P.P. 1861 XXI.1, 596.
65. B.P.P. 1861 XXI.2., 223, 247, 364.
66. Girls were in the majority in only 2 of the 165 registration districts in the industrial regions, compared with very nearly one-third of the registration districts of the east and south-east. Author's calculations, B.P.P. 1852–53, XC, 10–14, 20–2, 32–42.
67. In Gloucestershire, for example, a superior or equal percentage of the female population was at school in 1851 in 10 of 17 districts (Bristol, Gloucester, Cheltenham and other more urban areas excepted) and similar patterns were evident in other more agricultural counties. Author's calculations from tables of enrolment in Stephens, W. B., *Education, Literacy, and Society, 1830–1870: the geography of diversity in provincial England,* Manchester, 1987, Appendix F, pp. 326–38.
68. Author's calculations. B.P.P. 1861 XXI.i., 596. See also the report of the Revd J. Allen on schools in Bedfordshire, Cambridgeshire and Huntingdonshire. B.P.P. 1845, XXXV, 42.

6   Schooling for Domesticity? The Later Nineteenth Century

1. These were a record of daily activities, kept by the teacher in charge of the school. These records were required under the revised code of 1863, though the requirement only applied to those schools receiving financial support from the state and subject to inspection by Her Majesty's Inspectors; that is, the 'good' schools of the period.
2. This was laid down by a General Consolidated Order, cited in B.P.P. 1849, XLII, 73.
3. B.P.P. 1849, XLII, 34, 65, 159; B.P.P., 1850, XLIII, 111.
4. B.P.P. 1850, XLIII, 5–6.
5. B.P.P. 1849, XLII, 160. See also Digby, *Pauper Palaces,* London, 1981, pp. 183, 187, 189–90, for conditions in Norfolk workhouse schools.
6. B.P.P. 1849, XLII, 35–6, 81, 238.
7. B.P.P. 1852–53, LXXIX, 129.
8. B.P.P. 1850, XLIII, 4–7.
9. B.P.P. 1850, XLIII, 48.
10. Log-book entries for St Saviour's Girls and Infant school, Leeds, for 27/1/1863, 12/3/1863, 28/4/1863, 12/5/1863, 11/9/1863, 30/10/1863, 2/2/1864, 21/3/1866.
11. B.P.P. 1861 XXI. 2., 228.
12. B.P.P. 1870, XXII, appendix D, 104.

13. Newcastle Commission, 1861, XXI. 2., 230–1.
14. Reports of the Jubilee School for Girls, Manchester, 1856–70, 5, 14, 16–18, 22.
15. B.P.P. 1850, XLIII, 1, 8–9.
16. B.P.P. 1856, XLVii, 385.
17. Log-book, Ewell School for Girls, entry for 1/8/1866.
18. B.P.P., 1861, XXI.3., 63; 1856, XLVII, 386.
19. B.P.P., 1861, XXI.1., 663.
20. B.P.P., 1861, XXI.1., 662, 666.
21. Extensive reading has produced this as the sole example of a parent objecting to needlework – though Mrs Townsend's annoyance was probably prompted as much by the fact of her daughter having been sent home for cotton and to remove the 'hoops' from her skirt. Log-book, Norbiton St Peter's National School for Girls, entry for 8/6/1864.
22. B.P.P. 1857 XXXIII, 468, log-book, St Andrew's School, Derby, entries for 13/5/1865, 18/1/1866.
23. B.P.P. XXI. 2., 213.
24. Dyhouse, C., *Girls Growing Up in Late Victorian and Edwardian England*, London, 1981, pp. 89–90, Turnball, 'Learning Her Womanly Work: the elementary school curriculum, 1870–1914', in Hunt, F. (ed.), *Lessons for Life: the schooling of girls and women, 1850–1950*, Oxford, 1987, p. 95.
25. Turnball, *op. cit.*, pp. 96–7.
26. B.P.P. 1847, XLV, 17.
27. His remarks were made with particular reference to Wales, though they have a general applicability. B.P.P. 1861, XXI. 2., 545.
28. B.P.P. 1856, XLVII, 365.
29. B.P.P. 1861, XXI. I., 663–4.
30. B.P.P. 1854, LII, 442.
31. B.P.P. 1857, XXXIII, 481.
32. B.P.P. 1847, XLV, 303.
33. B.P.P. 1861, XXI.3., 135.
34. Annual Report of the National Society, 1840, 127–8.
35. B.P.P. 1843, XL, 138–9.
36. B.P.P. 1841, XX, 181 nn. 9, 13.
37. B.P.P. 1867–68, LIII, 101–2; 1861, XXI.1., 123; 1850, XLIII, 7.
38. B.P.P. 1856, XLVII, 521.
39. B.P.P. 1870, LIV, 514.
40. Log book, Almondsbury School for Girls, Wakefield. Entry for 23/8/1863.
41. B.P.P., 1857–58, XLV, 589–90.
42. Author's calculations, based on the reports of Inspectors Allen, Cook and Moseley in B.P.P., 1847, XLV, 40–67, 136–50, 112–33.
43. B.P.P. 1857, XXXIII, 240.
44. B.P.P. 1870, XXII, 143–4.
45. Committee Book, Mount Pleasant School. Liverpool, entry for May 1859.
46. B.P.P., 1861, XXI. 3., 137; Dyhouse, *op. cit.*, 102.
47. Report of the Ladies Committee, Hibernian Girls' school, August 1842; B.P.P. 1856, XLVIII, 413; 1852–53, LXXX, 464–7.
48. Second Annual Report of the Salford Ragged and Industrial Schools, 1836–37, 10.

49.   School Managers had to certify that the 'moral character of the candidates and their families justifies an expectation that the instruction and training of the school will be seconded by their own efforts and by the example of their parents'. 'With regard to girls the enquiries have been even stricter and more searching', stated Inspector Cook. Minute of 1846, B.P.P. 1847–48, L.31–2.

50.   Pupil teachers had to compete for Queen's scholarships to attend College, though, as a teaching post could be obtained on completion of apprenticeship, many girls did not attend College.

51.   *The Pupil Teacher*, 11, 1859, 81–2, quoted by Hurt, J., *Education in Evolution: church, state, society and popular education 1800–1870*, London, 1972, p. 125.

52.   B.P.P., 1854, LI, 482; 1857, XXXIII, 232; 1861 XXI.5., 231–2.

53.   See, for example, the Committee Book of Mount Pleasant School, Liverpool, January 1861; Minutes of St Paul's Bentinck School, London, 5/10/1863; Minutes of St Martin's National School, London, 6/10/1858; log-book, Holy Trinity School, Ipswich, January 1867.

54.   B.P.P., 1861, XXI.3., 86.

55.   National Society Monthly Papers 1862.

56.   B.P.P., 1856, XLVII, 385.

57.   Johnson, M., *Derbyshire Village Schools in the Nineteenth Century*, Newton Abbot, 1970, p. 95. B.P.P., 1847, XLV, 56–64. Also see B.P.P., 1870, XXII, 28.

58.   See, for example, B.P.P. 1856, XLVII, 384; 1857–58, XLV, 576.

59.   Log-book entries show a broad curriculum with Miss Hicks teaching geography and topics such as 'gunpowder'. The registers show that girls in particular might enjoy extended attendance, with Jane Barnham, for example, attending school for nine years. Log-book entries for the 1860s, register 1867–77, Little Glemham school, Suffolk. In the agricultural areas it was common for girls to stay at school for longer than boys. See, for example, Inspector Cook's report on schools in the east of England in B.P.P., 1846, XXII, 100–2.

60.   Calculated from log-book entries, Bramford school, Suffolk, 1865.

61.   The source of this information was an undated and anonymous contemporary survey of the parish, probably written by Professor Henslow. West Suffolk R.O.

62.   Log-book entries for St Peter's School for Girls, Derby, March and December 1864; St James's Girls' National School, Trowbridge, September 1864; Leeds Parish Church School for Girls, May 1865.

63.   In Northumberland, for example, the cookery grant was paid for only 24 girls. Turnball, *op. cit.*, p. 96.

64.   Log-book entries for Kingston Girls' school, October 1865, January and October 1866, March 1870.

65.   Kate Taylor, in Burnett, J., *Destiny Obscure*, London, 1983, p. 292.

66.   B.P.P. 1870, XLVII, 65.

67.   Annual Reports of the Ipswich Branch of the British and Foreign Schools Society, 1848–65.

68.   Stephens, W.B., *Education, Literacy, and Society, 1830–1870: the geography of diversity in provincial England*, Manchester, 1987, Appendix F, pp. 332–3.

69.   Figures taken from *ibid.*, Appendix D, pp. 322–33.

7 What a Woman Knows

1. A contemporary school reading book contained the phrase, 'What a woman knows is comparatively of little importance to what a woman is.' *A Reading Book for Use in Female Schools*, 1864, quoted in Beddoes, D., *Discovering Women's History: a practical manual*, London, 1983, p. 97. An earlier version of this chapter is in Gomersall, M., 'The Elementary Education of Females in England 1800–1870, with particular reference to the lives and work of girls and women in industrial Lancashire and rural Norfolk and Suffolk', unpublished Ph.D. thesis, Institute of Education, University of London, 1991.
2. Saraga, J., 'Determined Women', *The Times Educational Supplement* 13/9/1991, 43.
3. See 'Introduction'.
4. Lown, J. *Women and Industrialisation: gender at work in nineteenthcentury England*, Cambridge, 1990, p. 219.
5. Walby, S. *Theorizing Patriarchy*, Oxford, 1993 p. 4. Middleton and Roberts have shown, for example, that demarcations between the agricultural work of men and women have very early origins and that gender divisions of labour intensified with changes in farming from the sixteenth century. Middleton, C., 'Women's Labour and the Transition to Pre-industrial Capitalism', in Charles, L., and Duffin, L., *Women and Work in Pre-Industrial England*, Beckenham, 1985, pp. 181–206; Roberts, M., 'Sickles and Scythes: men's work and women's work at harvest time', *History Workshop*, 7, Spring 1979, 3–28; Roberts, M., '"Words they are Women, and Deeds they are Men": images of work and gender in early modern England', in Charles, L., and Duffin, L., *op. cit.*, pp. 122–80. For a detailed discussion of gender divisions of labour see 'The Weaker Vessel?' in Gomersall, 1991, *op. cit.*, pp. 33–88.
6. Lown, *op. cit.*, p. 217.
7. See, for example, Bryant, M., *The Unexpected Revolution*, London, 1979; Hollis, P., *Women in Public: the women's movement 1850–1900*, London, 1979.
8. This was said by a trade unionist at the end of the century in a comparison of women's wage rates with those of men. Quoted by Liddington, J., and Norris, J., *One Hand Tied Behind Us: the rise of the women's suffrage movement*, London, 1978, p. 36.

8 From the Past to the Present

1. This chapter draws on the work of Walby, in particular her discussion of the forms and structures of patriarchy, *Theorizing Patriarchy*, Oxford, 1992.
2. These general points subsume differences between the experiences of white women and those of Afro-Caribbean and Asian origin. Walby, *op. cit.*, 27–8, 42–5, 59.
3. Central Statistical Office, *Social Trends*, 24, 1994, pp. 59, 130.
4. Though a confidential report leaked to a newspaper suggests that, in the context of rising unemployment, the Confederation of British Industry no longer sees any necessity to support equal opportunities for women, ethnic

groups or others who may face additional barriers to employment. *The Independent on Sunday*, 14/2/93; Riley, K., Quality and Equality: promoting opportunities in schools, London, 1994, p. 16.

5. Professor Michael Barber in *The Times Educational Supplement*, 26/8/94.

6. Arnot, M., 'Male Hegemony, Social Class, and Women's Education', Boston, 1982, reprinted in Stone, L. (ed.), *The Education Feminism Reader*, London and New York, 1994, p. 97.

7. An earlier version of this argument can be seen in Gomersall, M., 'Education for Domesticity? a nineteenth-century perspective on girls' schooling and education', *Gender and Education*, 6, 3, 1994.

8. Walby, *op. cit.*, Chapter 8, pp. 173–201.

9. Bradley, H., *Men's Work, Women's Work*, Cambridge, 1989, 231.

10. Liddington, J., and Norris, J., *One Hand Tied Behind Us: the rise of the women's suffrage movement*, London, 1978; Liddington, J., *The Life and Times of a Respectable Rebel: Selina Cooper 1864–1946*, London, 1984.

11. Dyhouse, C., *Feminism and the Family in England 1880–1939*, Oxford, 1989; Banks, O., *Faces of Feminism: a study of feminism as a social movement*, Oxford, 1981.

12. Walby, *op. cit.*, pp. 50–1, 192; Walby, S., *Patriarchy at Work*, Cambridge 1986, pp. 157–8, 171–4

13. Walby, *Patriarchy*, pp. 207–17.

14. *Ibid.*, p. 221.

15. *Ibid.*, pp. 229–30; Walby, *Theorizing*, p. 26.

16. Her Majesty's Inspectorate, *The Preparation of Girls for Adult and Working Life*, DFE, 1992, p. 1.

17. Riley, *op. cit.*, pp. 17, 127–8.

18. Purvis, J., *A History of Women's Education in England*, Milton Keynes, 1991, p. 126.

19. DFE, 1992, 4–9.

20. Douglas, J. W., *The Home and the School*, London, 1964.

21. Riley, *op. cit.*, 44.

22. *Social Trends*, 24, 1994, pp. 46–7.

23. Riley, *op. cit.*, p. 45.

24. HMI, *op. cit.*, p. 11.

25. Arnot, *op. cit.*, p. 99.

26. Walby, *Theorizing*, p. 76. The higher rate of economic activity for Afro-Caribbean women that Walby found in the 1980s (74 per cent as compared with 46 per cent of white women) seems to have declined with 66 per cent of black women (Afro-Caribbean, African and others, but excluding Asians) being economically active compared with 71.9 per cent of white women, possibly as a result of recession, high unemployment and racism. *Social Trends*, p. 57.

27. Driver (1978, 1980) and Fuller (1980) in Riley, *op. cit.*, p. 52; *ibid.*, 57–83.

28. Walby, *Theorizing*, p. 76.

29. See also MacDonald, M., 'Schooling and the Reproduction of Class and Gender Relations', in Dale *et al.* (eds.), *Education and the State Vol. II: Politics, Patriarchy and Practice*, p. 169.

30. National Curriculum Council, *Education for Industrial Understanding*, Curriculum Guidance 4, York, 1990.

31. DFE, pp. 3, 11.
32. Riley, *op. cit.*, p. 27.
33. *Ibid.*, p. 10.
34. DFE, p. 7.
35. *Ibid.*, p. 2.
36. Riley, *op. cit.*, p. 128.

Bibliography

The bibliography is organised in two sections: section one lists pre-1900 primary sources; section two lists twentieth-century sources.
The place of publication is London unless otherwise stated.

1 PUBLICATIONS BEFORE 1900

BOOKS AND PAMPHLETS

Anonymous, *Extract from an Account of the Ladies Committee for Promoting the Education and Employment of the Female Poor*, Society for Bettering the Condition of the Poor, 1804.

Arnold, Matthew, *Reports on Elementary Schools 1852–1882*, 1889.

Austen, Mrs A., *Two Letters on Girls' Schools and on the Training of Working Women*, 1857.

Baines, E., *The Social, Educational and Religious State of the Manufacturing Districts*, 2nd edn, 1843.

Balfour, Clara, *Working Women of the last half Century*, 1836.

Barnard, Sir T., *The Education of the Poor: A Digest of the Reports of the Society for Bettering the Condition of the Poor*, 1809.

Bartley, Sir George C. T., *The Education Condition and Requirements of One Square Mile in the East End of London*, 1870.

—*The Schools for the People. Containing the History, Development and Present Working of Each Description of English School for the Industrial and Poorer Classes*, 1871.

Bodichon, Barbara, *Women and Work*, 1856.

Booth, James, *On the Female Education of the Industrial Classes*, 1855.

Bowles, W., *Thoughts on the Increase of Crimes and the Education of the Poor and the National Schools*, 1818.

Bremner, C. S., *Education of Girls and Women in Great Britain*, 1897.

Cappe, Catherine, *Account of Two Charity Schools for the Education of Girls*, York, 1800.

Carpenter, Mary, 'The Education of Pauper Girls', *Transactions of the National Association for the Promotion of Social Science*, 1852.

—'On the Importance of Statistics to the Reformatory Movement with Returns from Female Reformatories and Remarks on them', *Journal of the Statistical Society of London*, 20, 1857.

Engels, Frederick, *The Condition of the Working Class In England*, 1892, 1969 edn.

Fletcher, Joseph, 'Moral and Educational Statistics of England and Wales', *Journal of the Statistical Society of London*, 10, 1847.

—'Statistics of Attendance in Schools for Children of the Poorer Classes', *Journal of the Statistical Society of London*, 15, 1842.

Fry, Alfred, 'Report of the Inspector of Factories on the Effects of the Educational Provision of the Factories Act', *Journal of the Statistical Society of London*, 2, 1839.

Glyde, John, *The Moral, Social and Religious Condition of Ipswich*, Ipswich and London, 1850.

—*Suffolk in the Nineteenth Century: Physical, Moral, Social, Religious and Industrial*, 1851.

Grey, Mrs W., *On the Education of Women*, 1871.

Kay, James, *The Moral and Physical Condition of the Working Classes Employed in the Cotton Manufacture in Manchester*, 1832.

—'On the Establishment of County or District Schools for the Training of Pauper Children', *Journal of the Statistical Society of London*, 1, 1839.

—*The Education of the Poor in England and Europe*, 1846.

Kay-Shuttleworth, J., *Four Periods of Public Education*, 1862.

—*Memorandum on Popular Education*, 1868.

Kay-Shuttleworth, U. J., 'On the East Lancashire Union of Institutions having Evening Schools, on its Bearing on the Question of the Education of the Labouring Classes', *Transactions of the National Association for the Promotion of Social Science*, 1866.

Marshall, William, *The Review and Abstract of County Reports to the Board of Agriculture from the Several Agricultural Departments of England*, volume 3, Eastern Department, 1818, reprinted Newton Abbot, 1968.

Merryweather, Mary, *Experiences of Factory Life*, 3rd edn, 1862.

Mill, J. S., *On the Subjection of Women*, 1869.

Milne, J. D., *Industrial and Social Position of Women in the Middle and Lower Ranks*, 1857.

Parks, B. R., *Remarks on the Education of Girls, with reference to the Social, Legal and Industrial Position of Women in the Present Day*, 1856.

Porter, G. R., *Results of an Inquiry into the Condition of the Labouring Classes in the County of Norfolk*, Central Society of Education, 1839.

Raynbird, W., and Raynbird, H., *The Agriculture of Suffolk*, 1849.

Report of the Birmingham Statistical Society on the State of Education in Birmingham, *Journal of the Royal Statistical Society of London*, 3, 1840.

Report of the Education Committee of Finsbury, *Journal of the Royal Statistical Society of London*, vols. 3 and 6, 1840 and 1843.

St John, J. A., *On the Education of the People*, 1858.

Smith, M., *The Autobiography of Mary Smith, Schoolmistress and Nonconformist: a fragment of a life*, 1892.

Trimmer, S., *Reflections on the Education of Children in Charity Schools*, 1792.

—*The Oeconomy of Charity*, volume 1, 1801.

Ure, A., *The Cotton Manufacture of Great Britain*, 1836.

Wakefield, P., *Reflections on the Present Condition of the Female Sex with Suggestions for its Improvement*, 1798.

Zimmern, A., *The Renaissance of Girls' Education*: a record of fifty years' progress, 1892.

NEWSPAPERS

Bolton Chronicle and South Lancashire Advertiser 10/12/1853.
Hansard 15/3/1844.
Oldham Chronicle 7/4/1860.
The Pioneer 26/10/1833, 8/2/1834, 22/3/1834.
Preston Chronicle 12/11/1853.

PARLIAMENTARY PAPERS

Minutes of the Evidence before the Select Committee on the State of the Children Employed in the Manufactories, PP, 1816, III.

Reports of the Select Committee on the Education of the Lower Orders in the Metropolis, PP, 1816, IV.

Report of the Select Committee of the House of Commons on the Poor Laws, PP, 1817, VI.

A Digest of the Parochial Returns made to the Select Committee appointed to Inquire into the Education of the Poor, PP, 1819, IX.I, volumes 1 and 2.

Report from the Select Committee on Agricultural Labourers' Wages and the Condition and Morals of Labourers in that Employment, PP, 1824, VI.

Report of the Select Committee on the Bill to Regulate the Labour of Children in Factories, PP, 1831–32, XV.

Report of the Factory Inquiry Commission as to the Employment of Children in Factories, PP, 1833, XX.

Abstract of Answers and Returns relative to the State of Education in England and Wales, PP, 1835, XLIII.

Supplementary Report of the Factory Inquiry Commission on the Employment of Children in Factories, PP, 1834, XIX.

Reports of the Inspectors of Factories, PP, 1834, XLIII.

Report from the Commissioners on the Administration and Practical Operation of the Poor Laws, PP, 1835, VII. 2.

Report from the Commissioners on the Education of the Poorer Classes in England and Wales, PP, 1837–38, VII.

Report on the Effects of the Education Provision of the Factory Acts, PP, 1839, XLII.

Reports from the Commissioners: hand loom weavers, PP, 1840, XXIV.

First Report of the Commissioners for Inquiring into the Employment and Condition of Children in Mines and Manufactories, PP, 1842, XV.

Appendix to First Report, PP, 1842, XVI.

Report from the Select Committee on the Labouring Poor (Allotments of Land), PP, 1843, VII.

Reports from Commissioners on the Employment of Women and Children in Agriculture, PP, 1843, XII.

Reports of the Inspectors of Factories, PP, 1843, XXVII.

Reports of the Inspectors of Factories, PP, 1847, XV.

Reports of the Inspectors of Factories, PP, 1847–48, XXVI.

Education Census, PP, 1852–53, XC.

Reports of the Inspectors of Factories, PP, 1852–53, XL.

Report of the Committee on the State of Education in the Municipal Boroughs of Manchester and Salford, PP, 1852–53, XI.

Report from the Select Committee on Education in Manchester and Salford, PP, 1852–53, XXIX.

Reports of the Inspectors of Factories, PP, 1854, XIX.

Reports of the Inspectors of Factories, PP, 1856, XVIII.

Reports of the Inspectors of Factories, PP, 1859, XII.

Reports of the Inspectors of Factories, PP, 1860, XXXIV.

Reports of the Inspectors of Factories, PP, 1861, XXII.

Report of the Royal Commission on the State of Education in England (Newcastle Commission), PP, 1861, XX.I–XX.5.

Children's Employment Commission, PP, 1862, XVIII.

Children's Employment Commission, PP, 1864, XXII.

Children's Employment Commission, PP, 1865, XX.

Report on the Employment of Women and Children in Agriculture, PP, 1867–68, XVII.

Report on the Employment of Children, Young Persons and Women in Agriculture, PP, 1868–89, XIII.

Reports on Schools for the Poorer Classes in Birmingham, Leeds, Liverpool and Manchester, PP, 1870, LIV.

Minutes of the Committee of Council on Education

PP, 1841, XX; PP, 1843, XL; PP, 1845, XXXV; PP, 1846, XXXII; PP, 1847, XLV; PP, 1847–48, L; PP, 1849, XLII; PP, 1850, XLIII; PP, 1851, XLIV; PP, 1852, XXXIX; PP, 1852–53, LXXX; PP, 1853, XL; PP, 1854, LII; PP, 1854–55, XLII; PP, 1856, XLVII; PP, 1857, XXXIII; PP, 1857–58, XLV.

Reports of the Committee of Council on Education

PP, 1859, XXI; PP, 1860, LIV; PP, 1861, XLIX; PP, 1862, XLII; PP, 1863, XLVII; PP, 1864, XLV; PP, 1865, XLII; PP, 1866, XXVII; PP, 1867, XXII; PP, 1867–68, LV; PP, 1868–69, XX; PP, 1870, XXII; PP, 1871, XXII; PP, 1872, XXII; PP, 1872–73, XXIV; PP, 1873–74, XVIII; PP, 1874–75, XXIV; PP, 1875–76, XXIII; PP, 1876–77, XXIX; PP, 1877–78, XXVIII; PP, 1878–79, XXIII; PP, 1879–80, XXII; PP, 1880–81, XXXII; PP, 1881–82, XXIII; PP, 1882–83, XXV.

MANUSCRIPT AND OTHER COLLECTIONS

Societies

British and Foreign School Society Annual Reports, 1815–70.

Committee of Sunday Schools for Children of all Denominations in Manchester and Salford, Annual Reports of the Salford Branch, 1812–26.

Diocesan Society for the Archdeaconry of Suffolk:
  Annual Reports 1840–70.
  Church Schools Enquiry 1846–47.
District Committee of Education for the Deanery of Lothingland, Suffolk, Annual
  Reports, 1840, 1842–45, 1854–57, 1866.
Ipswich British School Society, Annual Reports, 1847–70.
Norfolk and Norwich National Society:
  Archdeacon's Questionnaire on the State of Education in each parish, 1812.
  Attendance Returns, 1817, 1818.
  Draft Report on the Archdeacon's Inquiry into schools (not dated).
  Minute Book, 1812–46.
  Pamphlet, 1812.
Norwich Diocesan Society for the Education of the Poor in the Principles of the
  Established Church, Annual Reports, 1840, 1852–53.
Manchester and District Sunday School Association Annual Report, 1848–49.
Manchester and Salford Education Aid Society Annual Reports, 1856–72.
Manchester and Salford Ragged School Union Annual Reports, 1859–1936.
Manchester Statistical Society Reports:
  Report on the State of Education in Bury, 1835.
  Report on the State of Education in Salford in 1835, 1836.
  Report on the State of Education in Liverpool in 1835–36, 1836.
  Report on the State of Education in Bolton, 1837.
  Report on the State of Education in York in 1836–37, 1837.
  Report on the State of Education in Pendleton in 1838, 1839.
  Report on the State of Education in the County of Rutland in the Year 1838, 1939.
  Report on the State of Education in Kingston upon Hull, 1840.
National Society for the Education of the Poor in the Principles of the Established
  Church, Annual Reports, 1820–70.
Societies in Union with the National Society, Annual Reports, 1813–18.
Suffolk Society for the Education of the Poor in the Principles of the Established
  Church, Minutes of the Foundation Meeting, 1812.
The Suffolk Society for the Education of the Poor, Annual Reports, 1812–40.

School and Local Records

Log-books:
  Barwick in Elmet Parochial School, Leeds, 1863–70.
  Bedford and Hatton National School, London, 1863–70.
  Bolsterstone Church of England School, Sheffield, 1863–70.
  Bradwell School, Suffolk, 1868–70.
  Bramford School, Suffolk, 1863–70.
  British Infants' School, Suffolk, 1863–70.
  Crookes Endowed School, Sheffield, 1863–70.
  Dorking British School, Kingston upon Thames, 1863–70.
  Ewell Girls' School, Kingston upon Thames, 1863–86.
  Fence in Pendle School, Lancashire, 1863–70.
  Halewood School, Lancashire, 1864–70.
  Helmingham School, Suffolk, 1863–70.

Holbeck St Matthew's Girls' School, Leeds, 1868–70.
Ixworth School, Suffolk, 1863–70.
Kingston Girls' School, Kingston upon Thames, 1862–70.
Leigh National School, Kingston upon Thames, 1862–70.
Little Glemham School, Suffolk, 1863–70.
Lower Norwood Wesleyan Day School, Lambeth, 1863–70.
Mitcham Girls' National School, Kingston upon Thames, 1863–91.
Neepsend National School, Sheffield, 1863–70.
New Wortley School, Leeds, 1865–70.
Norbiton St Peter's National Girls' School, Kingston upon Thames, 1863–70.
Rose Bridge Wesleyan School, Wigan, 1867–70.
St Andrew's Girls' School, Leeds, 1862–70.
St George's Girls' National School, Sheffield, 1862–70.
St James' Infant School, Westminster, 1863–70.
St Luke's Girls' School, Leeds, 1863–70.
St Margaret's School for Girls, Ipswich, Suffolk, 1863–70.
St Mary's National School, Widnes, Lancashire, 1863–70.
St Miles' Girls' School, Norwich, Norfolk, 1864–70.
St Oswalds' School, Collyhurst, Manchester, 1864–70.
St Peter's School for Girls, Derby, 1862–70.
St Saviour's School, Leeds, 1863–70.
Stocksbridge School, Sheffield, 1869–70.
Southall National School, London, 1863–81.
Surrey Road Girls' School, Norwich, Norfolk, 1863–70.
Swanwick Church of England School, Derby, 1864–70.
Walmersley National School, Lancashire, 1865–70.
Westleton National School, Suffolk, 1863–70.
Weston Parochial School, Bath, 1863–80.
Weymouth House Girls' School, Bath, 1863–70.
Weymouth House Infants' School, Bath, 1863–70.
Managers' Minute Books:
Almondsbury National Sunday and Infant School, Wakefield.
Archbishop Tennyson Parochial School, Lambeth, 1826–70.
Aughton Parochial School, Lancashire, 1835–62.
Bacup National School, Manchester, 1830–59.
Bath National Sunday Schools and Schools of Industry, Bath, 1804–14.
Belper National School, Derbyshire, 1847–70.
Blue Coat Charity School, Ipswich, Suffolk, 1800–70.
Burley School, Leeds, 1864–70.
Calvert Street Sunday School, Norwich, Norfolk, 1862–70.
Clifton Infants' School, Bristol, (Ladies' Committee) 1827–99.
Crompton's Charity School, Manchester, 1787–1868.
Dorking Parochial School, Kingston upon Thames, 1819–69.
Eccleshall National School, Sheffield, 1834.
Feather Hill School, Leeds, 1827–45.
Feltham National School, London, 1840–48.
Friern Barnet Charity School, London, 1809–36.
Friern Barnet Schools, London, 1854–70.
Hanworth National School, 1859–72.

Harrow Parochial School, London, 1864–78.
Harrow Wesleyan Sunday School, London, 1829–68.
Lady Rawlinson's Charity School, Ealing, London, 1820–73.
Lindale School, Lancashire, 1838–70.
Maberly Street Sunday School, Hackney, London, 1835–56.
Maghull Church of England School, Liverpool, 1859–70.
Manchester Poor School, Manchester, 1846–64.
Norbiton National School, Kingston upon Thames, 1840–70.
Rastrick National Infants' School, Wakefield, 1862.
Reigate Girls' British School (Ladies' Committee), 1853–83.
St George's Infant School, Hanover Square, Westminster, 1828–72.
St James' National School, Westminster, 1853–70 (Governors), 1859–70 (Committee).
St Leonard's Charity School for Girls, Shoreditch, London, 1791–1804, 1804–37, 1837–88.
St Mark's School, Westminster, 1855–70.
St Margaret's National School, Uxbridge, London, 1864.
St Martin's in the Fields School, Westminster, 1844–70.
St Mary's Girls' Sunday School, Ealing, London, (Teachers' Meetings) 1864–92.
St Paul's Beninck Schools, London, 1862–76.
St Paul's School, Bristol, 1851–72.
St Silas's School, Bristol, 1860–70.
St Thomas's National School, Hackney, 1828–51, 1851–61, 1861–90.
Temple Newsam National School, Leeds, 1867.
Todmorden National School, Wakefield, 1847–48.
Weymouth House School, Bath, 1804–14, 1827–38, 1839–49.
Weymouth House School, Bath, Girls' School Committee Minutes, 1836.
Windlesham National School, Kingston upon Thames, 1864–72.
Wrea Green School, Lancashire, 1848–70.

Reports

Bath District National Schools, Report of the Finance Committee Bath, 1842.
Charter Street Ragged School Annual Report, Manchester, 1870.
Great Bridgewater Street Ragged School Annual Report, Manchester, 1856.
Hackney Church of England School, Reports of the Committee of Management, 1831, 1837.
Hackney, Homerton and Clapton British Schools Association Report, 1820.
Hackney National Schools Annual Reports, 1836–43, 1846–48, 1851–55, 1859, 1862–63.
Jubilee Charity School Manchester Annual Reports, 1856–70.
Lees Zion British School Annual Report, Preston, 1856.
Manchester Juvenile Refuge and School of Industry Annual Reports, 1847–53.
Norwich Wesleyan Sunday Schools Annual Report, 1849–50.
St Thomas's National School Hackney, Annual Reports, 1854–55, 1859–60, 1860–61.
Salford Ragged and Industrial School Annual Reports, 1858–68.
South Hackney Charity Schools, Report of the Management Committee, 1840.

South Hackney Parochial School Annual Report, 1839.
Stockport Sunday School Annual Reports, 1806–14, 1818–20, 1822–24, 1830–31, 1834–37, 1840, 1843, 1844, 1847.
Stoke Newington Lancasterian Schools Annual Reports, Hackney, 1837–42.
Westminster Schools, printed reports 1834–70.
Westminster National Free School Annual Report, Westminster, 1818.
Weymouth House Schools, Bath, Report on an Examination of Branch Schools in Union, 1843.
Weymouth House Schools, Bath, Report of the Sub-Committee, 1861.
Weymouth House Schools, Bath, Management Committee Reports, 1835–38, 1840–41, 1843–44.

Miscellaneous

Beccles National School, Suffolk, rules for admission (undated).
Clare Sunday School, Suffolk, papers, 1811–46.
Elvedon, Suffolk, rules of the day and Sunday school, 1870.
Flempton Dame School, correspondence, 1819.
Glemsford School, Suffolk, attendance register.
Hitcham, Suffolk, survey of parish with information on individuals and families in the parish in the late 1860s and early 1870s (undated and anonymous).
Kirkhall Lane School, Wigan, attendance register 1851–52.
Lancashire Public Schools Association, collection of papers read at a meeting in 1850.
Lees Zion British School, Preston, Report on a Public Examination, 1860.

2   TWENTIETH-CENTURY SOURCES

Aldrich, R., 'Educating Our Mistresses', *History of Education*, 12, 2, 1983, 93–102.
Alexander, S., 'Women's Work in Nineteenth-Century London: a study of the years 1820–1850', Mitchell, J. and Oakley, A. (eds.) *The Rights and Wrongs of Women*, Harmondsworth, 1976, pp. 59–111.
—'Women, Class and Sexual Differences in the 1830s and 1840s: some reflections on the writing of a feminist history', *History Workshop*, 17, Spring 1984, 125–49.
Alexander, S., Davin, A., and Hostettler, E., 'Labouring Women: a reply to Eric Hobsbawn', *History Workshop*, 8, Autumn 1979, 174–82.
Anderson, M., *Family Structure in Nineteenth-Century Lancashire*, Cambridge, 1971.
—'Smelser Revisited: sociological history and the working-class family', *Social History*, 3, 1, Oct. 1976, 317–34.
—*Approaches to the History of the Western Family 1500–1914*, London and Basingstoke, 1980.
Arnot, M., 'Male Hegemony, Social Class, and Women's Education', in Stone, L. (ed.), *The Education Feminism Reader*, London and Boston, 1994, pp. 84–104.

Banks, O., *Faces of Feminism: a study of feminism as a social movement*, Oxford, 1981.

Barrett, M., and McIntosh, M., 'The Family Wage', in Whitelegg, E., Arnot, M., Bartels, E., Beechey, V., Birke, L., Himmelweit, Leonard, D., Ruehl, S., and Speakman, M. A. (eds.), *The Changing Experience of Women*, Oxford, 1982, pp. 71–87.

Beechey, V., 'On Patriarchy', *Feminist Review*, 3, 1979, 65–82.

Beddoes, D., *Discovering Women's History: a practical manual*, 1983.

Berg, M., *The Age of Manufactures: industry, innovation and work in Britain, 1700–1820*, 1985.

Best, G., *Mid-Victorian Britain, 1851–1875*, 1979.

Bradley, H., *Men's Work, Women's Work*, Cambridge, 1989.

Bryant, M., *The Unexpected Revolution*, 1979.

—Review of Purvis, J. 'Hard Lessons', *History of Education Quarterly*, 31, 1, 1991, 136–7.

Burnett, J., *Ueful Toil*, 1974.

—*Destiny Obscure*, 1983.

Burstyn, J., 'Women's Education during the Nineteenth Century: a review of the literature', *History of Education*, 5, 1, 1976, 11–19.

Central Statistical Office, *Social Trends*, 24, 1994.

Cruikshank, M., 'A Lancashire Handloom Weavers' School', *Journal of Educational Administration and History*, XI,1, 1979, 15–18.

Charlesworth, A. (ed.), *An Atlas of Rural Protest in Britain 1548–1900*, Beckenham, 1983.

Clarke, A., *A Working Life of Women in the Seventeenth Century*, 1919, 1968 edn.

Collier, F., *The Family Economy of the Working Classes in the Cotton Industry 1784–1833*, Manchester, 1964.

Cook, T. (ed.), *Local Studies and the History of Education*, 1972.

Davidoff, L., and Hall, C., *Family Fortunes. Men and women of the English middle class, 1780–1850*, 1987.

Davin, A., '"Mind That You Do As You Are Told": reading books for Board school girls', *Feminist Review*, 3, 1979, 89–98.

Delamont, S., and Duffin, L., *The Nineteenth-Century Woman: her cultural and physical world*, 1978.

Dick, M., 'The Myth of the Working-Class Sunday School', *History of Education*, 9, 1, 1980, 27–41.

Digby, A., 'The Labour Market and the Continuation of Social Policy after 1834: the case of the eastern counties', *Economic History Review*, XVIII, 1975, 69–83.

—*Pauper Palaces*, 1981.

Digby, A., and Searby, P., *Children, Schools and Society in Nineteenth-Century England*, London and Basingstoke, 1981.

Drake, B., *Women in Trade Unions*, 1920, 1984 edn.

Dobbs, A. E., *Education and Social Movements 1700–1850*, 1919.

Douglas, J. W., *The Home and the School*, 1964.

Dunabin, J. F. D. (ed.), *Rural Discontent in Nineteenth-Century Britain*, 1974.

Dutton, H. I., and King, J. E., 'The Limits of Paternalism: the cotton tyrants of North Lancashire, 1836–1854', *Social History*, 7, 1, 1982, 59–74.

Dyhouse, C., *Girls Growing Up in Late Victorian and Edwardian England*, 1981.

—*Feminism and the Family in England 1880–1939*, Oxford, 1989.

Engels, F., *The Condition of the Working Class in England*, 1892, 1969 edn.

Farningham, M., *A Working Woman's Life*, 1907.

Flett, K., 'The Theory and Practice of Really Useful Knowledge', unpublished M. Ed. dissertation, University of London, 1983.

Foster, J., *Class Struggle and the Industrial Revolution*, 1984.

Friefield, M., 'Technological Change and the "Self-Acting" Mule: a study of skill and the sexual division of labour', *Social History*, 11, 3, 1986, 319–43.

Frith, S., 'Socialisation and Rational Schooling: elementary education in Leeds before 1870', in McCann, P. (ed.), *Popular Education and Socialisation in the Nineteenth Century*, 1977, pp. 67–92.

Frow, E., and Frow, R., *The Half-Time System in Education*, Manchester, 1970.

Gardner, P., *The Lost Elementary Schools of Nineteenth-Century England*, Beckenham, 1984.

Glen, R., *Urban Workers and the Industrial Revolution*, Beckenham, 1984.

Goldstrom, J. M., *Education: Elementary Education 1780–1900*, Newton Abbot, 1972.

——'The Content of Education and the Socialisation of the Working-Class Child 1830–1860', in McCann, P. (ed.), *Popular Education and Socialisation in the Nineteenth Century*, 1977, pp. 93–110.

Gomersall, M., 'Ideals and Realities: the education of working-class girls, 1800–1870', *History of Education*, 17, 1, 1988, 37–53.

——'Women's Work and Education in Lancashire, 1800–1870: a response to Keith Flett', *History of Education*, 18, 2, 1989, 153–62.

——'The Elementary Education of Females in England 1800–1870, with particular reference to the lives and work of girls and women in industrial Lancashire and rural Norfolk and Suffolk', unpublished Ph.D. thesis, Institute of Education, University of London, 1991.

——'Education for Domesticity? A nineteenth-century perspective on girls' schooling and education', *Gender and Education*, 6, 3, 1994, 235–47.

——'Challenges and Changes? The education of Lancashire factory women in the later nineteenth century', *History of Education*, 24, 2, 1995, 165–72.

Gorham, D., *The Victorian Girl and the Feminine Ideal*, 1982.

Gray, R., *The Aristocracy of Labour in Nineteenth-Century Britain*, London and Basingstoke, 1981.

Hall, C., 'The Early Formation of Victorian Domestic Ideology', in Burman, S. (ed.), *Fit Work for Women*, 1979, 15–32.

Hall, C., 'The Butcher, the Baker, the Candlestick Maker: the shop and the family in the Industrial Revolution', in Whitelegg, E., Arnot, M., Bartels, E., Beechey, V., Birke, L., Himmelweit, Leonard, D., Ruehl, S., and Speakman, M. A. (eds.), *The Changing Experience of Women*, Oxford, 1982, 2–16.

——'The Home Turned Upside Down? The working-class family in cotton textiles 1780–1850', in Whitelegg, E., Arnot, M., Bartels, E., Beechey, V., Birke, L., Himmelweit, Leonard, D., Ruehl, S., and Speakman, M. A. (eds.), *The Changing Experience of Women*, Oxford, 1982.

Halevy, E., *England in 1815*, 1949.

Hartmann, H., 'The Unhappy Marriage of Marxism and Feminism: towards a more progressive union', in Dale, R., Esland, G., Ferguson, R., and MacDonald, M., *Education and the State volume II: Politics, Patriarchy and Practice*, Lewes, 1981, 191–210.

Henriques, U., *Before the Welfare State: social administration in early industrial Britain*, 1979.

Her Majesty's Inspectorate, *The Preparation of Girls for Adult and Working Life*, DFE, 1992.

Hewitt, M., *Wives and Mothers in Victorian Industry*, 1958.

Higgs, E., 'Domestic Service and Households in Victorian England', *Journal of Social History*, 8, 2, 1983, 201–9.

—'Domestic Service and Household Production', in John, A. (ed.), *Unequal Opportunities: women's employment in England 1800–1918*, Oxford, 1986, pp. 125–50.

—'Women, Occupations and Work in the Nineteenth-Century Censuses', *History Workshop Journal*, 23, Spring 1987, 59–79.

Hobsbawm, E., and Rudé, G., *Captain Swing*, 1968.

Horn, P., *Education in Rural England 1800–1914*, New York, 1978.

—*The Rural World 1780–1850*, 1980.

Hostettler, E., 'Gorlay Steel and the Sexual Division of Labour', *History Workshop*, 4, Autumn 1977, 95–101.

Huberman, M., 'The Economic Origins of Paternalism: Lancashire cotton spinning in the first half of the nineteenth century', *Social History*, 12, 2, 1987, 175–92.

Hunt, F. (ed.), *Lessons for Life: the schooling of girls and women 1850–1950*, Oxford, 1987.

Hurt, J., *Education in Evolution: church, state, society and popular education 1800–1870*, 1971.

—*Elementary Schooling and the Working Classes 1860–1918*, 1979.

Hutchins, B. L., and Harrison, A., *A History of Factory Legislation*, 2nd edn, 1911.

John, A., *By the Sweat of their Brow: women workers at Victorian coal mines*, Beckenham, 1980.

Johnson, M., 'The Education of Girls in Derby and Derbyshire 1800–1930', unpublished M. Ed. dissertation, University of Nottingham, 1966.

—*Derbyshire Village Schools in the Nineteenth Century*, Newton Abbot, 1970.

Johnson, R., 'Educational Policy and Social Control in Early Victorian England', *Past and Present*, 49, 1970, 96–119.

—'Notes on the Schooling of the English Working Class', in Dale, R., Esland, G., and MacDonald, M., *Schooling and Capitalism*, 1976, pp. 44–54.

—'Educating the Educators: "experts" and the state 1833–1839', in Donajgrodzki, A. P., *Social Control in Nineteenth-Century Britain*, 1977, pp. 23–36.

—Really Useful Knowledge: radical education and working-class culture 1790–1845', in Dale, R., Esland, G., Ferguson, R., and MacDonald, M., *Education and the State: vol. II: Politics, Patriarchy and Practice*, 1981, pp. 3–19.

Jones, D., 'Thomas Campbell Foster and the Rural Labourers: incendiarism in East Anglia in the 1840s', *Social History*, 1, 1976, 5–37.

—*Crime, Protest, Community and Police in Nineteenth Century Britain*, 1982.

Joyce, P., *Work, Society and Politics: the culture of the factory in later Victorian England*, 1980, 1982 edn.

Kirk, N., *The Growth of Working-Class Reformism in Mid-Victorian Britain*, Beckenham, 1985.

Kitteringham, J., *Country Girls in Nineteenth-Century England*, Oxford, 1973.

Laqueur, T. W., 'Debate: literacy and social mobility in the Industrial Revolution in England', *Past and Present*, 64, August 1974, 96–107.

—*Religion and Respectability: Sunday schools and working-class culture*, New Haven, 1976.

Lewenhak, S., *Women and Trade Unions*, 1980.

Liddington, J., and Norris, J., *One Hand Tied Behind Us: the rise of the women's suffrage movement*, 1978.

Liddington, J., *The Life and Times of a Respectable Rebel: Selina Cooper 1864–1946*, 1984.

Lown, J., 'Not so much a Factory, More a Form of Patriarchy: Gender and Class during Industrialisation', in Gamarnikow, E., Morgan, D., Purvis, J., and Taylorson, D. (eds.), *Gender, Class and Work*, 1983, pp. 28–45.

—*Women and Industrialisation: gender at work in nineteenth-century England*, Cambridge, 1990.

MacDonald, M., 'Schooling and the Reproduction of Class and Gender Relations', in Dale *et al.* (eds.), *Education and the State volume II: Politics, Patriarchy and Practice*, Lewes, 1981.

Madoc-Jones, B., 'Patterns of Attendance and their Social Significance: Mitcham National School 1830–1939', in McCann, P. (ed.), *Popular Education and Socialisation in the Nineteenth Century*, 1977, pp. 41–66.

Marks, P., 'Femininity in the Classroom: an account of changing attitudes', in Mitchell, J., and Oakley, A., *The Rights and Wrongs of Women*, Harmondsworth, 1976.

Marsden, W. E., 'Diffusion and Regional Variation in Elementary Education in England and Wales 1800–1870', *History of Education*, 11, 3, 1982, 173–94.

—*Unequal Educational Provision in England and Wales, the Nineteenth-Century Roots*, 1987.

Malmgreen, G., *Neither Bread nor Roses: Utopian feminism and the English Working Class 1800–1850*, Brighton, 1978.

Marx, K., *Capital*, vol. 1, 1867, New York, 1967 edn.

Middleton, C., 'Women's Labour and the Transition to Pre-Industrial Capitalism', in Charles, L., and Duffin, L., *Women and Work in Pre-Industrial England*, Beckenham, 1985, pp. 181–206.

Miller, C., 'The Hidden Workforce: female fieldworkers in Gloucestershire 1870–1901', *Southern History*, 6, 1984, 139–55.

Mitchell, G. (ed.), *The Hard Way Up: the autobiography of Hannah Mitchell, suffragette and rebel*, 1968.

Mitchell, J., and Oakley, A. (eds.), *The Rights and Wrongs of Women*, Harmondsworth, 1976.

Murphy, J., 'The Rise of Public Elementary Education in Lancashire', *Transactions of the Historic Society of Lancashire and Cheshire*, 118, 1966, 104–38.

National Curriculum Council, *Education for Industrial Understanding*, Curriculum Guidance 4, York, 1990.

Newton, J., Ryan, M. P., and Walkowitz, J., (eds.), *Sex and Class in Women's History*, 1983.

Osterud, N., 'Gender Divisions and the Organisation of Work in the Leicester Hosiery Industry', in John, A. (ed.), *Unequal Opportunities: women's employment in England 1800–1918*, Oxford, 1986, pp. 45–70.

Perkin, H., *The Origins of Modern English Society*, 1969, 1972 edn.

Pinchbeck, I., *Women Workers and the Industrial Revolution 1780–1850*, 1930, 1981 edn.

Prior, M. (ed.), *Women in English Society 1500–1800*, 1985.

Purvis, J., 'Working-Class Women and Adult Education in Nineteenth-Century Britain', *History of Education*, 9, 3, 1980, 193–212.

—'The Double Burden of Class and Gender in the Schooling of Working-Class Girls in Nineteenth-Century England, 1800–1870', in Barton, L., and Walker, S., *Schools, Teachers and Teaching*, Lewes, 1981, pp. 97–116.

—'Women and Teaching in the Nineteenth Century', in Dale, R., Esland, G., Ferguson, R., and MacDonald, M., *Education and the State vol. II: Politics, Patriarchy and Practice*, Lewes, 1981, pp. 359–75.

—'"Women's Life is essentially Domestic, Public Life being Confined to Men" (Comte): separate spheres and inequality in the education of working-class women, 1854–1900', *History of Education*, 10, 4, 1981, 227–43.

—*Hard Lessons: the lives and education of working-class women in nineteenth-century England*, Cambridge, 1989.

—*A History of Women's Education in England*, Milton Keynes, 1991

Rendall, J. (ed.), *Equal or Different: women's politics 1800–1914*, Oxford, 1987.

Richards, E., 'Women in the British Economy since about 1700: an interpretation', *History*, LIX, 1974, 237–57.

Riley, K., *Quality and Equality: providing opportunities in schools*, 1994.

Roberts, D., *Paternalism in Early Victorian Britain*, Beckenham, 1979.

Roberts, E., *Women's Work 1840–1940*, Basingstoke, 1988.

Roberts, M., 'Sickles and Scythes: women's work and men's work at harvest time', *History Workshop*, 7, Spring 1979, 3–28.

—'"Words they are Women, and Deeds they are Men": images of work and gender in early modern England', in Charles, L., and Duffin, L., *Women and Work in Pre-Industrial England*, Beckenham, 1985, 122–80.

Roberts, R., *A Ragged Schooling*, Glasgow, 1978.

Rose, S., 'Gender at Work: sex, class and industrial capitalism', *History Workshop*, 21, 1986, 113–31.

—*Limited Livelihoods: gender and class in nineteenth-century England*, 1992.

Rowbotham, S., *Hidden from History*, 1973.

Rule, J., *The Labouring Classes in Early Industrial England 1750–1850*, Harlow, 1986.

Samuel, R. (ed.), *Village Life and Labour*, 1975.

Sanderson, M., 'Education and the Factory in Industrial Lancashire', *Economic History Review*, 20, 2, 1967, 266–79.

—'Social Change and Elementary Education in Industrial Lancashire 1780–1840', *Northern History*, University of Leeds, vol. 3, 1968, 131–53.

—'Literacy and Social Mobility in the Industrial Revolution in England', *Past and Present*, 56, 1972, 75–104.

—'The National and British School Societies in Lancashire: the roots of Anglican supremacy', in Cook, T. (ed.), *Local Studies and the History of Education*, 1972.

—*Education, Economic Change and Society in England 1780–1870*, Basingstoke and London, 1983.

Saraga, J., 'Determined Women', *The Times Educational Supplement*, 13/9/1991.

Schwarzkopf, J., *Women in the Chartist Movement*, 1991.

Seccombe, W., 'Patriarchy Stabilised: the construction of the male breadwinner wage norm in nineteenth-century Britain', *Social History*, 11, 1, 1986, 53–76.

Silver, H., *Education as History*, 1983.

Simon, B., *Studies in the History of Education 1780–1870*, 1960.

Smelser, N., *Social Change and the Industrial Revolution*, Chicago, 1959.

Snell, K. D. M., *Annals of the Labouring Poor: social change and agrarian England 1660–1900*, Cambridge, 1985, 1987 edn.

Stephens, W. B., *Regional Variations in Education during the Industrial Revolution: the task of the local historian*, Leeds, 1973.

—*Adult Education and Society in an Industrial Town: Warrington 1800–1900*, Exeter, 1980.

—*Education, Literacy and Society, 1830–1870: the geography of diversity in provincial England*, Manchester, 1987.

Taylor, B., *Eve and the New Jerusalem*, 1983.

Thirsk, J. and Imray, J., *Suffolk Farming in the Nineteenth Century*, Ipswich, East Suffolk Record Society, 1958.

Thomis, M., and Grimmett, J., *Women in Protest 1800–1850*, 1982.

Thompson, D., 'Women and Nineteenth-Century Radical Politics: a lost dimension', in Mitchell, J., and Oakley, A., (eds.), *The Rights and Wrongs of Women*, Harmondsworth, 1976, pp. 112–38.

—*The Chartists*, 1984.

—'Women, Work and Politics in Nineteenth-Century England: the problem of authority', in Rendall, J. (ed.), *Equal or Different: women's politics 1800–1914*, Oxford, 1987, pp. 57–81.

Thompson, E. P., *The Making of the English Working Class*, Harmondsworth, 1968.

Thompson, F., *Lark Rise to Candleford*, 1954 edn.

Thompson, F. L. M., *The Rise of Respectable Society*, 1988.

Tilly, L., and Scott, J., *Women, Work and Family*, 1978.

Turnball, A., 'Learning Her Womanly Work: the elementary school curriculum, 1870–1914', in F. Hunt (ed.), *Lessons for Life: the schooling of girls and women, 1850–1950*, Oxford, 1987, 83–100.

Tylecote, M., *The Mechanics' Institutes of Lancashire and Yorkshire before 1851*, Manchester, 1957.

Vanes, J., *Apparelled in Red: the history of the Red Maids' School*, Bristol, 1984.

Vincent, D., *Bread, Knowledge and Freedom: a study of nineteenth-century working-class autobiography*, 1982.

Walby, S., *Patriarchy at Work*, Cambridge, 1986.

—*Theorizing Patriarchy*, Oxford, 1992.

Walkowitz, J., *Prostitution and Victorian Society: Women, Class and the State*, Cambridge, 1980.

Walvin, J., *A Child's World: a social history of English Childhood 1800–1914*, Harmondsworth, 1978.

Wardle, D., *Education and Society in Nineteenth-Century Nottingham*, Cambridge, 1971.

Widdowson, F., *Going Up to the Next Class: women and elementary teacher training 1840–1914*, 1980.

Index